7th Workshop on Argument Mining (ArgMining 2020)

Held online due to COVID-19

Barcelona, Spain
13 December 2020

ISBN: 978-1-7138-2822-8

COLING 2020

The 7th Workshop on Argument Mining (ArgMining 2020)

Proceedings of the Workshop

December 13, 2020
Barcelona, Spain (Online)

Introduction

Welcome to the 7th Workshop on Argument Mining (ArgMining 2020), collocated with COLING 2020 (online conference). The ArgMining workshop series is the premier research forum devoted to the mining, the assessment, and the generation of natural language arguments. Previous editions have been held annually at ACL (2014, 2016, 2019), NAACL (2015), and EMNLP (2017, 2018).

Argument(ation) mining is an emerging research area of computational linguistics. At its heart, it involves the automatic identification of argumentative structures in free text, such as the premises, conclusions, and inference schemes of arguments as well as their inter relations and counter-considerations. To date, researchers have investigated argument mining on various registers including legal texts, scientific papers, product reviews, news editorials, Wikipedia articles, persuasive essays, political debates, tweets, and online discussions.

Argument mining is tied to stance and sentiment analysis, since every argument carries a stance towards its topic, often expressed with sentiment. Recently, the quality assessment of arguments came into focus; it is considered as an important step to bring computational argumentation to practical impact. Another raising topic in this area is the generation of argumentative structures in natural language, with the goal of providing explanations. While solutions to basic steps such as component segmentation and classification slowly become mature, many tasks remain largely unsolved, particularly when facing more open genres and topics. Success in computational argumentation requires joint efforts integrating NLP, theories of semantics and pragmatics, discourse, artificial intelligence, information retrieval, argumentation theory, and computational models of argument.

Computational argumentation gives rise to various applications of great importance. It provides methods that can find and visualize the main pro and con arguments on a topic of interest in a corpus — or even in documents, formus, and debates on the web. In instructional and educational contexts, written and diagrammed arguments can be mined to convey and assess students' command of course material, while the retrieval of mined arguments is expected to play a salient role in the emerging field of conversational search. With IBM's Project Debater, technology based on computational argumentation recently received a lot of media attention.

The community around ArgMining is constantly growing, and this is demonstrated by the number of submissions on argument mining accepted also in top level international conferences in NLP and AI. Concerning the workshop, this year's edition had 30 valid submissions (27 in 2017, 32 in 2018 and 41 in 2019), despite the complex situation due to the covid-19 pandemic. Among the submitted papers, there were 22 full papers, 6 short papers, and 2 demo papers. The submissions came from institutions on 13 countries. Two submissions were withdrawn due to acceptance at other venues, indicating the quality of submissions. Thanks to the hard work of 36 program committee members, all authors got three reviews on time. 9 full papers, 2 short papers, and 2 demo papers have been accepted, resulting in an overall acceptance rate of 43%. All such papers are included in the proceedings at hand. Give the unusual online conference format, we decided to give to all authors the possibility to present their work orally. Each presentation is pre-recorded and the video is available to the workshop audience in advance. A QA session is then organized during the workshop to discuss each paper, allowing the authors to get feedback from the ArgMining community. Additionally, one paper accepted at the Findings of the ACL: EMNLP 2020 will also be presented orally at the workshop.

We are delighted to have Marco Guerini (researcher at Fondazione Bruno Kessler, Trento, Italy) as keynote speaker, expert in persuasive communication and counter narratives generation. The final program is announced on the official workshop website: https://argmining2020.i3s.unice.fr/

Elena Cabrio and Serena Villata (ArgMining 2020 co-chairs)

ArgMining 2020 chairs:

Elena Cabrio, Université Côte d'Azur, Inria, CNRS, I3S, France
Serena Villata, Université Côte d'Azur, Inria, CNRS, I3S, France

Program Committee:

Ranit Aharonov, IBM Research
Khalid Al Khatib, Bauhaus-Universität Weimar
Laura Alonso Alemany, Universidad Nacional de Cordoba
Roy Bar-Haim, IBM Research
Yonatan Bilu, IBM Research
Katarzyna Budzynska, Warsaw University of Technology
Oana Cocarascu, King's College London
Anette Frank, Heidelberg Universiy
Andrea Galassi, University of Bologna
Ivan Habernal, Technische Universität Darmstadt
Shohreh Haddadan, University of Luxembourg
Christopher Hidey, Google
Yufang Hou, IBM Research
John Lawrence, University of Dundee
Beishui Liao, Zhejiang University
Marco Lippi, University of Modena and Reggio Emilia
Diane Litman, University of Pittsburgh
Santiago Marro, Université Côte d'Azur
Tobias Mayer, Université Côte d'Azur
Sebastian Padó, Stuttgart University
Joonsuk Park, University of Richmond
Simon Parsons, University of Lincoln
Georgios Petasis, NCSR "Demokritos"
Ariel Rosenfeld, Bar-Ilan University
Federico Ruggeri, University of Bologna
Patrick Saint-Dizier, Retired from IRIT-CNRS
Jodi Schneider, UIUC
Noam Slonim, IBM Research
Manfred Stede, University of Potsdam
Benno Stein, Bauhaus-Universität Weimar
Nicolas Turenne, BNU HKBU United International College (UIC)
Henning Wachsmuth, Paderborn University
Vern R. Walker, Maurice A. Deane School of Law at Hofstra University
Zhongyu Wei, School of Data Science, Fudan University

Invited Speaker:

Marco Guerini, Fondazione Bruno Kessler, Trento, Italy

Table of Contents

DebateSum: A large-scale argument mining and summarization dataset
Allen Roush and Arvind Balaji 1

Annotating Topics, Stance, Argumentativeness and Claims in Dutch Social Media Comments: A Pilot Study
Nina Bauwelinck and Els Lefever 8

Semi-Supervised Cleansing of Web Argument Corpora
Jonas Dorsch and Henning Wachsmuth 19

Exploring Morality in Argumentation
Jonathan Kobbe, Ines Rehbein, Ioana Hulpuș and Heiner Stuckenschmidt 30

Aspect-Based Argument Mining
Dietrich Trautmann 41

Annotation and Detection of Arguments in Tweets
Robin Schaefer and Manfred Stede 53

News Aggregation with Diverse Viewpoint Identification Using Neural Embeddings and Semantic Understanding Models
Mark Carlebach, Ria Cheruvu, Brandon Walker, Cesar Ilharco Magalhaes and Sylvain Jaume . . 59

ECHR: Legal Corpus for Argument Mining
Prakash Poudyal, Jaromir Savelka, Aagje Ieven, Marie Francine Moens, Teresa Goncalves and Paulo Quaresma 67

Argument from Old Man's View: Assessing Social Bias in Argumentation
Maximilian Spliethöver and Henning Wachsmuth 76

Use of Claim Graphing and Argumentation Schemes in Biomedical Literature: A Manual Approach to Analysis
Eli Moser and Robert E. Mercer 88

Annotating argumentation in Swedish social media
Anna Lindahl 100

Style Analysis of Argumentative Texts by Mining Rhetorical Devices
Khalid Al Khatib, Viorel Morari and Benno Stein 106

Creating a Domain-diverse Corpus for Theory-based Argument Quality Assessment
Lily Ng, Anne Lauscher, Joel Tetreault and Courtney Napoles 117

Workshop Program

The ArgMining 2020 workshop will take place on December 13, 2020. Due to the Covid-19 pandemic and the related emergency situation, the program may be subject to last-minute change. The updated workshop program is available at `https://argmining2020.i3s.unice.fr/`

DebateSum:
A large-scale argument mining and summarization dataset

Allen Roush
University of Oregon
gedboy2112@gmail.com

Arvind Balaji
Texas A&M University
arvindb02@gmail.com

Abstract

Prior work in Argument Mining frequently alludes to its potential applications in automatic debating systems. Despite this focus, almost no datasets or models exist which apply natural language processing techniques to problems found within competitive formal debate. To remedy this, we present the DebateSum dataset[1]. DebateSum consists of 187,386 unique pieces of evidence with corresponding argument and extractive summaries. DebateSum was made using data compiled by competitors within the National Speech and Debate Association over a 7-year period. We train several transformer summarization models to benchmark summarization performance on DebateSum. We also introduce a set of fasttext word-vectors trained on DebateSum called debate2vec. Finally, we present a search engine for this dataset which is utilized extensively by members of the National Speech and Debate Association today. The DebateSum search engine is available to the public here: http://www.debate.cards

1 Introduction and Background

American competitive debate's increasingly technical nature leads its competitors to search for hundreds of thousands of pieces of evidence every year. While there are many types of competitive debate that can be assisted by Argument Mining technologies, some types of formal debate are easier to automate than others. In the United States, the National Speech and Debate Association (NSDA) organizes the majority of competitive debates held in secular high schools. The NSDA sanctions four different types of debate and many different speaking events. The NSDA-sanctioned debate format most suited to being assisted by Natural Language Processing technologies is called "Cross Examination Debate" (CX) or "Policy Debate". This is because Policy Debate is significantly more popular and evidence-intensive than the other debate forms that the NSDA offers. Unlike other forms of debate, which have narrow topics that rotate per tournament or per month, Policy Debate maintains one extremely broad topic over a whole year. This encourages extremely deep and thorough amounts of preparation. Significantly more evidence (and subsequently, training data) is produced by NSDA Policy Debaters than by other types of debaters.

Most debaters are encouraged to keep their cases and evidence secretive and hidden from their opponents. However, due to the extreme research burdens which policy debaters face, many universities hold "debate camps" which students attend to prepare for the year's topic. The primary goal of debate camp is for attendees to produce as much evidence as they can before the competitive season starts. These debate camps attract thousands of coaches, competitors, and staff, and function as an effective crowed sourcing platform. At the end of the summer, these debate camps release all evidence gathered by the attendees together on the Open Evidence Project[2]. The Open Evidence Project hosts thousands of debate cases and hundreds of thousands documents. The Open Evidence Projects extensive case library gives any policy debater access to a wide variety of debate cases, allowing for novices and competitors with limited amounts of preparation time to present effective arguments.

The Open Evidence Project is a fantastic hidden-gem resource for argument mining. A diverse range of highly motivated high school students and their coaches produce high quality arguments and evidence

---

[1] The DebateSum dataset is available here: https://github.com/Hellisotherpeople/DebateSum

[2] The Open Evidence Project is hosted here: https://openev.debatecoaches.org/Main/

Proceedings of the 7th Workshop on Argument Mining, pages 1–7
Barcelona, Spain (Online), December 13, 2020.

to support each argument made. Policy debate does not focus on the speaking style or delivery of the speech as much as other types of debate do. Policy debates are instead extremely intricate and technical and most unexpectedly to lay-people, the debaters deliver them *fast*[3]. Since rounds are usually decided by technical details of evidence, competitors are encouraged to present the maximal amount of evidence for their position in their speeches. This evidence is always available to be reviewed later by the judge before a decision is made. This leads to a phenomenon known as speed-reading (colloquially referred to as "spreading" within the debate community) which is done by the majority of serious competitors for strategic benefits. To casual observers, spreading seems completely absurd, but the competitive advantages that it confers are significant. The desire to present as much evidence as possible motivates competitors to research extremely deeply and to produce/deliver the maximum amount of evidence possible. It is due to these factors that DebateSum is such a large dataset.

Conditions on arms sales create effective leverage for advancing foreign policy goals, most countries have and will change their problematic policies to continue to get access to US weapons.

Miller, Project on Middle East Democracy deputy director, Binder, Project on Middle East Democracy advocacy officer, 19

[Andrew, 5-10-2019, War on the Rocks, "The Case for Arms Embargoes Against Uncooperative Partners," https://warontherocks.com/2019/05/the-case-for-arms-embargoes-against-uncooperative-partners/, accessed 7-7-2019, //EJA]

The efficacy of withholding military assistance, including grant aid and arms sales, to modify the behavior of recipient countries is a hotly debated topic in the U.S. foreign policy community. Last month, War on the Rocks published another contribution to this discussion. In "The Case Against Arms Embargos, Even for Saudi Arabia," Raymond Rounds opposes what he calls an "arms embargo" on Saudi Arabia, arguing that suspending U.S. arms sales as leverage over policy disagreements will only backfire by driving the kingdom to purchase arms from other countries. He contends that suspending sales to Saudi Arabia will fail to alter objectionable Saudi conduct, whether in Yemen or domestically, while "[damaging] ties with Saudi Arabia." According to Rounds, this dynamic is not unique to Saudi Arabia, but a general proposition that applies to all U.S. arms recipients.

If he is correct, arms embargoes — a regular tool of U.S. foreign policy — are quixotic attempts to shape the behavior of foreign governments and put the United States at a strategic disadvantage to global competitors. While this argument seems reasonable, if depressing, it suffers from two principal and serious flaws.

First, the empirical record does not support Rounds' contention that arms embargoes do not deliver. While these suspensions are not a silver bullet, there is ample evidence to demonstrate that they can be effective in changing the policy of a target country. For example, in 2005, the United States successfully used the suspension of a joint weapons project to persuade Israel to cancel a proposed sale of drone equipment to China. In another example, then-Secretary of State Rex Tillerson secured commitments from Egypt to resolve a longstanding criminal case against 41 foreign NGO workers, including Americans and Europeans, and to suspend military cooperation with North Korea in exchange for releasing $195 million in suspended military aid. More recently, the legislative hold Sen. Robert Menendez placed on an arms sale to Saudi Arabia and the United Arab Emirates, when combined with threatened legislation to impose further restrictions on transfers to Saudi Arabia, helped pressure the Saudi-led coalition in Yemen to re-engage in negotiations with the Houthis, resulting in an imperfect but still important deal on the port of Hodeidah.

The author's argument that arms embargoes do not work cites the 2013 suspension of U.S. military aid to Egypt following that country's military coup. This policy clearly failed to reverse the military coup

Figure 1: An example of an argument-evidence-summary triplet from the DebateSum dataset as presented in its original form before parsing. The argument is highlighted in blue (lines 1-4), and would be presented by debaters as part of their case. Metadata, such as the date, title and author of the evidence are highlighted in green (lines 5-9). The evidence consists of all text after the blue and green-highlighted sections. The extractive summary consists of all underlined text within the document. The highlighted sections of the underlined text are the extracts which the debater chooses to read out-loud alongside their argument. Note that the argument can also be used an abstractive summary or as a query in query-focused summarization

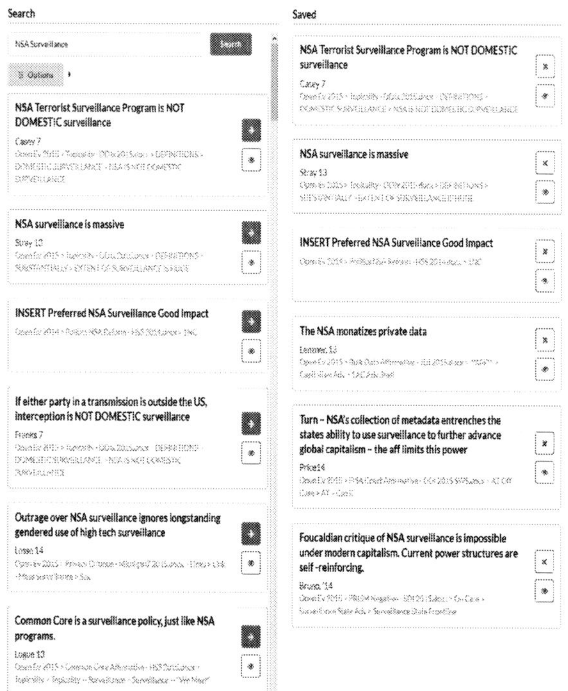

Figure 2: The debate.cards search engine. Debaters can quickly search for evidence by keywords. They can pick evidence to view in detail with the eyeball icon, or move it to the "saved" column with the arrow icon. When a debater has moved all of the evidence that they need to the "saved" column, they can click the download button (not shown) to download a properly formatted word document with all of the saved evidence in it. Policy Debaters extensively use this download feature before or in debate rounds to compile evidence for their case.

---

[3] It truly must be seen to be believed, an example of this can be found here, and it is the norm within the activity: `https://youtu.be/Q5iJ7mRONNs?t=754`

This uniquely technical style of debate has thus far been largely unassisted by natural language processing technologies. Debaters would find that effective information retrieval, summarization (especially query-focused summarization), and classification systems could automate, supplement, and/or assist them in their research work. The primary reason for this lack of effective systems within competitive debate was the lack of domain specific training data available. DebateSum remedies this problem by introducing the largest (to our knowledge) dataset of document-argument-summary triplets in existence and we believe that it is one of the largest argument mining datasets ever gathered.

2 Innovations Introduced

We introduce three innovations: the DebateSum dataset (and summarization models trained on it), debate2vec word embeddings, and the "debate.cards" argument search engine.

Open Evidence stores tens of thousands of debate cases as Word documents. Some debate cases can have thousands of documents within them. DebateSum was gathered by converting each word document into an html5 file using pandoc[4]. This allows for easy parsing of documents, allowing for them to have their arguments, document, and summary extracted.

DebateSum consist of argument-evidence-summary triplets. Policy Debaters colloquially refer to these triplets as "cards". Each card consist of a debater's argument (which acts as a biased abstractive summary of the document), a supporting piece of evidence and its citations, and a word-level extractive summary produced by "underlining" and/or "highlighting" the evidence in such a way to support the argument being made. Figure 1 shows an example of one of these cards before parsing. Thousands of competitors and coaches manually produced and annotated DebateSum's triplets. We train transformer-based token-level extractive summarization models to form strong baselines and to act as a blueprint for performance benchmarking summarization models on DebateSum.

Debate2vec is a set of fasttext (Bojanowski et al., 2016) word vectors produced for study on word analogy and word similarity tasks. It is trained on the evidence in DebateSum along with additional evidence (which was not included in DebateSum due to missing or malformed arguments or summaries). Debate2vec is trained on 222485 documents. Debate2vec is 300 dimensional, with a vocabulary of 107555 lowercased words. It was trained for 100 epochs with a learning rate of 0.10. No subword information is included to keep the memory consumption of the model down. Debate2vec is particularly well suited for usage in domains related to philosophy, law, government, or politics.

Debate.cards is an argument search engine which indexes DebateSum (and additional evidence gathered by college level debaters or contributed by users later in the year). Debate.cards was designed as a research tool for Policy Debaters. Prior to debate.cards, competitors would have to painstakingly search through potentially thousands of word documents for specific pieces of evidence. Debate.cards allows competitors to search for evidence by keyword match within the argument, evidence or the citation. Figure 2 shows a sample of the debate.cards search engine.

3 Prior Work

We are not the first to utilize Natural Language Processing techniques to assist debaters with summarization. Abstractive summarization of political debates and arguments has been studied for quite some time (Egan et al., 2016), (Wang & Ling, 2016). The most well-known application of argument mining to debate comes from IBM's Project Debater. Recent work from IBM research has shown the impressive capabilities of automatic argument summarization (Bar-Haim et al., 2020). They utilize a crowd-sourced argument dataset of 7000 pro/con claims scraped from the internet and then they abstractivly synthesize key-points which summarizes the arguments made by the participants. Our work and dataset focuses instead on word-level extractive summarization of debate documents. There is work related to retrieving extractive "snippets" in support of an argument, but this work is query-independent and extracts summaries at the sentence level rather than the word level (Alshomary et al., 2020). Other work related to debate summarization exists, but is trained on limited datasets or restricted to significantly less technical debating styles and formats (Sanchan et al., 2017).

One notable feature that would be extremely useful to members of the Policy Debate community is the ability to generate an extractive summary of their evidence which is *biased towards supporting their*

---

[4] Available here: `https://pandoc.org/`

argument. Some evidence will make arguments for both sides, but only the portions which support a particular position would ideally be read aloud. Some authors have explored this unique problem which they call *query focused* or *query based* summarization, notably (Baumel et al., 2018), (Xu & Lapata, 2020) and (Nema et al., 2017). These systems are somewhat similar to our work, but they deal with abstractive rather than extractive summarization, and are trained on comparatively small datasets like the DUC 2007 or Debatepedia dataset. Luckily, a queryable word-level extractive summarization system exists and is used among the community[5]. This summarizer is called "CX_DB8" (to celebrate the "cross examination" debate community) and is unsupervised, which makes it unable to be directly trained on DebateSum (though it can use word embedding's which are trained on it). It also gets inferior ROUGE scores compared to supervised models. The summarization models we train on DebateSum are not que-ryable, but they follow the tradition of supervised extractive summarization models being benchmarked using ROUGE scores.

Before our work, there were (to our knowledge) no pre-trained word embedding's or language models publically available for Policy Debate. The closest pre-trained language model that we could find to our domain is the publically available Law2Vec[6] set of legal word embedding's. A significant proportion of policy debaters end up becoming lawyers, in no small part due to the similarity between competitive debate and litigation. Our Debate2Vec[7] word embedding's are trained on the entirety of the DebateSum document dataset. They are (to our knowledge) the largest publically available set of word vectors trained on a non-legal argumentative corpus

Finally, there is prior work related to argumentation search engines and information retrieval systems for debaters. Websites such as debate.org, procon.org, and debatepedia.org serve as useful search engines for arguments in support or opposition of a topic. Argument search engines which match or exceed the scale of DebateSum's arguments have been built by crawling these sorts of websites (Wachsmuth et al., 2018), but these indexed arguments do not have corresponding evidence and extracts associated with them. No dedicated search engine for competitive policy debate evidence existed prior to our work. Furthermore, we believe that no dedicated search engine for *any* type of debate argument-evidence-summary triplets exists that matches the scale or breadth of the Debate-Cards search engine.

4 Analysis

The DebateSum dataset consists of 187,386 unique documents that are larger than 100 words. There are 107,555 words which show up more than 10 times in the corpus. There are 101 million total words in DebateSum. Each document consists of on average 520 words. Each argument is on average 14 words long, and each summary consist of 198 words on average. The mean summary compression ratio is 0.46 and the mean argument compression ratio is 0.06.

DebateSum is made from evidence pertaining to each of the yearly policy debate resolutions. Since DebateSum consists of 7 years of evidence, there are 7 resolutions which it covers. Affirmative debate cases almost always advocate for a particular "plan" which implements a resolution. There are potentially an infinite number of topical plans. Negative teams can read a potentially infinite number of counter-plans or counter-advocacies alongside evidence for why the affirmative plan is bad. Debaters will be expected to prepare cases for both the affirmative and negative side and debate each side an equal number of times throughout a tournament. As a result, a considerable amount of evidence gathered in a particular year will be only tangentially related to the resolution as it must be generic enough to answer any type of plan or counterplan. There is a consistent "metagame" of popular and strong arguments which are crafted to be used for any topic on either side. Many of them have their roots in philosophical critiques of the plan or even the state itself which may appear to have little or no relevance to the reso-lution. One can get insights into the specific list of arguments made available by looking at the corre-sponding years page of Open Evidence and inspecting the DebateSum debate cases in their original form. A table which lists the official resolution and its year is presented below:

YEAR	RESOLUTION
2013-2014	Resolved: The United States federal government should substantially increase its economic engagement toward Cuba, Mexico or Venezuela.
2014-2015	Resolved: The United States federal government should substantially increase its non-military exploration and/or development of the Earth's oceans.
2015-2016	Resolved: The United States federal government should substantially curtail its domestic surveillance.
2016-2017	Resolved: The United States federal government should substantially increase its economic and/or diplomatic engagement with the People's Republic of China.
2017-2018	Resolved: The United States federal government should substantially increase its funding and/or regulation of elementary and/or secondary education in the United States.
2018-2019	Resolved: The United States federal government should substantially reduce its restrictions on legal immigration to the United States.
2019-2020	Resolved: The United States federal government should substantially reduce Direct Commercial Sales and/or Foreign Military Sales of arms from the United States.

5   Experiments and Result

We train transformer architecture neural network language models on word-level extractive summarization using the simple-transformers[8] framework. We formulate this problem as a token classification problem between "underlined" and "not-underlined" tokens. We fine-tune the existing weights for 5 epochs using early stopping and the adam (Kingma & Ba, 2015) optimizer. Fp16 is enabled for training. We evaluate our models on a test split of 18,738 documents. The ROUGE metric is used for measuring summarization quality. We evaluate using the default settings of py-rogue[9] on our models. We report the ROUGE F1 scores of these transformer models.

Model	ROUGE-1	ROUGE-2	ROUGE-L
BERT-Large (Devlin et al., 2018)	56.32	35.20	49.98
GPT2-Medium (Radford et al., 2019)	52.07	34.20	53.23
Longformer-Base-4096 (Beltagy et al., 2020)	**60.21**	**38.53**	**57.21**

Table 1: Comparison of different token classification transformer models fine-tuned on the training split of the DebateSum dataset.

6   Conclusion

In this paper, we presented a new large-scale argument mining and summarization dataset called DebateSum. Each row of DebateSum consists of a piece of debate evidence, a word-level extractive summary of that evidence, and the argument made with the evidence. The argument can also be used as an abstractive summary or as a query in tandem with the extract for query-focused extractive summarization. We also trained word vectors on the debate evidence subset of DebateSum. We showcased an innovative search engine for DebateSum which is extensively utilized by competitive debaters today. Finally, we fine-tuned several transformer models on word-level extractive summarization of DebateSum documents and measured their performance using the ROUGE metric. We observe that Longformer is superior to competitor models, likely because of the significantly larger sequence length allowing long-range context to assist in choosing which tokens to include in a summary. We release all code and data to the public.

---

[8] Found here: https://github.com/ThilinaRajapakse/simpletransformers
[9] Available here: https://github.com/Diego999/py-rouge

References

Alshomary, M., Düsterhus, N., & Wachsmuth, H. (2020). Extractive Snippet Generation for Arguments. *SIGIR 2020 - Proceedings of the 43rd International ACM SIGIR Conference on Research and Development in Information Retrieval*, 1969–1972.

Bar-Haim, R., Eden, L., Friedman, R., Kantor, Y., Lahav, D., & Slonim, N. (2020). From Arguments to Key Points: Towards Automatic Argument Summarization. *Proceedings of the 58th Annual Meeting of the Association for Computational Linguistics*, 4029–4039.

Baumel, T., Eyal, M., & Elhadad, M. (2018). *Query Focused Abstractive Summarization: Incorporating Query Relevance, Multi-Document Coverage, and Summary Length Constraints into seq2seq Models*. Retrieved from http://arxiv.org/abs/1801.07704

Beltagy, I., Peters, M. E., & Cohan, A. (2020). *Longformer: The Long-Document Transformer*. Retrieved from http://arxiv.org/abs/2004.05150

Bojanowski, P., Grave, E., Joulin, A., & Mikolov, T. (2016). Enriching Word Vectors with Subword Information. *Transactions of the Association for Computational Linguistics*, *5*, 135–146. Retrieved from http://arxiv.org/abs/1607.04606

Devlin, J., Chang, M.-W., Lee, K., & Toutanova, K. (2018). BERT: Pre-training of Deep Bidirectional Transformers for Language Understanding. *NAACL HLT 2019 - 2019 Conference of the North American Chapter of the Association for Computational Linguistics: Human Language Technologies - Proceedings of the Conference*, *1*, 4171–4186. Retrieved from http://arxiv.org/abs/1810.04805

Egan, C., Siddharthan, A., & Wyner, A. (2016). Summarising the points made in online political debates. *Proceedings of the Third Workshop on Argument Mining (ArgMining2016)*, 134–143.

Kingma, D. P., & Ba, J. L. (2015). Adam: A method for stochastic optimization. *3rd International Conference on Learning Representations, ICLR 2015 - Conference Track Proceedings*. Retrieved from https://arxiv.org/abs/1412.6980v9

Nema, P., Khapra, M. M., Laha, A., & Ravindran, B. (2017). Diversity driven attention model for query-based abstractive summarization. *ACL 2017 - 55th Annual Meeting of the Association for Computational Linguistics, Proceedings of the Conference (Long Papers)*, *1*, 1063–1072.

Radford, A., Wu, J., Child, R., Luan, D., Amodei, D., & Sutskever, I. (2019). *Language Models are Unsupervised Multitask Learners*. Retrieved from https://github.com/codelucas/newspaper

Sanchan, N., Aker, A., & Bontcheva, K. (2017). Automatic Summarization of Online Debates. *Proceedings of the International Conference Recent Advances in Natural Language Processing, RANLP 2017*, 19–27.

Wachsmuth, H., Potthast, M., Al Khatib, K., Ajjour, Y., Puschmann, J., Qu, J., … Stein, B. (2018). Building an Argument Search Engine for the Web. *Proceedings of the 4th Workshop on Argument Mining*, 49–59.

Wang, L., & Ling, W. (2016). Neural Network-Based Abstract Generation for Opinions and Arguments. *Proceedings of the 2016 Conference of the North American Chapter of the Association for Computational Linguistics: Human Language Technologies*, 47–57.

Xu, Y., & Lapata, M. (2020). *Query Focused Multi-Document Summarization with Distant Supervision*. Retrieved from http://arxiv.org/abs/2004.03027

This page intentionally left blank.

Annotating Topics, Stance, Argumentativeness and Claims in Dutch Social Media Comments: A Pilot Study

Nina Bauwelinck and Els Lefever
LT3, Language and Translation Technology Team
Department of Translation, Interpreting and Communication – Ghent University
Groot-Brittanniëlaan 45, 9000 Ghent, Belgium
`firstname.lastname@ugent.be`

Abstract

One of the major challenges currently facing the field of argumentation mining is the lack of consensus on how to analyse argumentative user-generated texts such as online comments. The theoretical motivations underlying the annotation guidelines used to generate labelled corpora rarely include motivation for the use of a particular theoretical basis. This pilot study reports on the annotation of a corpus of 100 Dutch user comments made in response to politically-themed news articles on Facebook. The annotation covers topic and aspect labelling, stance labelling, argumentativeness detection and claim identification. Our IAA study reports substantial agreement scores for argumentativeness detection (0.76 Fleiss' kappa) and moderate agreement for claim labelling (0.45 Fleiss' kappa). We provide a clear justification of the theories and definitions underlying the design of our guidelines. Our analysis of the annotations signal the importance of adjusting our guidelines to include allowances for missing context information and defining the concept of argumentativeness in connection with stance. Our annotated corpus and associated guidelines are made publicly available.

1   Introduction

User-generated content (UGC) such as can be found in the comment sections of newspapers and social media sites is a valuable resource for the collection of argumentative texts written in natural language. According to Manosevitch and Walker (2009), user comments offer a "substantial amount of factual information, and [demonstrate] a public process of weighing alternatives via the expression of issue positions and supporting rationales". The field of argumentation mining, which forms a part of Natural Language Processing (NLP) research, uses this type of data as a resource to train and test automatic detection systems for the purpose of extracting the various components making up the argumentation expressed by the users (Park and Cardie, 2014; Villalba and Saint-Dizier, 2012). Training the systems requires annotating the data, for example labelling claims and reasons for those claims in the text. The various annotation tasks required for producing such data have proven to be very difficult for human annotators. Defining a good set of annotation guidelines is essential towards advancing the field of argumentation mining on UGC data such as social media comments. Currently, the myriad of theoretical perspectives on how to analyse argumentation as well as the unpredictable nature of UGC data have lead to a lack of current consensus on reliable guidelines for the various argumentation annotation tasks.

This paper presents a pilot annotation study for the identification of the topics, topic aspects and stance expressed by the comments, as well as the detection of argumentativeness and the main claim or conclusion presented. This study assesses the suitability of our current guidelines by measuring the Inter Annotator Agreement (IAA) for all tasks and analyses some specific cases which proved most challenging to our annotators. Our aim is to adjust the guidelines based on these results and analysis (Bauwelinck and Lefever, 2020), which will then serve as the basis for an extensive annotation study on a more substantial corpus and including more annotation tasks required for a full analysis of the

---

Proceedings of the 7th Workshop on Argument Mining, pages 8–18
Barcelona, Spain (Online), December 13, 2020.

argumentation presented in the comments (a.o., this will include premise and argumentative relation annotation).

In Section 2, we briefly discuss some of the relevant research. In Section 3, we give an overview of the theoretical frameworks which form the basis of our annotation scheme. In Section 4, we describe our pilot corpus and in Section 5 we give an overview of the annotation procedure, as well as more information on the rationale underlying our guidelines. In Section 6, we first present the results of the IAA study. In Section 7, we then present our analysis of the annotations. We end with Section 8 on concluding remarks as well as indications for future research.

2 Related Research

In the field of argumentation mining, many different problems related to the analysis of argumentation in texts are being treated as different subtasks for automatic detection. Many of these tasks relate more generally to the processing of various aspects of texts within the broader field of NLP. For example, as a preliminary step towards the more argumentation-specific detection tasks, the tasks of topic and stance detection are often performed. Users, especially when arguing on controversial topics, tend to emphasize specific aspects of the topic, a concept called "framing" (Entman, 1993). Therefore, both the more general topics and the more fine-grained topic aspects need to be identified. A major challenge still lies in determining how the different aspects relate to each other and to the major topic under discussion (Saint-Dizier, 2016). This challenge relates to the issue of determining how fine-grained the targets of the users' stance needs to be. There is still no consensus on this issue, but the findings have confirmed that the more fine-grained the stance target, the more difficult it is to automatically classify the stance, and stance targets that are defined too broadly may not be specific enough to become associated with each respective side (*pro/con*) of the debate target (Wojatzki and Zesch, 2016). Most authors therefore opt for a predetermined list of topics, in which topics either take the form of single words (more coarse-grained approach) or phrases (fine-grained). The latter approach was used by Saint-Dizier (2016), who defined controversial issues as evaluative statements (e.g., "Climate action is necessary") as this would aid in mining pro/con arguments for these specific controversies. As a preliminary step for the annotation of different argument components (Stab and Gurevych, 2014; Peldszus and Stede, 2015), the text needs to be split into smaller segments. This step is often skipped in argumentation mining research, in favour of departing from pre-segmented text (Ajjour et al., 2017). The segmentation of user-generated comments is not straightforward, as they contain many irregularities in the use of punctuation, capitalization and other orthographic markers of sentence boundaries. Determining the boundaries of argumentative segments is challenging but necessary for argumentation mining, as it forms the preliminary step both towards identifying the claim and premises as well as more fine-grained components of the argument. Textual indicators of argumentativeness such as discourse markers are often used as features for the automatic detection of argumentative segments (Eckle-Kohler et al., 2015). An important caveat of using argumentative words or phrases for the task of argumentativeness detection is that they may also occur in non-argumentative text (van Eemeren and Houtlosser, 2006). Argumentation mining research has produced some work on the linguistic cues which may be helpful for the identification of argumentativeness (Nguyen and Litman, 2015), especially the detection of discourse markers has been explored to serve as signallers of argumentativeness to aid the automatic detection of arguments (Somasundaran et al., 2008; Tseronis, 2011; Eckle-Kohler et al., 2015). The detection of segments representing the claim or conclusion of an argument in texts is an important prerequisite for applications involving fact checking (Vlachos and Riedel, 2014). It is a very challenging task, especially when applied to an extremely varied resource, like online discourse (Habernal and Gurevych, 2017). There is no current consensus on what exactly constitutes a claim, leading to many different annotation approaches (Daxenberger et al., 2017).

3 Theoretical Frameworks

For the annotation of topics in comments, it is difficult to predetermine a list of possible topics. The comments in our corpus were made in response to newspaper articles shared via Facebook, so we can safely assume they will often refer to the newspaper content (Manosevitch and Walker, 2009). In order to capture all the available topic information, the distinction between structuring and interactional topics is useful. The *structuring topics* are those found in the surrounding context; the *interactional topics* are those which form the topics of discussion and are found in the immediate context of interaction (Stromer-Galley and Martinson, 2009). This distinction has been applied by Rowe (2015), who used the two categories for the topic annotation of user comments to newspaper articles shared via Facebook and comments made on the same articles, via the official newspaper website. In their study, the structuring topic is that which is reported on in the article and the interactional topics are present in the individual comments. This approach seems feasible for our corpus, since the data type is so similar.

For some interactional topics and aspects in the comment, the user expresses a stance reflecting his personal opinion towards the specific topic or aspect. Not all topics and aspects touched upon in the comment will be the target of the users' opinion, as some will only be mentioned in passing, or to set up the context for the argumentation. The typical stance annotation labels include *pro*, *contra* and *none*, where the last one represents a topic or aspect which is not used as a target for the opinion of the user (Küçük and Can, 2020). Parallel to the distinction between the broader (discussion-wide) structuring topic label and the narrower interactional topic label (based on the comment text itself), the distinction between a debate stance and explicit stance is made by Wojatzki and Zesch (2016). The debate stance is the stance towards the target of the whole debate. It is often implicit and inferrable from the explicit stance(s) which rely on textual evidence. This distinction has proven successful for stance annotation on noisy social media data and has even helped model implicit argumentation (Wojatzki and Zesch, 2016).

Given the difficulty of the automatic segmentation of argumentative texts (Al-Khatib et al., 2016) and our focus on the segment-level annotation of argumentativeness and claims, we also perform a preliminary manual segmentation step before handing the data to the annotators to avoid the error percolation which an added segmentation annotation task would inevitably introduce.

While discourse markers are considered useful indicators of argumentativeness (Eckle-Kohler et al., 2015), Tseronis (2011) proposed the more specific concept of the *argumentative marker* which is a lexical item signalling the presence of an argumentative move (e.g., marking a standpoint). The argumentative marker may consist of a single word, phrase or sentence. A distinction is made between those markers which are syntactically part of the main constituents of the phrase and those that are independent on a semantic and syntactic level (Tseronis, 2011). The concept of *shell language* developed by Madnani et al. (2012) is similar to the *argumentative markers*, in the sense that they may be used as signallers of argumentativeness and may consist of longer sequences of words than is the case for discourse markers. Shell language includes organizational phrases, such as ones marking the expression of an opinion (e.g., "I think that"), but also ones marking argumentative structures (such as "after all"). Du et al. (2014) have used shell language for the task of automatically separating topical contents from organizational language and have demonstrated the usefulness of this task, for instance to improve topic detection. They evaluated their fully unsupervised Shell Topic Model on argumentative UGC sourced from online forums. Ducrot (1982) contends that argumentativeness is present in an utterance even if it does not contain a linguistic expression it may explicitly be linked to. The first major challenge lies in defining what exactly constitutes argumentativeness. The distinction between the argumentative and informative components of utterances (Anscombre, 1995) provides one possible answer. The informative component corresponds to the propositional content of the sentence. The argumentative component signals the utterance's *argumentative orientation*: whether or not it has the potential of being used as a premise for a given conclusion. This perspective helps to circumvent the difficulty of reconstructing the intentions of the author of an argumentative text, as it emphasizes the text itself as the locus of the author's intention.

Biran and Rambow (2011)'s concept of the claim consists of any utterance conveying subjective information and anticipating the question "why are you telling me that?". Daxenberger et al. (2017) have criticized Biran and Rambow's (2011) annotated dataset of online comments from blog threads for containing noisy sentences annotated with claims. However, we hypothesize this is not necessarily caused by the definition of the claim concept. Instead, it is a characteristic of this type of data. Our annotation guidelines employ a very similar definition of the claim concept as the one used in Biran and

Rambow (2011).

The current pilot study represents the first phase of our aim to define the annotation guidelines on a corpus of 100 Dutch user-generated comments sourced from the social media platform Facebook. All comments were made in response to an online newspaper article being shared via the official Facebook page of a Flemish newspaper. In this first phase, we focus on measuring agreement and finding edge cases for the annotation tasks of topic and stance labelling, segmentation of the text into argumentative units and claim identification. The second phase will consist of an agreement study on the same corpus sample of 100 comments and will focus on the tasks of premise and argumentative relation identification.

4 Corpus

Facebook is by far the most popular platform for accessing news (Rowe, 2015). However, given the difficulty in collecting this data automatically and assumptions about the lack of argumentation in shorter texts (Habernal and Gurevych, 2017), this platform is rarely used to source data for argumentation mining purposes. Our corpus of 100 Dutch comments was sourced from the official Facebook page of Het Laatste Nieuws (HLN), a popular Flemish newspaper. As is the case for many news outlets (Rowe, 2015), the Facebook page is used to share news articles with a wider audience, often linking to the official website of the newspaper. The corpus was collected manually and contains comments made on posts published in the second and third weeks of June 2020. We did not predetermine a list of topics to filter the Facebook posts. Instead, we chose to collect the first ten comments of each most recent post on the page which was topically related to a political or controversial topic. This included news stories related to policy decisions, party politics, but also related to topics like health care, poverty and racism. We filtered out duplicate comments and comments in other languages than Dutch, but did not filter out multiple comments made by the same user. Aside from the 100 comments, we also collected the 30 associated article texts and gathered 30 screenshots of the Facebook posts commented upon.

5 Annotation

Six annotators participated in this study. All of them were Dutch native speakers and linguists who received the same annotation guidelines (Bauwelinck and Lefever, 2020) to follow[1]. They each annotated a total of 100 Dutch user comments, all 100 were the same set for each annotator and were used to measure inter-annotator agreement.

We performed two preliminary steps to prepare the corpus for the annotators. First, to prepare for the topic annotations we annotated the structuring topics and aspects contained in the Facebook posts and the news article texts. For the topic annotations of the Facebook posts, we labelled the topic information as present on screenshots of the post in question, thus including information like the title of the article, the accompanying image and description text in our decision making. For the topic annotations of the article texts, we limited ourselves to the title and the first three paragraphs of each article. The second preparatory step was to manually segment all the comments in order to prepare for the argumentativeness and claim annotation tasks, which were to be performed on a segment-level. We segmented the comments based on the shell language expressions we found (Madnani et al., 2012; Du et al., 2014), but only if they were also set apart from other segments in a syntactical way (Tseronis, 2011). If the expression occurred syntactically embedded in the phrase, we considered it a part of the larger segment. This approach allowed us to distinguish organizational segments from content segments. We did not consider markers of opinion (such as "I don't think that") as part of shell language, since we only wanted to focus on separating organizational phrases marking argumentative structures from content segments, leaving markers of subjectivity to remain a part of the content segments. Thus, our segmentation approach is more coarse-grained. Other researchers like Nguyen and Litman (2015) have used shell-like concepts for the task of detecting argument components in persuasive essays, also allowing shell language (in Nguyen and Litman's (2015) terms "argument words") to occur in the argument content (in Nguyen and Litman's (2015) terms "domain words").

---

[1]Both the corpus (consisting of comments, article texts and Facebook screenshots) and the associated annotation guidelines can be found at https://www.lt3.ugent.be/resources/platos_pilot-study/.

For the segmentation of comments containing rhetorical questions, we decided to follow the perspective of Speech Act Theory, which contends that this special type of questions only has the surface structure of a question, but realizes the speech act of making a statement (Walton, 2007). Thus, every rhetorical question which was followed by an explicit answer was considered as one segment together with that answer. Our approach resulted in a total number of 504 segments across the whole corpus. The highest number of segments for a single comment is 19; the lowest is 1. The comments in our corpus contained an average number of 5 segments.

We divided our annotators into two groups of three. Each group was assigned different annotation tasks:

1. The first group had to annotate the *topics* and *topic aspects* contained in the comment (*interactional topics*), as well as the *stances* expressed towards those topics and aspects. This task was performed on the level of the entire comment text. The annotators could select the topics and aspects from the list of structuring topics identified in the preliminary step for all the articles and Facebook posts. They were allowed to create additional topic and aspect labels if they could not find a suitable one in the list.

2. The second group was tasked with labelling the predefined segments of each comment as *argumentative unit (AU)* or *non-argumentative unit (NAU)*. Organizational elements which did not carry any argumentatively relevant information were to be marked as *NAU*. Then, the annotators had to indicate which segment best represented the *claim* of the argument. Only segments marked as *AU* were eligible to receive the claim label.

We provide an example of an annotated comment from our corpus to help clarify the annotation tasks. We refer the reader to the guidelines for a more detailed description of the labels. For the comment "And in the stores everyone touches all the fruit and vegetables with their hands better to monitor everything that is in the store, people even open packages and eat the product", the topic-aspect combinations *corona (measures, spread of disease), enforcement* and *shops* were labelled by one of our annotators. Three stance labels were identified: *pro* towards the topic of *enforcement* and the aspect of *measures* and *contra* towards the aspect of *spread of disease*. The segmented comment was shown to the second group of annotators as follows: "1[And] 2[in the stores everyone touches all the fruit and vegetables with their hands] 3[better to monitor everything that is in the store,] 4[people even open packages and eat the product]". In a first round, the annotator determined for each segment whether it was argumentatively relevant or not, resulting in the following labels: argumentative (segments 2, 3 and 4); non-argumentative (segment 1). In a second round, the annotator was given the segments prelabelled for argumentativeness. The annotator then had to determine which of the segments labelled as argumentative best represented the central claim/conclusion of the user comment. In this example, segment 3 was labelled as the claim. All other segments marked argumentative in this comment are therefore seen to support or to be otherwise argumentatively relevant leading up to this claim.

6   Inter-annotator Agreement Results

For the first annotation tasks, viz. assigning topics, aspects and stance, the annotators could assign multiple labels to the same comment. As standard IAA scoring mechanisms (such as Cohen's pairwise kappa) assume the assignment of one category label per unit of annotation, these metrics are not suitable for measuring IAA for multiple labels per annotator. Therefore other metrics, such as Krippendorff's *Alpha* (Krippendorff, 1970; Krippendorff, 2004), have to be used to calculate disagreement (or distance) between sets of assigned labels. Krippendorff's *Alpha* considers difference in annotation on all possible annotation units, irrespective of the number of labels and the type of annotation (categorical, numeric, ordinal). To calculate the distance between two sets of annotation labels, we followed the implementation of Passonneau (2006), using MASI (Measuring Agreement on Set-valued Items). The resulting distance is 0 when sets are overlapping, and 1 when sets are disjoint.

The first annotation tasks appeared to be challenging, resulting in a total of 88 different topics, 245 aspects and 197 stance labels. As a lot of the disagreement for stance is caused by the choice of different

| Alpha/MASI distance | | | #comments perfect agreement | | |
Ann1 - Ann2	Ann1 - Ann3	Ann2 - Ann3	Ann1 - Ann2	Ann1 - Ann3	Ann2 - Ann3
Topics					
0.36	0.64	0.66	55	20	19
Aspects					
0.61	0.76	0.81	29	14	10
Topic/Aspect Stance					
0.66	0.84	0.82	30	12	11
Stance					
0.39	0.51	0.47	56	39	43

Table 1: Krippendorff's Alpha values using the MASI distance metric for each pair of annotators and the number of instances with total label agreement for topics, aspects, stance at the topic/aspect level and stance at the comment level.

aspects of the same topic, we also calculated the distance when only considering the sets of stance labels disregarding the specific topic or aspect they were attached to. Table 1 lists the distance between the sets of labels assigned per pair of annotators and the number of instances with total label agreement for topics, aspects, stance at the topic/aspect level and stance labels ignoring the aspect/topic.

In the following step, annotators were charged with labeling each segment as (1) either an argumentative unit (AU) or non-argumentative unit (NAU) and (2) a claim or no claim. As annotators could only assign one label per task, we could apply more traditional IAA metrics for these tasks such as Cohen's pairwise kappa (Cohen, 1960), which measures agreement between two raters, and Fleiss' kappa (Fleiss, 1971), that can be used for measuring agreement between multiple raters. Note that the Fleiss kappa is a multi-rater generalization of Scott's pi statistic, not Cohen's kappa. Table 2 lists the agreement scores for these two tasks. For the interpretation of the kappa scores, we refer to Landis and Koch (1977), who consider kappa scores ranging between 0.21 and 0.40 as *fair* agreement, between 0.41 and 0.60 as *moderate* agreement, between 0.61 and 0.80 as *substantial* agreement and between 0.81 and 0.99 as *almost perfect* agreement.

| Cohen's kappa | | | Fleiss' kappa |
Ann1 - Ann2	Ann1 - Ann3	Ann2 - Ann3	All annotators
Argumentativeness /vs/ non-argumentativeness			
0.74	0.82	0.71	0.76
Claim detection			
0.45	0.48	0.41	0.45

Table 2: Cohen's kappa agreement scores for pairs of annotators and Fleiss' kappa agreement for all three annotators for the tasks of argumentativeness and claim detection.

7 Analysis

7.1 Comment-level annotation tasks (topic, aspect, stance detection)

We reached moderate agreement for the topic and aspect labelling tasks, considering the Krippendorff's distance is rather high between all pairs of annotators. This is partly due to errors percolating from the topic labelling step to the aspect labels. When we consider only the stance labels per comment, without taking into account the topic and aspects they are linked to, we see that on average, almost half the comments show perfect agreement. In addition, annotators sometimes assign similar (sub)topics or additional (sub)topics, resulting in fairly large distance scores: e.g. [travel, Corona, aviation] vs [Corona, aviation] results in a distance of 0.55, and [police, politician] vs [politician] results in a distance of 0.665. Perfect agreement on the stance labelling task was reached for only 8 comments, all three annotators agreeing on the "none" stance label for those comments. When considering partial agreement (defined here with the following condition satisfied: all three annotators share at least one stance label towards the same topic, e.g. "(politics)contra"), we noted partial agreement for 19 comments.

In the following, we briefly discuss some concrete annotation examples for the annotation tasks which were performed on the comment level. When considering the distance metric between the stance labels only, we noted some recurring labelling errors.

(1)   Feeling ill = stay at home! Easy! There are people who can't stand wearing the mask due to breathing problems! Wearing a mask in this heat is asking for trouble for those people. Keep your distance, sanitize your hands and stay AT HOME when ill. EASY...[2]

In some cases, the annotator identified the stance towards a specific topic, while the others identified only the stance towards the broader related topic. In Example 1, Annotator 1 identified a contra stance towards the *mouth mask obligation* topic, while Annotator 2 identified only a pro stance towards the more general topic of *corona measures*. Annotator 3 did identify both stances. One possible explanation for this confusion is that the annotators may have made a distinction between main topics and more peripheral topics in the comment. In future guidelines, it will be necessary to emphasize the need for identifying both the stance towards the broader topics and more specific ones.

(2)   Just have them all write a protest letter, you won't be receiving much mail.

Comments containing irony such as Example 2 seem to complicate the stance annotation in some cases (perfect agreement for stance labelling amounting only to 8% of the total of 25 ironic comments and partial agreement reaching 28% (7/25)). Two of the annotators indicated doubts in cases such as these and were subsequently instructed to use the *NONE* label in case of doubt. This instruction will also be added to the future guidelines. Additionally, we will ask the annotators to mark the instances of irony and context-related understandability issues, a strategy also applied by Wojatzki and Zesch (2016) in their stance annotation study.

(3)   And the people who kept working from home every day and entertained the kids at the same time, also don't get anything from the government. The energy bill has nevertheless seriously increased in the past 3 months .. This decision was not well considered at all!

Some specific topic labels frequently caused disagreement. In Example 3, disagreement is caused by the fact that one annotator has interpreted the user's stance as being in favour of the government handing out a financial compensation to those in need, resulting in the stance label *(compensation)PRO*. Another annotator has interpreted the stance as being against the lack of compensation for specific groups of the population, resulting in the label *(compensation)CONTRA*. The third annotator has circumvented the issue by adding the extra labels *(government)CONTRA* and *(aid)PRO*. In any case, the future guidelines will still include the option of defining extra labels wherever called for.

(4)   1[Feeling ill = stay at home!] 2[Easy!] 3[There are people who can't stand wearing the mask due to breathing problems!] 4[Wearing a mask in this heat is asking for trouble for those people.] 5[Keep your distance, sanitize your hands and stay AT HOME when ill.] 6[EASY...]

7.2   Segment-level annotation tasks (argumentativeness, claim detection)

Considering the difficulty of the annotation task, we reached substantial agreement scores for the task of argumentativeness detection (0.76 Fleiss' kappa). For the argumentativeness labelling task, non-argumentative segments were defined as those having primarily an organizational function in the comment (for example, to introduce a particular component of the argumentation). Two annotators expressed their doubts as to how to annotate segments which in addition to the organizational function, also seemed to express the stance of the user, such as segments 2 and 6 in Example 4. To avoid mislabelling of such segments which are stance-bearing (and should thus be labelled as AU), we will add this specification to the guidelines.

---

[2]All examples from the corpus given here have been translated from the original Dutch.

(5) 1[She's right.] 2[But no matter what she says or does, it will never be enough.] [...]

Segments occurring at the very start of the comment caused disagreement for argumentativeness labelling, especially in cases like Example 5 where the segment appeared to interact with the surrounding context (for instance, the title or the content of the newspaper article). Since the information in these segments often consists of an evaluative comment on the article content, they are considered stance-bearing and should be labelled as AU. We found a total of 45 comments in our corpus in which the first segment interacted with the context. In 77.8% of these cases (35/45 comments), perfect agreement was reached across all three annotators for the argumentativeness labelling task. When we compare this to the 52% of comments reaching perfect agreement for this task on the whole corpus, we see that the influence of the lack of context information available to our annotators was moderate for this task on our current corpus. We will ensure such segments are flagged in future annotations. This will help us to determine which types of comments may require context features for the automatic detection system.

Additionally, it will be useful to ensure our future guidelines are more explicit on the possible guises of argumentativeness (defined in our guidelines as "all information relevant to the support or expression of the author's position"). Therefore, we will explicitly state that this then includes background information (e.g., "In 1400, a virus was considered an illness") and (parts of) personal narratives ("Just the other day I saw a whole family with no mouth masks on"). In our corpus, we found a total of 44 comments contained at least one of these less obviously argumentative segments (corresponding to 19% or 98/504 total segments in our corpus). Since the annotators themselves raised the question of whether or not such segments were to be considered argumentative fairly quickly, we were able to achieve perfect agreement across all three annotators for 80% (79/98) of segments. However, perfect agreement was only reached for 43% (19/44) of all comments containing this type of segment, meaning that there were few comments in which they were all captured. Therefore, we will include more examples of what sequences of less obviously argumentative segments may look like (such as the first segment of Example (6) in the guidelines). In Example (6), while both segments are argumentative (since together they form evidence for the user's claim that the experts are distributing confusing information about the usefulness of mouth masks), we found disagreement on the argumentative relevance of the first segment.

(6) 1[During the acute phase the experts said that wearing mouth masks wasn't useful .] 2[Now that the virus has been seriously reduced, we do have to wear them .] [...]

Maar (English: but) (29 instances) and *en (English: and)* (23 instances) were the most frequently occurring shell language expressions and proved indicative of argumentativeness (*But* preceded an AU segment for 23/29 instances and *And* preceded an AU segment for 15/23 instances for all annotators). This is not surprising, since *maar* (English: but) is a connective often used to signal a contrasting reason in argumentation and *en* (English: and) can be used to signal an additional reason. An important type of shell language expression we found in our corpus (*I shouldn't be saying this*; *There is not much more to say about this*) corresponds to the so-called "discourse markers of standpoint continuity", identified by Craig and Sanusi (2000) as a common characteristic of group discussions on controversial issues. They are commonly used to specify argumentative standpoints as well as to avoid disagreement while saving face (Craig and Sanusi, 2000). However, a clear distinction should be introduced in the guidelines between such markers and segments like *I do understand his point* or *I get that*, which are indicative of the stance of the author and should be annotated as AU (all three annotators currently annotated these segments as NAU). The presence of the verbs of understanding as well as the first person singular may help distinguish such segments.

We reached moderate agreement for the claim labelling task (0.45 Fleiss' kappa). For 33 comments full agreement was reached on the claim annotation task. Many of the claims identified are elliptical, e.g.: *Belgium doomed, Mayor not capable.* This is typical of the nature of our data. From Daxenberger et al.'s (2017) analysis of claim segments in various argumentation mining corpora, the presence of policy claims (Schiappa and Nordin, 2014) emerged as a common characteristic in multiple corpora (e.g., of the Wikipedia Talk Page Corpus (Biran and Rambow, 2011) and the Microtext corpus of Peldszus and Stede (2015)). In our corpus, such policy claims, which are often characterized by the presence of the modal verb "should" (Daxenberger et al., 2017), were present in 32 comments, for example: *Everyone should just decide for themselves what they find important, taking care of yourself or blending in with the crowd.* Since the policy claim expresses a wish for things to be done differently, it may be expressed in the form of an advice (*We can stop driveling about the mouth masks now*), or as a strong imperative (*if your heart isn't in it, don't do it*), the latter of which seems to be particularly indicative of claim segments. Perfect agreement for the claim labeling task was reached on 44% of comments (14/32) (corresponding to 22 segments containing at least one segment with "should" or an imperative form.

Aside from the occurrence of policy claims, when comparing the claims annotated in our corpus to those found in the Web Discourse corpus (Habernal and Gurevych, 2017), our claims are more often anaphoric in the sense that they express the stance of the author, but without specific lexical reference to the given topic ("I personally find it really sad it's not obligatory,"). Many claims contain expressions signalling beliefs (such as "in my opinion", "personally", "I find"), which according to Daxenberger et al.'s (2017) analysis, is characteristic of the claims found in persuasive student essays (such as the corpus of Stab and Gurevych (2017)). In general, the claim of an argument is more likely to carry stance-taking words toward the topic. This aspect has been identifed as a useful feature for the automatic detection of claims (Ajjour et al., 2019).

The fact that we can find many correspondences with existing corpora of different genres and domains, strengthens our assumption that general markers of claim presence may still be found across genres. Adding these markers in the guidelines for the annotation can help create a more unified approach towards the annotation of claims, which appeared to be absent in the field (Daxenberger et al., 2017). We will investigate the presence and usefulness of such general markers of argumentativity in our more extended corpus, including more domains and platforms to source UGC data from.

8   Conclusion and Future Research

The insights we gained from this pilot annotation study will be used to improve our annotation guidelines. In this study, we pre-segmented all the comments in a preliminary step. This was done to avoid too much error percolation from the annotation results of the segmentation into the claim annotation task, which would make calculating the agreement on claim identification a difficult matter. However, we realize this pre-segmentation may introduce more bias when considering the annotation of other argumentative components like premises and relations between segments. Since the automatic segmentation of texts into argumentative and non-argumentative segments is still very challenging and advances in the field are still being developed, we will use Al-Khatib et al.'s (2016) rule-based algorithm for the automatic pre-segmentation of the corpus as a step prior to the manual annotation. In this way, the annotators will be asked to correct the automatic segmentation by merging incorrectly split segments.

We believe the low agreement results for the first set of annotation tasks (topic, aspect and stance detection) may be improved by reducing the number of possible structuring topic labels for the annotators to choose from. This will require pruning the list of structuring topics and aspects we identified to include only the most frequently occurring ones. Since we are aware of the risk of bias entering our annotation process in providing the structuring topic and aspect labels for the annotators to choose from when deciding on the interactional labels, we will include an evaluation step (removing duplicate labels and becoming aware of ambiguities in certain labels) in our revised annotation guidelines to be performed by a separate annotator. From our analysis of the results for the argumentativeness annotation task, we conclude that our guidelines need more incorporation of stance expressions as an important indicator of argumentativeness.

Since most of our annotators indicated that they had trouble annotating comments due to missing context, we want to explore the impact of context on the various annotation tasks we have performed in this study. First of all, our new guidelines will have to supply more examples of information that is considered argumentatively relevant, e.g., background or context setting information. In particular, we want to investigate whether there are "triggering devices" which are used to evoke context (Nyan, 2017) in the comment. Since the function of context is often defined as narrowing down the range of possible understandings of a text or utterance (Nyan, 2017), we are interested in studying how supplying the annotators with various degrees of context information will for instance impact their understanding of the argumentativeness and the claim of a comment.

References

Y. Ajjour, W. Chen, J. Kiesel, H. Wachsmuth, and B. Stein. 2017. Unit segmentation of argumentative texts. In *Proceedings of the 4th Workshop on Argument Mining*, pages 118–128, Copenhagen, Denmark. Association for Computational Linguistics.

Y. Ajjour, M. Alshomary, H. Wachsmuth, and B. Stein. 2019. Modeling frames in argumentation. In *Proceedings of the 2019 Conference on Empirical Methods in Natural Language Processing and the 9th International Joint Conference on Natural Language Processing (EMNLP-IJCNLP)*, pages 2922–2932, Hong Kong, China. Association for Computational Linguistics.

K. Al-Khatib, H. Wachsmuth, J. Kiesel, M. Hagen, and B. Stein. 2016. A news editorial corpus for mining argumentation strategies. In *Proceedings of COLING 2016, the 26th International Conference on Computational Linguistics: Technical Papers*, pages 3433–3443, Osaka, Japan.

J.C. Anscombre. 1995. De l'argumentation dans la langue à la théorie des topoï. In *La théorie des topoï*, pages 11–47. Kimé, Paris.

N. Bauwelinck and E. Lefever. 2020. Annotation Guidelines for Labeling Topics, Aspects, Stance, Argumentativeness and Claims in Dutch social media comments, version 1.0. Technical report, Ghent University, LT3 15-01.

O. Biran and O. Rambow. 2011. Identifying justifications in written dialogs. In *Proceedings of the 2011 IEEE Fifth International Conference on Semantic Computing*, ICSC '11, pages 162–168, USA. IEEE Computer Society.

J. Cohen. 1960. A coefficient of agreement for nominal scales. *Educational and Psychological Measurement*, 20:37–46.

R.T. Craig and A.L. Sanusi. 2000. 'i'm just saying...': Discourse markers of standpoint continuity. *Argumentation*, 14(4):425–445.

J. Daxenberger, S. Eger, I. Habernal, C. Stab, and I. Gurevych. 2017. What is the essence of a claim? cross-domain claim identification. In *Proceedings of the 2017 Conference on Empirical Methods in Natural Language Processing*, pages 2055–2066, Copenhagen, Denmark. Association for Computational Linguistics.

J. Du, J. Jiang, L. Yang, D. Song, and L. Liao. 2014. Shell miner: Mining organizational phrases in argumentative texts in social media. *2014 IEEE International Conference on Data Mining*, pages 797–802.

O. Ducrot. 1982. Note sur l'argumentation et l'acte d'argumenter in concession et consécution dans le discours. In *Cahiers de linguistique française, 4*, pages 143–163, Genève. Université de Genève.

J. Eckle-Kohler, R. Kluge, and I. Gurevych. 2015. On the role of discourse markers for discriminating claims and premises in argumentative discourse. In *Proceedings of the 2015 Conference on Empirical Methods in Natural Language Processing*, pages 2236–2242, Lisbon, Portugal. Association for Computational Linguistics.

R. Entman. 1993. Framing: Toward clarification of a fractured paradigm. *Journal of Communication*, 43(4):51–58.

J.L. Fleiss. 1971. Measuring nominal scale agreement among many raters. *Psychological Bulletin*, 76:378–382.

I. Habernal and I. Gurevych. 2017. Argumentation mining in user-generated web discourse. *Computational Linguistics*, 43(1):125–179.

K. Krippendorff. 1970. Bivariate agreement coefficients for reliability of data. *Sociological methodology*, pages 139–150.

K. Krippendorff. 2004. Measuring the reliability of qualitative text analysis data. *Quality quantity*, 38:787–800.

D. Küçük and F. Can. 2020. Stance Detection: A Survey. *ACM Computing Surveys*, 53(1).

J.R. Landis and G.G. Koch. 1977. The measurement of observer agreement for categorical data. *Biometrics*, 33:159–174.

N. Madnani, M. Heilman, J. Tetreault, and M. Chodorow. 2012. Identifying high-level organizational elements in argumentative discourse. In *Proceedings of the 2012 Conference of the North American Chapter of the Association for Computational Linguistics: Human Language Technologies*, pages 20–28, Montréal, Canada. Association for Computational Linguistics.

E. Manosevitch and D. Walker. 2009. Reader comments to online opinion journalism: A space of public deliberation. In *10th International Symposium on Online Journalism*, Austin, Texas.

H. Nguyen and D. Litman. 2015. Extracting argument and domain words for identifying argument components in texts. In *Proceedings of the 2nd Workshop on Argumentation Mining*, pages 22–28, Denver, Colorado, USA. Association for Computational Linguistics.

T. Nyan. 2017. Re-contextualising argumentative meanings: An adaptive perspective. *Argumentation*, 31:267–299.

J. Park and C. Cardie. 2014. Identifying appropriate support for propositions in online user comments. In *Proceedings of the First Workshop on Argumentation Mining*, pages 29–38, Baltimore, Maryland. Association for Computational Linguistics.

R. Passonneau. 2006. Measuring agreement on set-valued items (MASI) for semantic and pragmatic annotation. In *Proceedings of the Fifth International Conference on Language Resources and Evaluation (LREC'06)*, Genoa, Italy. European Language Resources Association (ELRA).

A. Peldszus and M. Stede. 2015. An annotated corpus of argumentative microtexts. In *Proceedings of the First Conference on Argumentation*, Lisbon, Portugal.

I. Rowe. 2015. Deliberation 2.0: Comparing the deliberative quality of online news user comments across platforms. *Journal of Broadcasting & Electronic Media*, 59(4):539–555.

P. Saint-Dizier. 2016. Challenges of argument mining: Generating an argument synthesis based on the qualia structure. In *Proceedings of the 9th International Natural Language Generation conference*, pages 79–83, Edinburgh, UK. Association for Computational Linguistics.

E. Schiappa and J.P. Nordin. 2014. *Argumentation: Keeping Faith with Reason*. Pearson.

S. Somasundaran, J. Wiebe, and J. Ruppenhofer. 2008. Discourse level opinion interpretation. In *Proceedings of the 22nd International Conference on Computational Linguistics (Coling 2008)*, pages 801–808, Manchester, UK.

C. Stab and I. Gurevych. 2014. Identifying argumentative discourse structures in persuasive essays. In *Proceedings of the 2014 Conference on Empirical Methods in Natural Language Processing (EMNLP)*, pages 46–56, Doha, Qatar. Association for Computational Linguistics.

J. Stromer-Galley and A.M. Martinson. 2009. Coherence in political computer-mediated communication: analyzing topic relevance and drift in chat. *Discourse & Communication*, 3(2):195–216.

A. Tseronis. 2011. From Connectives to Argumentative Markers: A Quest for Markers of Argumentative Moves and of Related Aspects of Argumentative Discourse. *Argumentation*, 25(4):427–447.

F. van Eemeren and P. Houtlosser. 2006. Strategic maneuvering: A synthetic recapitulation. *Argumentation*, 20(4):381–392–802.

M.P.G. Villalba and P. Saint-Dizier. 2012. Some facets of argument mining for opinion analysis. *COMMA*, 245:23–34.

A. Vlachos and S. Riedel. 2014. Fact checking: Task definition and dataset construction. In *Proceedings of the ACL 2014 Workshop on Language Technologies and Computational Social Science*, pages 18–22, Baltimore, MD, USA. Association for Computational Linguistics.

D.N. Walton. 2007. *Dialog theory for critical argumentation*. John Benjamins, Amsterdam.

M. Wojatzki and T. Zesch. 2016. Stance-based Argument Mining – Modeling Implicit Argumentation Using Stance. In *Proceedings of the KONVENS*, pages 313–322.

Semi-Supervised Cleansing of Web Argument Corpora

Jonas Dorsch
Faculty of Media, Webis Group
Bauhaus-Universität Weimar
Weimar, Germany
`jonas.dorsch@uni-weimar.de`

Henning Wachsmuth
Department of Computer Science
Paderborn University
Paderborn, Germany
`henningw@upb.de`

Abstract

Debate portals and similar web platforms constitute one of the main text sources in computational argumentation research and its applications. While the corpora built upon these sources are rich of argumentatively relevant content and structure, they also include text that is irrelevant, or even detrimental, to their purpose. In this paper, we present a precision-oriented approach to detecting such irrelevant text in a semi-supervised way. Given a few seed examples, the approach automatically learns basic lexical patterns of relevance and irrelevance and then incrementally bootstraps new patterns from sentences matching the patterns. In the existing args.me corpus with 400k argumentative texts, our approach detects almost 87k irrelevant sentences, at a precision of 0.97 according to manual evaluation. With low effort, the approach can be adapted to other web argument corpora, providing a generic way to improve corpus quality.

1 Introduction

Computational argumentation research lays the ground for applications that support opinion formation, including argument search engines (Wachsmuth et al., 2017b), collective deliberation (Uszkoreit et al., 2017), and debating technologies (Toledo et al., 2019). Such applications rely on large pools of up-to-date arguments, which can hardly be found anywere but on the web. One of the most used web argument sources are debate portals where people jointly collect arguments or debate each other on defined issues. Debate portals, and similar web platforms, are rich of argumentatively relevant content and structure, including arguments as well as facts, background information, and similar. This enables researchers to crawl large-scale argument corpora in a distantly-supervised manner (Al-Khatib et al., 2016).

However, the texts found on debate portals also comprise debate-specific language and boilerplate text that is likely to be irrelevant, if not even detrimental, to the mentioned applications. In the text in Figure 1, for instance, the author defines the debated issue (sentence #2), states a thesis (#3–5), and presents two arguments (#6–8, #9–13) — all of which can be considered argumentatively relevant. In contrast, sentences #1, #14, and #15 add nothing of importance, merely making meta-comments and expressing gratitude. In other cases, irrelevant text includes salutations, insults, purely rhetorical moves, and spam. As detailed in Section 2, finding such text differs from finding non-argumentative text segments, since the latter may still be relevant as context for the argumentative segments, as in the case of sentence #2 in Figure 1. Many existing approaches relying on debate portals do not clean the crawled arguments from irrelevant text. Until now, for example, the argument search engine *args.me* (Wachsmuth et al., 2017b) has just returned the full shown text as one pro argument for the query "gay marriage". This at least harms user experience, and it might even corrupt the support of opinion formation in some cases.

In this paper, we study how to find irrelevant text in web arguments such as those from debate portals automatically, in order to clean respective corpora on this basis. In particular, we develop a semi-supervised learning approach that aims to detect as many irrelevant sentences as possible with very high precision, i.e., hardly any relevant sentence should be classified as irrelevant (Section 3). Given a seed set of sentences, the approach learns basic lexical n-gram patterns that frequently match text in either relevant or irrelevant

Proceedings of the 7th Workshop on Argument Mining, pages 19–29
Barcelona, Spain (Online), December 13, 2020.

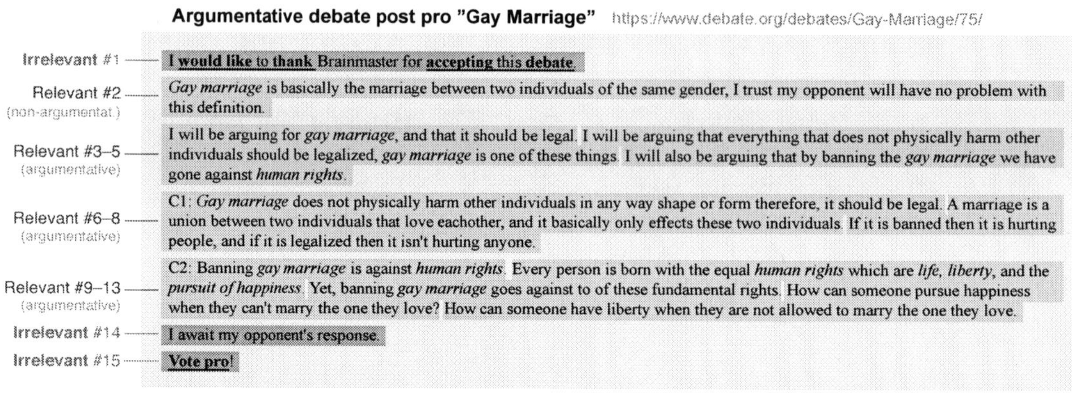

Figure 1: Example text taken from a debate portal. Sentences #1, #14, and #15 can be considered irrelevant to the arguments made by the author. Our approach learns basic lexical patterns to detect such sentences, here shown bold and underlined. Italicized phrases indicate patterns in sentences learned to be relevant.

sentences, and it keeps all patterns with some minimum precision (estimated on all matching sentences). Based on all matching sentences in a given corpus, it then bootstraps new patterns, revises previous ones, and incrementally repeats the process. The final set of irrelevance patterns is used to cleanse the corpus.

We analyze our approach on the args.me corpus (Ajjour et al., 2019), consisting of 387,606 arguments from four debate portals, more than any other available corpus to our knowledge (Section 4). Exploring different types of lexical patterns, we find that word n-grams ignoring stopwords serve best to distinguish relevant from irrelevant sentences. From the most frequent such n-grams, we manually select a set of seed sentences. Then, we run the bootstrapping process, analyze the patterns found by the approach over its different iterations, and evaluate its precision both in an automatic way and in a manual annotation study with three human annotators on 600 sentences (Section 5). At a Fleiss' κ agreement of 0.50, our approach detects irrelevant sentences with a precision of 0.97, in total 86,916 of them in 68,814 arguments from the args.me corpus. We provide a cleaned version of the corpus to the community.[1]

Finally, we discuss how to adopt our approach to improve the quality of web argument corpora, beyond the one studied (Section 6). Altogether, the contribution of this paper is three-fold:

- A semi-supervised approach to detect argumentatively irrelevant sentences in web arguments.
- Several common lexical patterns of relevance and irrelevance in web arguments.
- A cleaned version of the largest available argument corpus, with notably less irrelevant text.

2   Related Work

Initially, research on tasks such as argument mining has largely been carried out on small, well-curated collections of texts, including Wikipedia articles (Aharoni et al., 2014), student essays (Stab and Gurevych, 2014), pure arguments (Peldszus and Stede, 2015), and presidential debates (Lawrence and Reed, 2017). Major real-world applications of computational argumentation, however, need to scale up to web contexts to fulfill their purpose. This includes search engines that oppose pro and con arguments on controversial issues (Wachsmuth et al., 2017b), technologies that debate humans (Toledo et al., 2019), and more.

To obtain web arguments, many works have relied on crawled debate portals and similar web platforms, often in a distant-supervision manner where argumentative structure and similar annotations are directly derived from available meta-information (Al-Khatib et al., 2016). Corpora have been built in such a way based on several debate portals, including *4forums.com* (Walker et al., 2012), *idebate.org* (Cabrio and Villata, 2012), *createdebate.com* (Habernal and Gurevych, 2016), *debate.org* (Durmus and Cardie, 2019), and *reddit.com/r/changemyview* (Egawa et al., 2020). Naturally, less curation of the acquired web texts comes at the cost of more noise, which in turn calls for a cleansing of the resulting corpus.

---

[1]Both the original and the cleaned args.me corpus are found at: `https://webis.de/data.html#args-me-corpus`

Cleansing processes are described in several publications on argument corpora, mostly only referring to the acquired annotations though (Habernal and Gurevych, 2016; Toledo et al., 2019; Gretz et al., 2020). In contrast, the paper at hand targets the cleansing of the corpus texts themselves. Only few works describe respective cleansing steps in detail. Among these, Al-Khatib et al. (2016) deleted special symbols and debate-specific phrases such as "this house" from crawled arguments, and Habernal and Gurevych (2017) removed quotations of previous posts in debate posts. Wachsmuth et al. (2017b) discarded certain types of noisy instances completely for the argument search engine args.me, but the texts in the original associated corpus (Ajjour et al., 2019) still contain much irrelevant text, as our experiments will reveal. Applying our approach has led to an improved version of that corpus.

In this paper, we introduce a semi-supervised learning approach for corpus cleansing. In general, we follow the bootstrapping idea of successful pattern mining methods, such as *DIPRE* (Brin, 1998), *Snowball* (Agichtein and Gravano, 2000), and *Espresso* (Pantel and Pennacchiotti, 2006). While these methods aim at semantically relevant information, we distinguish *pragmatically* relevant from irrelevant text within an author's argumentative discourse. We are not aware of any other approach in this direction.

It is noteworthy in this regard that the cleansing task at hand differs notably from the unit segmentation of argumentative texts (Ajjour et al., 2017). While all argumentative units match the notion of relevance considered here (defined in Section 3), also non-argumentative units may be seen as relevant, if they give facts, definitions, or other background information serving as context for the argumentative units. As such, our notion of relevance relates to the local relevance with respect to some conclusion rather than the global relevance of an argumentative statement in the discussion of an issue (Wachsmuth et al., 2017a).

3   Approach

This section presents our semi-supervised learning approach to detecting irrelevant text in web arguments as well as to clean a respective corpus on this basis. The approach aims to find as many irrelevant text units as possible at an estimated precision beyond a threshold τ (in Section 5, we use $\tau = 0.95$). To this end, it learns linguistic patterns that occur often in irrelevant units and rarely in relevant units (or vice versa). Later, we consider each sentence as one unit, but other granularities would work in principle, too. Figure 2 gives an overview of the three main stages of the approach, each of which will be detailed below:

(a) *Seed Pattern Selection.* Given a corpus as input, a pool of common linguistic patterns is mined from its units, from which seed patterns indicating irrelevance and relevance are selected manually.

(b) *Pattern Bootstrapping.* All units matching any seed irrelevance (relevance) pattern are retrieved, new candidate patterns are mined from the units and added to the pool. Then, only high-precision irrelevance (relevance) patterns are kept in the pool, i.e., those found nearly only in irrelevant (relevant) units. This process is repeated until no new patterns are found or k iterations have passed.

(c) *Corpus Cleansing.* The final pool of irrelevance patterns is used to automatically remove irrelevant units from the corpus.

It is important to see that the relevance patterns are eventually *not* used for the actual cleansing. They serve to distinguish relevant from irrelevant units only, thereby aiding the identification high-precision irrelevance patterns.

While we have designed our approach for web arguments in particular, notice that the outlined processed is largely generic and could easily be transferred to other cleansing tasks where relevant and irrelevant units can be distinguished. What makes our approach specific to web arguments is what we mean by argumentative relevance and irrelevance.

3.1   Argumentative Relevance and Irrelevance

We consider relevance here from the perspective of using the individual arguments in a corpus for empirical analysis of how people argue or for applications such as argument search and debating technologies. For such use cases, portal-specific debate structure emerging from sequences of arguments as well as purely rhetorical moves related to the underlying debates are not of interest. We thus define irrelevance as follows:

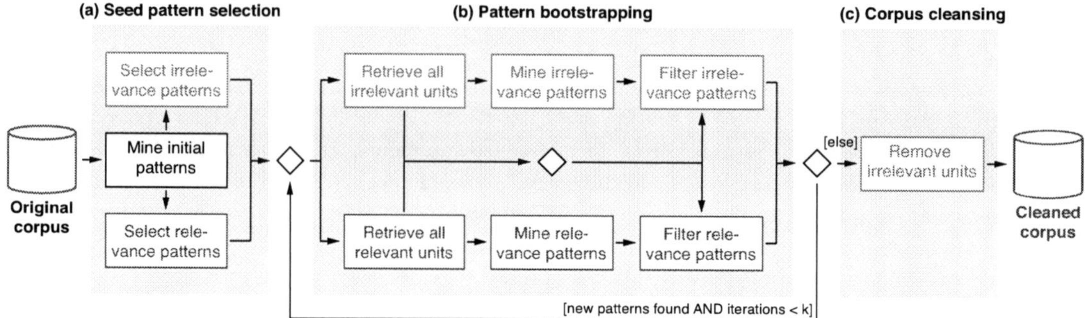

Figure 2: Conceptual process of our semi-supervised bootstrapping approach: (a) Seed (ir)relevance patterns are selected manually from intially mined candidates. (b) New (ir)relevance patterns are mined and filtered automatically from text units matching the existing patterns, until no new patterns are found or k iterations have passed. (c) The corpus is cleaned by removing units matching the irrelevance patterns.

Argumentative Irrelevance. A unit of a web argument is said to be irrelevant, if and only if it does not represent any claim, evidence, fact, background information, or similar statement related to the issue discussed by the author of the text. Examples of irrelevant units include meta-comments on a debate, salutations, expressions of gratitude, personal insults, purely rhetorical moves, and spam.

Any unit not matching the definition is considered to be relevant. While we could have also defined argumentative relevance instead, we decided to focus on irrelevant units, since they constitute the target concept to be detected. In other words, given that we target argument corpora, we expect irrelevant units to be the exception rather than the default. An estimation of the proportion of irrelevant units for the data processed in our experiments follows in Section 4.

3.2 Seed Pattern Selection

The goal of stage (a) is to acquire a pool of linguistic patterns matching text units that can be considered either irrelevant or relevant. The set of all units matching any of these seed patterns then represents the ground-truth data that the pattern bootstrapping starts from. The selection of seed patterns is the only step that requires some level of supervision within our approach. To minimize manual effort, we propose to tackle the selection semi-automatically, i.e., we first mine the most promising candidate patterns automatically from sample data (we use a random 10% sample of the given corpus in Section 5). Then, we manually classify a subset of them to be seed patterns either of irrelevance or of relevance. To do so, however, we need to first define what is considered to be a candidate pattern.

Candidate Patterns. In general, any type of linguistic pattern may be mined from corpus texts, for which respective mining methods are available. Since we expect the given notion of relevance to be largely assessable based on a unit's words only, we restrict our view to basic *lexical* patterns here. For simplicity, we just look for n-grams, but we explore four types of patterns that emerge from making two choices:

- *Counts vs. TF-IDF.* In case of counts, we simply see the m most frequent n-grams as candidates for each n. In case of TF-IDF, we take those n-grams with the highest TF-IDF score in the sample data (each unit being one document). In our experiments, we use $m = 100$ and $n \in \{1, \ldots, 5\}$.

- *W/ stopwords vs. w/o stopwords.* We determine either n-grams based on the full unit texts (w/ stopwords) or we apply stopword removal before (w/o stopwords).

Since high TF-IDF scores usually indicate content, respective patterns are likely to be more useful for relevant than irrelevant sentences. Whether they outperform count-based patterns there is hard to predict, though. In Section 5, we compare the four pattern types against each other. Given all m candidates of the preferred pattern type (say, *Counts w/o stopwords*) for each n, the authors of this paper then manually agree for each candidate on whether to select it as an irrelevance pattern, a relevance pattern, or neither.

3.3 Pattern Bootstrapping

The goal of stage (b) is to incrementally extend the pool of irrelevance and relevance patterns using bootstrapping, i.e., by deriving new patterns from units matching the current patterns in the pool. This fully automatic process continues until no new patterns are found anymore or until a maximum number k of iterations has passed, e.g., if running time is a factor (in Section 5, we continue until the end).

In particular, the first step is to retrieve the sets of all units matching any irrelevance patterns and of all units matching any relevance pattern from the corpus.[2] As sketched in Figure 2, these unit sets are used for two purposes: First, new candidate irrelevance (relevance) patterns are mined from the set of irrelevant (relevant) units and added to the pattern pool. Second, only those patterns are filtered and kept in the pool that indicate an irrelevant (relevant) unit with an estimated precision $p \geq \tau$. We estimate p as follows:

Estimated Precision. Let tp be the number of all retrieved irrelevant (relevant) units that matches a specific irrelevance (relevance) pattern, and let fp be the number of all relevant (irrelevant) units matching this pattern. Then the precision of the pattern is estimated as $p = tp \, / \, (tp + fp)$.

For the mining step, one parameter to decide upon is the minimum frequency of a pattern to consider it a candidate. We suggest to derive this parameter's value from the seed pattern frequencies. For example, if all seed patterns have at least 20 matches in the sample, and the full corpus has 10 times the sample size, then a reasonable value may be $20 \cdot 10 = 200$. For the filtering step, it is favorable that the sizes of the two unit sets remain balanced, because imbalanced sizes decrease the comparability of the values tp and fp. We therefore suggest to adjust the minimum numbers based on the estimated proportion of irrelevant units. For example, if there are about 10 times as many relevant as irrelevant units, reasonable values may be 200 for irrelevance and $200 \cdot 10 = 2000$ for relevance (the numbers given here exemplarily are those we use in Sections 4 and 5). An alternative is to test and adjust these parameters empirically.

An important characteristic of the outlined bootstrapping process is that patterns added to the pool in previous iterations may be removed later from the pool again. This is because the sets of retrieved relevant and irrelevant units change during the process, which in turn may change the precision estimations of the patterns. This can be understood as an internal revision mechanism of our approach that optimizes the precision of the final pool. We see the effect of this mechanism in our experiments in Section 5.[3]

3.4 Corpus Cleansing

The goal of stage (c) is to actually clean the given corpus, based on the final pool of irrelevance patterns. Relevance patterns play no role anymore in this stage; they are used only before, to be able to help identify irrelevance patterns with high precision, as described.

A simple cleansing way would be to just remove all units from the corpus that match any irrelevance patterns. Instead, however, we suggest to restrict the removal to only those irrelevant units before the first and after the last relevant unit. As long as only units are removed that are actually irrelevant, we thereby avoid to negatively affect the coherence of arguments. Moreover, as for the example of Figure 1, we will see below that most irrelevant units are indeed found in the beginning and ending of texts, i.e., the suggested restriction reduces recall to some extent only. Notice that this does not mean that most units in the beginning and ending are irrelevant; in line with our discussions above, we expect the majority of texts to contain no irrelevant unit at all. The following section supports that this is true for the corpus at hand.

4 Data

The presented approach targets argumentative language of varying quality, as often observed in web-based corpora. Below, we assess its impact on the *args.me corpus* (Ajjour et al., 2019), which is to our knowledge the largest available argument corpus to this date, about 7.3 GB in file size. The corpus represents the database underlying the argument search engine args.me (Wachsmuth et al., 2017b). It contains 387,606

---

[2] We include units that match both relevance and irrelevance patterns, since the subsequent filtering step accounts for them. Also, other performance optimizations are useful, such as storing previously found units. We leave them out here for simplicity.

[3] Depending on what sentences match the patterns, it is theoretically possible that a pattern first belongs to the relevance pool and later to the irrelevance pool (or vice versa). We did not observe notable cases in this regard, though.

Pattern type	n-gram	Patterns of Relevant Sentences		Patterns of Irrelevant Sentences	
		Most frequent pattern	**Score**	**Most frequent pattern**	**Score**
Counts	1-gram	people	36 287	opponent	29 088
w/ Stopwords	2-gram	the world	6 210	my opponent	27 149
	3-gram	the fact that	4 206	my opponent s	3 983
	4-gram	in the united states	977	thank my opponent for	1251
	5-gram	has nothing to do with	494	i thank my opponent for	682
Counts	1-gram	people	36 287	opponent	29 088
w/o Stopwords	2-gram	united states	3 906	thank opponent	1 494
	3-gram	big bang theory	251	first round acceptance	617
	4-gram	life liberty pursuit happiness	102	would like thank opponent	359
	5-gram	make law respecting establishment religion	69	round 1 acceptance round 2	82
TF-IDF	1-gram	chronicled	1.00	—	—
w/ Stopwords	2-gram	and weaponry	0.56	actually forfeiting	1.00
	3-gram	an infinite regression	1.00	—	—
	4-gram	abusive education and domestic	1.00	—	—
	5-gram	acceptance of metapyhsical space that	1.00	—	—
TF-IDF	1-gram	abortions	1.00	—	—
w/o Stopwords	2-gram	americans like	1.00	—	—
	3-gram	able kill others	1.00	—	—
	4-gram	accidentally killing equivalent purposely	1.00	—	—
	5-gram	able disprove evolution instead creationists	1.00	—	—

Table 1: The top n-gram patterns agreed upon to indicate relevant and irrelevant sentences respectively, for each evaluated pattern type, along with their score (count or TF-IDF) in the 10% sample of the args.me corpus. We left out spam patterns, such as "kfc ... kfc", as they would have shadowed most other patterns. Based on the full lists (see supplementary material), we decided to use the type *Counts w/o Stopwords*.

arguments that were mined from four debate portals using distant supervision: *debate.org*, *debatewise.org*, *idebate.org*, and *debatepedia.org*. Each argument consists of a mostly very short conclusion as well as a mostly notably longer premise, the latter containing the actual argumentative text. In total, the corpus spans around seven million sentences. We see each sentence as one unit in our approach.

Many texts in the args.me corpus include sentences that are irrelevant to the actual argument, such as the example in Figure 1. Needless to say, no ground-truth information on irrelevance is given, though. For a rough estimation of the proportion of irrelevant sentences, we conducted a pilot study where the two authors of this paper independently decided about the relevance of a set of sentences, following the definition in Section 3. In particular, we considered a corpus sample used previously by Alshomary et al. (2020), which contains the top five pro and the top five con arguments each for the top 10 queries.

From the 1294 sentences in the 100 sample arguments, one of us classified 147 (11.3%) to be irrelevant, the other one 139 (10.7%). In terms of Cohen's κ, we had a substantial inter-annotator agreement of 0.75. In total, 175 sentences (13.5%) were seen as irrelevant by either of us, 111 (8.5%) by both. Since we believe that, in doubt, a sentence should be deemed relevant, we take 8.5% as our estimation. In the whole corpus, we thus expect around 600,000 sentences to be irrelevant. The 111 sentences come from only 39 of the 100 arguments. Assuming this number is representative, about 150k arguments in the corpus should contain irrelevant sentences. In the following experiments, these numbers will give us a rough idea of the recall of our approach. There, we use a random 10% sample of all corpus arguments for the seed pattern selection, and the whole corpus for all subsequent steps.

5   Evaluation

We now report on the step-by-step application of our approach from Section 3 to the corpus from Section 4 and on the manual evaluation of the obtained results. The goal was to assess the impact of the approach on the quality of web-based argument corpora. We hypothesized that the approach is able to detect a large number of irrelevant sentences with a precision as high as its internal precision threshold τ.[4]

---

[4]Source code and supplementary material can be found here: `https://github.com/webis-de/ArgMining-20`

Type	n-grams	Seed Patterns
Relevance	1-grams	government (94198), states (85388), state (68123), law (59609), society (58695), money (54314), death (52327), universe (49412)
	2-grams	big bang (9370), minimum wage (8650), human rights (8592), god exists (7959), health care (7537), years ago (7165), global warming (6399), high school (6235), opponent claims (6160), believe god (6151), human beings (6136), video games (6051), god exist (5810), existence god (5636), jesus christ (5592), supreme court (5513), new york (4890), human life (4838), old testament (4640), years old (4632), god created (4621), god would (4495), self defense (4089), merriam webster (2015)
	3-grams	new york times (1071), world war ii (1062)
	4-grams	life liberty pursuit happiness (791), (aw respecting establishments religion (370), make law respecting establishment (352), shall surely put death (192)
Irrelevance	2-grams	first round (10113), thank opponent (10018), vote con (6048), round acceptance (4698), vote pro (4585), new arguments (4056), accepting debate (4040), accept debate (3432), kfc kfc (15), thinking bee (3), wonyou wonyou (1), ham ham (1)
	3-grams	debate good luck (335), debate look forward (863), hi hi hi (1), dan small penis (1)
	5-grams	every one wrong every one (2)

Table 2: The full lists of positive and negative and seed patterns used for each n-gram type, along with the number of different sentences they match in the corpus (in parentheses), ordered by number of matches.

5.1 Insights into Seed Pattern Selection

To learn what pattern type is best to detect irrelevant sentences, we compared all four candidates emerging from the two choices discussed in Section 3 (Counts vs. TF-IDF, w/ or w/o stopwords). For each type, we retrieved the top 100 n-grams, $n \in \{1, \ldots, 5\}$, covering a large variety of issues debated in the underlying arguments. Then, the two authors of this paper both judged all 2000 resulting patterns as to whether they likely indicate always irrelevant sentences or always relevant ones. Based on the patterns that we both agreed upon, the most promising type was chosen for the seed patterns.

Exemplarily, Table 1 lists the top 1- to 5-gram of each pattern type that indicate relevance or irrelevance respectively. We left out spam patterns such as "wonyou wonyou wonyou" and "kfc kfc", though, as they would limit insights, dominating the top positions; the full lists for each pattern type are given in the supplementary material. For both *TF-IDF* pattern types, we find the relevance patterns to clearly serve their purpose, relating to the content of arguments. Many such patterns are found in the full lists. However, rarely any TF-IDF pattern seemed to reliably indicate irrelevance. This matches the intuition that phrases with high TF-IDF scores are specific to a document's content rather than reflecting general language. In contrast, the two *Counts* pattern types yielded several irrelevance patterns, as the table demonstrates. We decided for *Counts w/o Stopwords*, since it produced patterns that clarified many cases which *Counts w/ Stopwords* left ambiguous. For example, "would like thank opponent" reveals irrelevance knowing the source debate portals (here, debate.org), whereas respective patterns with stopwords ("would like to thank", "like to thank my") leaves more doubts regarding the irrelevance of respective sentences.

Table 2 presents the full set of 38 relevance and 17 irrelevance seed patterns for the type *Counts w/o Stopwords*. A pattern was not included if being redundant, i.e., if it was already covered by a shorter one, e.g., "first round acceptance" was covered by "first round". We observe that no 1-gram made it into the pool of irrelevance patterns; a single word seems not enough to be sure about irrelevance. As of length 2, however, we judged several patterns to be sufficiently reliable indicators of irrelevance, the most frequent ones occurring over 10,000 times in the corpus, namely, "first round" and "thank opponent".

5.2 Insights into Pattern Bootstrapping

As indicated in Section 3, we set τ to 0.95, kept all mined relevance patterns with at least 2000 matches as candidates and all mined irrelevance patterns with at least 200 matches. Given the seed patterns, we then ran the bootstrapping process until no new pattern was found anymore, which happened in iteration 6. On a standard computer (Intel Core i7, 2.7 GHz, 16 GB RAM), the whole process took about two hours.

Table 3 shows key statistics for each iteration (and the seed pattern selection). In case of the *relevance*

Iteration	Relevance Patterns			Irrelevance Patterns			
	Patterns	Matches	Auto. Prec.	Patterns	Matches	Auto. Prec.	Man. Prec.
Seed	38	600 469	1.00	17	41 619	0.97	1.00 (0.99)
1	10	7 602	0.99	74	5 849	0.98	1.00 (0.96)
2	0	−57	n/a	19	3 606	0.98	1.00 (0.94)
3	0	−15	n/a	4	956	0.97	0.96 (0.93)
4	0	−10	n/a	3	594	0.98	0.97 (0.93)
5	0	−6	n/a	5	225	0.98	0.88 (0.79)
Total	48	607 983	0.98	122	52 849	0.98	0.97 (0.92)

Table 3: Counts of relevance and irrelevance patterns, counts of different sentences they match, their automatically estimated mean precision, and their manually evaluated mean precision (majority agreement, full agreement in parentheses) in each iteration of our approach. The last row shows the results at the end.

patterns, the 38 seed patterns already match more than 600k *different* sentences, with a mean estimated precision of 1.00, i.e., they virtually never matched any sentence retrieved for the seed irrelevance patterns. Already in iteration 2, the revision effect discussed in Section 3 starts: 57 relevant sentences were removed there, because they also matched newly mined irrelevance patterns. Still, the set of relevance patterns remained stable, and this behavior continued in subsequent iterations. For the *irrelevance patterns*, we observe a monotonous growth of the pattern pool in the first five iterations, with more than 10k different sentences being detected as irrelevant in iterations 1–5 in addition to the seed sentences. In total, 122 patterns were found; their mean estimated precision remained at least 0.97 in all iterations.

To analyze the behavior of our approach during the bootstrapping process, we chose a random sample of 600 irrelevant sentences for manual evaluation (found in the supplementary material): 100 matching the seed irrelevance patterns, and 100 each for the irrelevance patterns from the five iterations. Relevant patterns were disregarded, as they are not needed for corpus cleansing. We randomized the ordering of all sentences and gave them independently to three annotators with background on computational argumentation, none being an author of this paper (one master and two PhD students; two male, one female; one each from Europe, the Middle East, and East Asia). We asked the annotators to classify each sentence as relevant or irrelevant, based on the definition from Section 3. The annotators got some intuitive guidelines (see supplementary material) and could ask questions beforehand.

We observed an inter-annotator agreement of 0.50 in terms of Fleiss' κ, which seems reasonable given that relevance assessment is inherently subjective (Croft et al., 2009). Given the annotations, we computed the mean precision of our approach in detecting irrelevant sentences for each iteration, once in terms of majority agreement (irrelevance correct if two annotators say so) and once for full agreement (all three say so). The right-most column in Table 3 shows the results, revealing that the majority-agreement precision is perfect until the end of iteration 2. While the next two iterations remain promising, the precision decreases to 0.88 in the final iteration (0.79 under full agreement), suggesting that patterns get worse over time. An early termination may thus be favorable, but the best moment is naturally unknown in practice.

52,849 different sentences are matched by the detected irrelevance patterns eventually, at an overall precision of 0.97. Some of them occur multiple times, resulting in 86,916 irrelevant sentences in total that come from 68,814 arguments. Under the roughly estimated irrelevance proportion from Section 4, the recall would hence be around 0.15 for irrelevant sentences and around 0.46 for arguments with irrelevance sentences. The seed step alone found 71,926 irrelevant sentences in total, i.e., a recall of roughly 0.12. If we consider the seed step as a baseline for the full approach, we see that precision decreases by 3% (1.00 to 0.97), but recall increases by about 20% (0.12 to 0.15). While there is arguably room for optimization, we still conclude that the results support the impact of our approach and, by that, our hypothesis.

5.3 Insights into Corpus Cleansing

Based on the final pool of 122 irrelevance patterns, we explored the cleansing potential for the given corpus. Figure 3(a) shows a histogram of the corpus texts with a certain number of detected irrelevant sentences. We see that most texts contain one such sentence only, in all but six cases seven or less. These

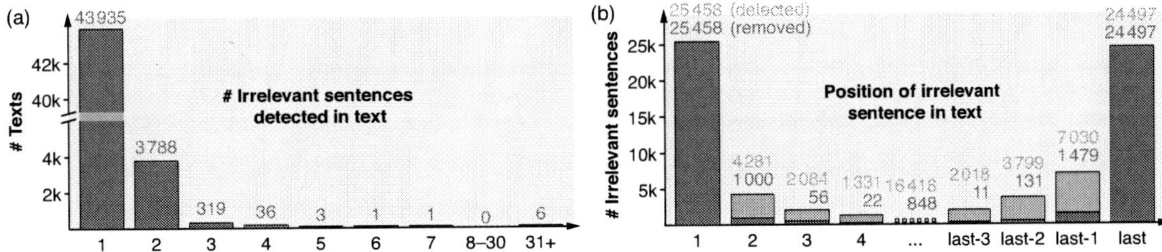

Figure 3: (a) Histograms of the number of texts in the args.me corpus with a certain a number of irrelevant sentences, as detected by our approach. (b) Histogram of the number of detected (upper number) and removed (lower number) irrelevant sentences over the different sentence positions of a text.

six cases all have more than 30 irrelevant sentences; manual inspection revealed that they all contain spam where the same word sequence repeats itself. In Figure 3(b), we plot the positions of irrelevant sentences in the corpus texts. As expected, most of them are found in the beginning or the end. Due to our discussed restriction of discarding only these, the final number of sentences removed from the args.me corpus sums up to 53,502 (found in 48,089 arguments). In addition to the original args.me corpus, we now also provide the cleaned corpus version at `https://webis.de/data.html#args-me-corpus`.

6   Conclusion

Web-based argument corpora play an important role in computational argumentation research and its applications. Not all text in such corpora is relevant to the arguments, though. In this paper, we have presented an approach that detects irrelevant text units in argumentative texts with low supervision. The approach iteratively bootstraps linguistic patterns of irrelevance and relevance from units matching known patterns. On the 387k arguments in the args.me corpus, the approach detected 87k irrelevant sentences at a precision of 0.97, from which at least 53k can be removed without notably reducing the arguments' coherence. These results demonstrate the potential of our approach to improve corpus quality.

Naturally, the approach has limitations. On one hand, the results revealed that, under the employed configuration, a large proportion of detected sentences came from the seed patterns. To obtain good seed patterns, manual effort is needed. On the other hand, the recall of our approach seems not so high, as far as we can estimate from the data inspected. While not all irrelevant units can be captured by the simple patterns we considered, another reason may lie in the restriction that only new candidate patterns are found which occur in sentences matching previous patterns. Particularly patterns that show up only in short units may thus be overlooked, if they are not covered by the seed patterns already. Improvements might, e.g., consider units adjacent to irrelevant units, but this may come at the cost of reduced precision. In this regard, notice that the impact our approach to some extent depends on the availability of a reliable unit boundary detector (say, a sentence splitter), which is not a trivial requirement for noisy web data.

Finally, an arising question may be how complex it is to apply the approach to other than the data processed here. Following our proposed process to obtain frequent candidate seed patterns automatically, the main manual effort boils down to finding reliable seed patterns among these candidates. In our case, this took no more than a few hours, which seems negligible given the potential impact on corpus quality. Besides, only some initial tuning of the approach parameters to the data at hand may be needed. We are thus confident that the approach can be easily adopted to clean other argument corpora (including transcribed corpora with spoken argumentative language) as well as to many other cleansing tasks where the irrelevance of text units can be defined in a measurable way.

Acknowledgments

We thank Milad Alshomary, Wei-Fan Chen, and Jana Puschmann for their participation in the manual evaluation, and the anonymous reviewers for their helpful comments. Thank you also to Johannes Kiesel as part of the Webis Group for the technical support and the integration of the results into args.me.

References

Eugene Agichtein and Luis Gravano. 2000. Snowball: Extracting relations from large plain-text collections. In *Proceedings of the Fifth ACM Conference on Digital Libraries*, DL '00, pages 85–94, New York, NY, USA. Association for Computing Machinery.

Ehud Aharoni, Anatoly Polnarov, Tamar Lavee, Daniel Hershcovich, Ran Levy, Ruty Rinott, Dan Gutfreund, and Noam Slonim. 2014. A benchmark dataset for automatic detection of claims and evidence in the context of controversial topics. In *Proceedings of the First Workshop on Argumentation Mining*, pages 64–68, Baltimore, Maryland, June. Association for Computational Linguistics.

Yamen Ajjour, Wei-Fan Chen, Johannes Kiesel, Henning Wachsmuth, and Benno Stein. 2017. Unit segmentation of argumentative texts. In *Proceedings of the 4th Workshop on Argument Mining*, pages 118–128. Association for Computational Linguistics.

Yamen Ajjour, Henning Wachsmuth, Johannes Kiesel, Martin Potthast, Matthias Hagen, and Benno Stein. 2019. Data acquisition for argument search: The args.me corpus. In *KI 2019: Advances in Artificial Intelligence - 42nd German Conference on AI, Kassel, Germany, September 23-26, 2019, Proceedings*, pages 48–59.

Khalid Al-Khatib, Henning Wachsmuth, Matthias Hagen, Jonas Köhler, and Benno Stein. 2016. Cross-domain mining of argumentative text through distant supervision. In *Proceedings of the 2016 Conference of the North American Chapter of the Association for Computational Linguistics: Human Language Technologies*, pages 1395–1404. Association for Computational Linguistics.

Milad Alshomary, Nick Düsterhus, and Henning Wachsmuth. 2020. Extractive snippet generation for arguments. In *43nd International ACM Conference on Research and Development in Information Retrieval*, SIGIR '20, pages 1969–1972, New York, NY, USA. Association for Computing Machinery.

Sergey Brin. 1998. Extracting patterns and relations from the world wide web. In *Selected Papers from the International Workshop on The World Wide Web and Databases*, WebDB '98, pages 172–183, Berlin, Heidelberg. Springer-Verlag.

Elena Cabrio and Serena Villata. 2012. Combining textual entailment and argumentation theory for supporting online debates interactions. In *Proceedings of the 50th Annual Meeting of the Association for Computational Linguistics (Volume 2: Short Papers)*, pages 208–212. Association for Computational Linguistics.

Bruce Croft, Donald Metzler, and Trevor Strohman. 2009. *Search Engines: Information Retrieval in Practice*. Addison-Wesley, USA, 1st edition.

Esin Durmus and Claire Cardie. 2019. A corpus for modeling user and language effects in argumentation on online debating. In *Proceedings of the 57th Annual Meeting of the Association for Computational Linguistics*, pages 602–607, Florence, Italy, July. Association for Computational Linguistics.

Ryo Egawa, Gaku Morio, and Katsuhide Fujita. 2020. Corpus for modeling user interactions in online persuasive discussions. In *Proceedings of The 12th Language Resources and Evaluation Conference*, pages 1135–1141, Marseille, France, May. European Language Resources Association.

Shai Gretz, Roni Friedman, Edo Cohen-Karlik, Assaf Toledo, Dan Lahav, Ranit Aharonov, and Noam Slonim. 2020. A large-scale dataset for argument quality ranking: Construction and analysis. In *Proceedings of the Thirty-Fourth AAAI Conference on Artificial Intelligence*, pages 7805–7813. AAAI.

Ivan Habernal and Iryna Gurevych. 2016. Which argument is more convincing? Analyzing and predicting convincingness of web arguments using bidirectional lstm. In *Proceedings of the 54th Annual Meeting of the Association for Computational Linguistics (Volume 1: Long Papers)*, pages 1589–1599. Association for Computational Linguistics.

Ivan Habernal and Iryna Gurevych. 2017. Argumentation mining in user-generated web discourse. *Computational Linguistics*, 43(1):125–179, April.

John Lawrence and Chris Reed. 2017. Using complex argumentative interactions to reconstruct the argumentative structure of large-scale debates. In *Proceedings of the 4th Workshop on Argument Mining*, pages 108–117, Copenhagen, Denmark, September. Association for Computational Linguistics.

Patrick Pantel and Marco Pennacchiotti. 2006. Espresso: Leveraging generic patterns for automatically harvesting semantic relations. In *Proceedings of the 21st International Conference on Computational Linguistics and 44th Annual Meeting of the Association for Computational Linguistics*, pages 113–120, Sydney, Australia, July. Association for Computational Linguistics.

Andreas Peldszus and Manfred Stede. 2015. Joint prediction in MST-style discourse parsing for argumentation mining. In *Proceedings of the 2015 Conference on Empirical Methods in Natural Language Processing*, pages 938–948, Lisbon, Portugal, September. Association for Computational Linguistics.

Christian Stab and Iryna Gurevych. 2014. Annotating argument components and relations in persuasive essays. In *Proceedings of COLING 2014, the 25th International Conference on Computational Linguistics: Technical Papers*, pages 1501–1510. Dublin City University and Association for Computational Linguistics.

Assaf Toledo, Shai Gretz, Edo Cohen-Karlik, Roni Friedman, Elad Venezian, Dan Lahav, Michal Jacovi, Ranit Aharonov, and Noam Slonim. 2019. Automatic argument quality assessment - New datasets and methods. In *Proceedings of the 2019 Conference on Empirical Methods in Natural Language Processing and the 9th International Joint Conference on Natural Language Processing (EMNLP-IJCNLP)*, pages 5625–5635. Association for Computational Linguistics.

Hans Uszkoreit, Aleksandra Gabryszak, Leonhard Hennig, Jörg Steffen, Renlong Ai, Stephan Busemann, Jon Dehdari, Josef van Genabith, Georg Heigold, Nils Rethmeier, Raphael Rubino, Sven Schmeier, Philippe Thomas, He Wang, and Feiyu Xu. 2017. Common round: Application of language technologies to large-scale web debates. In *Proceedings of the Software Demonstrations of the 15th Conference of the European Chapter of the Association for Computational Linguistics*, pages 5–8, Valencia, Spain, April. Association for Computational Linguistics.

Henning Wachsmuth, Nona Naderi, Yufang Hou, Yonatan Bilu, Vinodkumar Prabhakaran, Tim Alberdingk Thijm, Graeme Hirst, and Benno Stein. 2017a. Computational argumentation quality assessment in natural language. In *Proceedings of the 15th Conference of the European Chapter of the Association for Computational Linguistics: Volume 1, Long Papers*, pages 176–187. Association for Computational Linguistics.

Henning Wachsmuth, Martin Potthast, Khalid Al-Khatib, Yamen Ajjour, Jana Puschmann, Jiani Qu, Jonas Dorsch, Viorel Morari, Janek Bevendorff, and Benno Stein. 2017b. Building an argument search engine for the web. In *Proceedings of the 4th Workshop on Argument Mining*, pages 49–59. Association for Computational Linguistics.

Marilyn Walker, Jean Fox Tree, Pranav Anand, Rob Abbott, and Joseph King. 2012. A corpus for research on deliberation and debate. In *Proceedings of the Eighth International Conference on Language Resources and Evaluation (LREC'12)*, pages 812–817, Istanbul, Turkey, May. European Language Resources Association (ELRA).

Exploring Morality in Argumentation

Jonathan Kobbe, Ines Rehbein, Ioana Hulpuș, Heiner Stuckenschmidt
University of Mannheim
`{jonathan,ines,ioana,heiner}@informatik.uni-mannheim.de`

Abstract

Sentiment and stance are two important concepts for the analysis of arguments. We propose to add another perspective to the analysis, namely *moral sentiment*. We argue that moral values are crucial for ideological debates and can thus add useful information for argument mining. In the paper, we present different models for automatically predicting moral sentiment in debates and evaluate them on a manually annotated test set. We then apply our models to investigate how moral values in arguments relate to argument quality, stance, and audience reactions.

1 Introduction

Argumentation mining is a new research field that is closely related to the subfields of stance detection and sentiment analysis (Stede, 2020), since "every argument carries a stance towards its topic, often expressed with sentiment".[1] In addition to stance and sentiment, there is another dimension that can play an important role in debates, namely *moral beliefs*. A debater's moral beliefs go beyond stance and can be expressed with varying sentiment. They play an important role in ideological debates and cannot be resolved by simply comparing facts but often involve a battle of ideas and a clash of different belief systems. Consider the following arguments on whether or not gay marriage should be legal.[2]

(1) The institution of marriage has traditionally been defined as being between a man and a woman.

(2) Denying some people the option to marry is discriminatory and creates a second class of citizens.

Both arguments are based on moral belief systems. The first argument refers to moral values that promote respect for tradition, while the second focuses on fairness and equal rights. Arguments that express an opposite stance towards the topic usually differ concerning their moral framing. On the other hand, we observe that arguments expressing a similar stance towards a certain topic may still differ with regard to how the argument is framed, as illustrated in example (3) and (4) below. While (3) opposes the legalization of prostitution because it is considered as a harmful form of oppression targeting women, example (4) depicts prostitution as increasing the danger of diseases and contamination. This makes moral framing an interesting ingredient for argument mining.

(3) Prostitution and human trafficking are forms of gender-based violence.

(4) Prostitution is the biggest vector of sexually transmitted diseases.

In the paper, we argue that identifying moral values in debates has the potential to support argument analysis and to help with different subtasks related to argument mining. Being able to distinguish between arguments with similar stance and sentiment but framed according to different moral categories can help to identify new arguments and can improve camp detection, thus supporting more fine-grained modeling of debaters beyond stance. Furthermore, moral framing is of particular interest for the analysis of political debates (Lakoff, 1997; Roggeband and Vliegenthart, 2007).

---

[1]Cited from the workshop website (`https://argmining2020.i3s.unice.fr/`).

[2]From `https://gaymarriage.procon.org` (accessed August 25, 2020).

Proceedings of the 7th Workshop on Argument Mining, pages 30–40
Barcelona, Spain (Online), December 13, 2020.

In practice, however, predicting moral sentiment from text poses several challenges. First, morality is a fuzzy concept, and it is difficult to find an operationalization that turns it into measurable data. Moral sentiment is often expressed implicitly and thus hard to detect, based merely on the presence of lexical cues. In addition, human coders might be biased by their own belief systems, which casts doubt on the validity of the annotations used to train or evaluate automatic systems.

In the paper, we present work in progress where we evaluate different models for the prediction of moral framing in text on two datasets and assess the benefits of these predictions for the analysis of arguments. Based on three datasets with argumentative text, we investigate whether we can find correlations between moral values and different aspects of argumentation, such as argument quality, stance, or audience approval. We are interested in the following research questions:

RQ1: Do debaters that produce high-quality arguments make more or less frequent use of moral framing?
RQ2: Is moral framing more strongly related to a positive or negative stance?
RQ3: Can we find a positive correlation between the audiences' approval and the use of moral frames?

Our main contributions are the following: (i) We augment the ArgQuality Corpus of Wachsmuth et al. (2017) with annotations for moral values, as a first test set for the evaluation of moral sentiment in argumentation; (ii) We evaluate two methods for the prediction of moral sentiment on the new dataset; (iii) We present a correlation study investigating the relation between moral framing and argument quality, stance, and audience reactions.

The paper is structured as follows. We first review work on quantifying moral sentiment in text (§2). In §3, we describe the annotation of our test set and present different approaches to the automatic detection of moral sentiment in debates. Then we discuss our correlation analysis (§4), and in §6 we summarise our results and conclude.

2   Related Work

As an operationalisation for the concept of moral sentiment, we refer to Moral Foundations Theory (MFT) (Haidt and Joseph, 2004; Graham et al., 2013). MFT has its roots in social and cultural psychology and assumes the existence of innate and universally available psychological systems that build the foundations of intuitive ethics. These foundations are augmented by culture-specific constructs of virtues and backed up by personal narratives "that people construct to make sense of their values and beliefs" (Graham et al., 2013)[p.17], and are also reinforced by institutional environments. MFT assumes that all moral issues can be described along the following dimensions: *Care-Harm, Fairness-Cheating, Loyalty-Betrayal, Authority-Subversion,* and *Purity-Degradation.*[3]

Dictionary-based approaches to MFT   The first version of the Moral Foundations Dictionary (MFD) was presented by Graham et al. (2009) and has been used for a content analysis of christian sermons held in liberal and conservative congregations. Each of the five moral foundations listed above has been further split into a *vice* and a *virtue* subcategory, reflecting the positive and negative ends of each dimension. Examples are *peace*, protect*, compassion** for $Care_{virtue}$ and *suffer*, crush*, killer** for $Care_{vice}$. The MFD includes, on average, 32 words per moral subcategory. Frimer et al. (2019) presents a new version of the MFD with more entries per MF subcategory, selected according to prototypicality estimates for each MF, based on cosine similarity for Word2Vec embeddings for each item in the dictionary. While the authors admit that the construct validity of the MFD 2.0 is not better than for the original MFD, they recommend the use of the MFD 2.0 due to its improved coverage. Other work on expanding the MFD includes Rezapour et al. (2019) who increase the original size of the dictionary to over 4,600 lexical items, using a quality controlled, human in the loop process.[4]

The MF dictionary has been used in several studies in the political and social sciences, psychology, and related fields (Takikawa and Sakamoto, 2017; Matsuo et al., 2018; Lewis, 2019). Dictionary-based approaches to measuring moral values in text, however, have severe shortcomings. They can neither

---

[3]Another foundation currently under discussion is *Liberty-Opression.*

[4]Arguably, a comparison of size is not meaningful, given that the original MFD includes regular expressions that can match an unknown number of instance types while the expanded lexicon includes word forms for unigrams and word compounds.

	Care	Fairness	Loyalty	Authority	Purity	Moral
Cohen's κ	.469	.407	.529	.363	.280	.434
Krippendorff's α	.459	.400	.530	.356	.255	.402
Absolute Agreement (positive/negative)	60/187	16/267	10/294	12/274	13/257	165/68
Absolute Disagreement	73	37	16	34	50	87

Table 1: Inter-Annotator Agreement for the five MFs and for a binary label (*Moral*: yes/no).

account for unknown words or the different meanings a word can take, nor do they consider that shifter words and negation can change the polarity of an expression. In addition, we expect that moral vocabulary might vary considerably, depending on the speaker's age and other geopolitical, social, and cultural variables. Garten et al. (2016) address the coverage problem of dictionary-based approaches by replacing the terms in the MF dictionary with their averaged vector representations in distributional space. They show that predicting moral foundations based on the cosine similarity of the words in a text to the distributional representations outperforms a naive method that predicts MF based on word counts.

Machine learning-based approaches   Recent work has applied the framework of MFT to research questions in the social and political sciences (Fulgoni et al., 2016; Johnson and Goldwasser, 2018; Reza-pour et al., 2019; Xie et al., 2019), replacing dictionary-based counts with more sophisticated methods. Johnson and Goldwasser (2018) model moral framing in politicians' tweets, using probabilistic soft logic (Bach et al., 2013). Lin et al. (2018) improve the prediction of moral foundations by acquiring additional background knowledge from Wikipedia, using information extraction techniques such as entity linking and cross-document knowledge propagation. Xie et al. (2019) study the change of moral sentiment in longitudinal data, presenting a parameter-free model that predicts moral sentiment on three different levels: (i) moral relevance, (ii) moral polarity, and (iii) the ten moral subclasses of the MFD encoding the virtue/vice dimension for each MF. Finally, Resapour et al. (2019) show that using dictionary counts for moral sentiment as features in a supervised classification setup can increase results for stance detection.

3   Predicting Moral Sentiment in Tweets and Debates

3.1   A New Test Set for Moral Framing in Argumentation

As a test set for evaluating moral framing in English argumentative text, we use the Dagstuhl ArgQuality Corpus (Wachsmuth et al., 2017). The dataset contains 320 arguments with approx. 22,600 tokens, covering 16 topics, and is balanced for stance. The data was extracted from two online debate platforms by Habernal and Gurevych (2016).[5] Each instance has been annotated by three coders, using a fine-grained scheme to assess the arguments' quality. The data also provides a majority score for each dimension of argument quality (Wachsmuth et al., 2017). The authors report a low agreement for the individual annotations (.51 Krippendorff's α) but a high majority agreement (94%).

We further augment the ArgQuality corpus with annotations for moral foundations, manually coded by two of the authors.[6] We chose not to annotate the 10 subclasses encoded in the dictionary but considered the two ends of each dimension (virtue/vice) as one category. The motivation behind this decision is that both are closely related, and it is often unclear which end of the dimension is addressed, particularly for negated sentences. E.g., "I could never hurt you" could either be considered as an instance of Harm as it uses vocabulary related to this dimension or could be annotated as the opposite, Care, as it talks about *not* being able to harm somebody, thus being more strongly related to the *virtue* class.

Table 1 shows inter-annotator agreement (IAA) scores for individual MFs on the ArgQuality dataset. As expected, IAA is low, being roughly in the same range as agreement scores reported for the annotation of emotions (Schuff et al., 2017; Wood et al., 2018), thus giving evidence for the subjectivity of the task. Our IAA is not directly comparable to Hoover et al. (2020) as they report Fleiss' κ for the 10 fine-grained subclasses, with an avg. of .315 κ over all 10 classes.

---

[5] www.createdebate.com and convinceme.net.

[6] All resources created for this paper are available at https://github.com/dwslab/Morality-in-Arguments

3.2 Methods for the Prediction of Moral Sentiment

We model moral sentiment prediction as a text classification task and propose two distinct methods for feature generation. The first method is based on a *sense-disambiguated* version of the MFD and extends its coverage by exploiting relations in Wordnet (WN) (Fellbaum, 2010). The second method uses the MFD as seed data to learn BERT sequence embeddings that encode moral sentiment. The representations created by each method are fixed-sized vectors that can easily be combined by concatenation.

I. Sense-disambiguated features (WN-PPR) The MFD has two main disadvantages that we try to overcome with this method. First, the lexicon contains many words with different word senses, where the moral value only applies to one specific sense. Thus, we link the dictionary entries to their corresponding WN synsets. This way, *fair* is only considered to be related to the MF *fairness-cheating* if used as synonym to *just* or *honest*, but not if used as synonym to *carnival, funfair* or *attractively feminine*. Also, this way we overcome the problems resulting from the use of regular expressions in the MFD (e.g., *defenestration* would belong to the MF *Care* because of the entry *defen**, and *Churchill* would trigger *Purity* because of the entry *church**). The second disadvantage of the MFD is its low coverage, which we extend by running Personalized Pagerank (Haveliwala, 2003) on the set of WN synsets that have been linked to dictionary entries.

    a) Linking MFD entries to WN To create a word sense disambiguated version of the MFD, one expert annotator was presented with the following information: a specific moral foundation; a WN synset whereof at least one word in the synset is part of the respective MF in the MFD; and its definition. With this information, the annotator decided whether the synset is relevant for the moral foundation in question or not. Overall, the resulting lexicon contains, on average, 61 synsets per MF.

    b) Extending the disambiguated Lexicon We extend the disambiguated lexicon by exploiting relations between synsets in WN, such as *hypernym* or *similar to*. Concretely, we run personalized pagerank on the graph consisting of the WN synsets and the relations between them for every MF, using the corresponding lexicon entries as seed nodes. This way, each WN synset is assigned a fixed-sized vector containing scores for each MF, including the category *GeneralMorality*.[7] We expect that higher scores reflect a stronger correspondence between the synset and the respective MF.

    c) Extracting features from text Given a short English text, we first extract WN 3.0 synsets using the disambiguation method by Tan (2014). Then we link these synsets to WN 3.1, using the official Wordnet Search Engine[8] and, if necessary, resolving the final mapping manually. For instance, a variety of offensive terms have been removed in WN 3.1, and thus, we had to link terms like *darky* or *tom* to *black (noun.person)* manually.[9] As each of the synsets is assigned a fixed-size score vector in our lexicon, any function to aggregate these vectors is conceivable. To obtain vectors that do not depend on the input text's length, we decided to take their mean. The result is a vector consisting of 6 entries, where each entry represents a MF, including *GeneralMorality*.

II. Contextualized MF sequence embeddings (SBERT-Wiki) Our second method uses Sentence-BERT (SBERT) (Reimers and Gurevych, 2019) to obtain text representations that encode moral sentiment. SBERT is a modification of the original transformer model, based on siamese networks. The modified SBERT encodes sentence similarity in a human interpretable way where similar sentence pairs can be retrieved efficiently, based on cosine similarity. While previous work has computed BERT-based embeddings for text sequences (i) by averaging (or summing) over all word embeddings for this particular text or (ii) by using the network output at the position of the [CLS] token, Reimers and Gurevych (2019) show that those representations are not well suited to encode sentence similarity and often yield inferior results as compared to using averaged Glove embeddings (Pennington et al., 2014).

---

[7] *GeneralMorality* includes terms related to moral concepts that do not fit into one of the five MFs (e.g. *ethic, good, evil*).

[8] `http://wordnet-rdf.princeton.edu/json/pwn30/...`

[9] We are aware that this treatment is not optimal. A better solution would link those terms to a synset that captures their offensive usage, similar to the one for *Kraut: offensive term for a person of German descent.*

SBERT can also be applied to tasks where an anchor text is compared to a positive and a negative text sample, thus learning to maximize a score based on the similarity of the anchor text to the first sentence (the positive sample) and its distance to the second text (the negative sample). For that, SBERT uses the triplet objective function (equation 1) where d is a distance metric (here: Euclidean distance), and the margin is set to 1.

$$L = max(d(s_{anchor} - s_{pos}) - d(s_{anchor} - s_{neg}) + margin, 0) \tag{1}$$

We fine-tune SBERT embeddings so that they encode different moral foundations. First, we download all short Wikipedia abstracts from DBpedia[10] and label them with their corresponding MF (if any), using weak supervision. Our approach is based on the MFD and proceeds as follows: For each dictionary entry, we search in Wikipedia for corresponding articles to get a set of candidates consisting of articles whose title is a lexicon entry (including redirections) and articles that are linked by the lexical entry's disambiguation page. From these candidates, we manually select the ones related to the MF and label their abstracts accordingly.

This approach yields 317 short abstracts from Wikipedia, labeled with moral foundations, extracted from a pool of 4,935,596 unlabelled short Wikipedia abstracts. We iterate over each abstract in the annotated dataset, considering the abstract as the anchor text. First, we retrieve all other abstracts labeled with the same moral foundation as the anchor and create pairs of (anchor, positive sample). Then, for each pair, we randomly select 3 labeled abstracts that belong to a different moral foundation as well as 7 abstracts from the unlabelled pool as negative samples, assuming that the unlabelled abstracts also do, more often than not, either belong to a different moral foundation or do not express any moral content. This gives us a total of 10 negative samples for each pair and results in a weakly supervised dataset with 107,940 instances. We then fine-tune the model on the data, using the same settings as reported in Reimers and Gurevych (2019). After the training is completed, we use the learned model to retrieve representations for new text sequences from different argumentation datasets, expecting that the fine-tuned embeddings will now capture some aspects of moral sentiment. We compare our approach with the pretrained SBERT embeddings (bert-base-nli-stsb-mean-tokens) of Reimers and Gurevych (2019), trained without the fine-tuning step on the weakly supervised Wikipedia abstracts.

3.3 State of the Art and Baselines

multi-label BERT   To compare our lexicon-based methods with a state-of-the-art approach to text classification, we train a multi-label text classifier based on BERT. We use a publicly available implementation in pytorch[11] that replaces the cross-entropy loss with a binary cross-entropy with logits to adapt the BERT sequence classifier to the multi-label setup.

The model includes an input embedding layer for the pretrained BERT embeddings, the BERT encoder with 12 attention layers, and, as final layer, a linear transformation, with one dimension for each class. This gives us six output dimensions: the five moral foundations + one class for tweets with non-moral content. Our model uses the pretrained English uncased BERT base embeddings with a vocabulary size of around 30,000. We use the same data splits and preprocessing in all experiments (for details, see §3.4). In contrast to our other models, however, BERT further segments the input text into subword tokens (WordPiece tokenization), which might increase coverage for words not seen in the training data.

Random baseline   The *Random* baseline assigns labels randomly but respecting the class distribution in the training data. Results are averaged over 100 trials.

MFD baseline   Given a text, we compute frequency counts for each MF, based on the entries in the MFD, and normalize by text length. We use these count-based vectors as features for the text classifier. Similar to WN-PPR, we derive one feature per MF, including general morality.

---

[10] https://wiki.dbpedia.org/downloads-2016-10

[11] The code was adapted from https://medium.com/huggingface/multi-label-text-classification-using-bert-the-mighty-transformer-69714fa3fb3d and is based on the HuggingFace library (https://github.com/huggingface/pytorch-pretrained-BERT).

Method	Moral	Care	Fairness	Loyalty	Authority	Purity	Average (excl. Moral)
Random baseline	.519	.173	.169	.100	.099	.055	.119
MFD baseline	.630	.332	.213	.166	.231	.141	.217
multi-label BERT	.669	**.510**	**.573**	**.437**	**.377**	**.363**	**.452**
WN-PPR	.628	.334	.379	.311	.210	.088	.264
SBERT-Base	.685	.434	.511	.372	.327	.214	.372
SBERT-Wiki	**.697**	.463	.516	.377	.341	.220	.383
WN-PPR + SBERT-Wiki	.689	.446	.520	.387	.346	.230	.386

Table 2: Binary F1-scores on the MFTC for individual MFs (F1 for the positive class). The last column shows the average over the F1 scores for the five MFs (excluding *Moral*).

Method	Moral	Care	Fairness	Loyalty	Authority	Purity	Average (excl. Moral)
Random baseline	.658	.257	.179	.096	.134	.105	.154
MFD baseline	**.853**	.056	.237	.043	.200	.086	.124
multi-label BERT	.444	**.517**	**.519**	**.138**	.157	.208	**.308**
WN-PPR	.756	.118	.253	.049	.105	.029	.111
SBERT-Base	.703	.280	.342	.065	.148	.133	.194
SBERT-Wiki	.730	.339	.246	.125	**.233**	**.318**	.252
WN-PPR + SBERT-Wiki	.686	.298	.351	.067	.040	.135	.178

Table 3: Binary F1-scores on the Dagstuhl ArgQuality Corpus for individual MFs (F1 for the pos. class).

3.4 Data

We now present the data used for the evaluation of the methods described above (§3.2) for the prediction of moral sentiment in tweets and debates. As training data for our MF classifiers, we use the Moral Foundations Twitter Corpus (Hoover et al., 2020), a collection of approximately 35,000 tweets covering seven controversial topical threads: All Lives Matter, Black Lives Matter, the Baltimore protests, the 2016 Presidential election, hate speech & offensive language (Davidson et al., 2017), Hurricane Sandy, and #MeToo. Each tweet has been annotated with MF by at least three trained annotators. The authors report Fleiss' κ and PABAK, a measure adjusted for prevalence and bias (Sim and Wright, 2005). IAA is relatively low (with a Fleiss κ in the range of 0.24 - 0.46 and PABAK ranging from 0.65 - 0.85) and shows considerable variation across the different moral domains and threads.

We follow the procedure described in Hoover et al. (2020) to create a gold standard from the annotated tweets and consider a label as *gold* if it was assigned by at least half of the annotators. Thus, our gold standard includes 6 labels: one for each MF and a sixth one for GeneralMorality. Note that in the MFTC, this label is called *Non-moral* while we report results for its inverse, which we call *Moral*. We normalized the tweets using the script available from the Glove website.[12] We noticed that the dataset includes many near-duplicates (e.g., 96 instances of *homosexuality is a sin*). To ensure that these near-duplicates do not appear in both training *and* test set, we split the data into the different threads and present results for a seven-fold cross-validation where we train the models on six threads and evaluate on the remaining one. We also evaluate the models trained on the MFTC on out-of-domain data from the ArgQuality Corpus, where we consider all labels assigned by each of the two annotators as ground truth.[13]

3.5 Results for MF Prediction on Tweets and Debates

We conduct experiments on the Twitter corpus, testing different traditional classification methods, and report results for the best performing classifiers only. For WN-PPR and MFD-Features, this was a k-nearest-neighbors classifier, and for SBERT-Base, SBERT-Wiki, as well as for WN-PPR + SBERT-Wiki a Linear Discriminant Analysis.[14] All other results, as well as the correlations reported in §4, refer to these classification methods.

Table 2 shows results on the MFTC for our different methods. Not surprisingly, multi-label BERT outperforms all other methods on the Twitter data. However, our lexicon-based methods outperform the random baseline for each category, with the best results obtained by the concatenation of SBERT-Wiki

---

[12] https://nlp.stanford.edu/projects/glove/preprocess-twitter.rb

[13] As the data has been annotated by two of the authors, we can be sure that we do not have to eliminate spammers.

[14] We use the scikit-learn implementation for these methods. Other methods we tried include Logistic Regression, Decision Trees, Naïve Bayes, Support Vector Machines.

with WN-PPR. WN-PPR on its own only yields poor results, barely outperforming the constant and the MFD baseline.

When applying the classifiers to the out-of-domain data from the ArgQuality corpus (Table 3), multilabel-BERT still yields best results, but now SBERT-Wiki outperforms BERT on the *Authority, Purity* and *Moral* categories. The lower performance for the *Moral* class can be explained by the differences in class distribution between the two datasets. In the MFTC, this class makes up for approximately 57% of the training instances, while the amount of moral instances in the debate corpus is much higher (79%). The lexicon-based methods are not sensitive to the class distribution in the training data, which, in this case, makes them more robust. Still, all systems fail to beat the majority baseline for the Moral class which has a binary F1-score of 0.881.[15] WN-PPR again performs poorly with results below the Random baseline, and results for the MFD baseline also fail to outperform Random. This time, results for the concatenation of WN-PPR and BERT-Wiki are considerably worse than for BERT-Wiki alone.

4 Correlation Studies

To study the impact of moral framing in argumentation, we investigate the correlation between moral sentiment and other properties of argumentative text, namely argument quality, stance, and audience reactions. For this, we use the multilabel-BERT model that yielded the best results on both datasets.

4.1 Data

The **Dagstuhl ArgQuality Corpus** contains arguments that are annotated with different dimensions of argument quality, such as *cogency* and *credibility*, as well as a score for *overall quality*. Some of the dimensions are also interesting for contexts other than argument quality, such as *clarity* and *emotional appeal*.

The **IBM Argument Quality Ranking Corpus** (Gretz et al., 2019) is used to triangulate our findings on the Dagstuhl ArgQuality Corpus and to investigate the correlation between moral sentiment and an argument's stance. The corpus contains more than 30,000 arguments on 71 topics, labelled for quality (*good* or *bad*) and stance (*pro* or *con*) by crowd annotators. To obtain ranks for argument quality, the authors apply two different strategies, which both give more weight to the answers of reliable annotators.

We use **CORPS** (Guerini et al., 2013) to investigate whether moral sentiment in political speeches has an impact on the audience. CORPS includes >3,600 political speeches held by more than 203 different speakers, tagged for audience reactions such as *applause, laughter* or *booing*. The motivation for creating the corpus was that such tags might highlight passages in the speech where an attempt has been made by the speaker to persuade the audience, either successful or not. We expect to find a correlation between text passages that triggered a positive audience reaction (i.e. *applause*) and moral framing, but not for *laughter* (we focus on these two tags as the other tags are relatively rare in comparison[16]). We also exclude mixed tags that mark two different reactions for the same text passage (*laughter; applause*). To test our hypothesis, we predict moral sentiment for the speech passages directly before an audience reaction was triggered. We consider up to 360 tokens of speech context and omit all speech passages where another tag occurs within this context.

4.2 Results for the Correlation Analysis

Table 4 shows Spearman correlations between argument quality, stance, and audience reactions and a) human annotations (HU) and b) labels predicted by multi-label BERT (BM). We observe a weak positive correlation between argument quality and moral sentiment for the two most frequent categories (*Moral, Care*) on the ArgQuality data. For the other MFs, there are no significant effects. On the IBM-AQR Corpus, we see a consistent and significant positive correlation for *Care* and *Fairness*. However, the effect is very weak. For the subdimensions of argument quality, the correlations tend to be similar to the ones for overall quality and are highest for *emotional appeal*, which seems plausible. Concerning argument stance, we again find slightly positive correlations for *Care* and *Moral*. Results on the CORPS

---

[15]The majority baseline is not included in tables 2 and 3 because its binary F1-score is zero for all classes except *Moral*.

[16]Applause: 23,095; Laughter: 5,857; Booing: 532; Cheers: 80; Sustained applause: 61; Spontaneous demonstration: 16.

	Care		Fairness		Loyalty		Authority		Purity		Moral	
	HU	BM	HU	BM	HU	BM	HU	BM	HU	BM	HU	BM
Dagstuhl ArgQuality Corpus												
overall quality	**.25**	**.15**	.10	.08	.05	**.10**$^-$	-.09	.05$^+$	.03	.07$^-$	**.19**	.21
local acceptability	**.18**	.09	.00	-.04$^+$	.00	.04$^-$	**-.15**	-.01$^+$	-.03	.07$^-$	.03	.09
appropriateness	**.30**	**.17**	-.01	.03	-.02	.05$^-$	-.09	.00$^+$	.01	.02	**.19**	**.15**
arrangement	**.24**	**.16**	.08	.03	.03	.08$^-$	-.06	-.01$^+$	.04	.05	**.16**	**.17**
clarity	**.17**	**.17**	.02	.02	.05	**.12**$^-$	-.03	-.01$^+$	.03	.06	.09	**.21**$^-$
cogency	**.24**	**.16**	.05	.06	-.02	.03$^-$	-.10	.05$^+$	.01	.03$^-$	**.10**	**.18**
effectiveness	**.25**	**.17**	.09	.09	-.05	.07$^-$	-.10	-.02$^+$	.04	.04	**.21**	**.17**
global acceptability	**.23**	**.12**	.05	.05	-.01	.07$^-$	**-.12**	.02$^+$	.01	.04	**.12**	**.13**
global relevance	**.15**	.06	**.11**	.09	.02	.07$^-$	-.11	.00$^+$	.04	.05	**.12**	**.11**
global sufficiency	**.19**	.11	**.11**	.11	-.01	.06$^-$	-.04	-.03$^+$	.07	.05$^-$	**.19**	**.14**$^+$
reasonableness	**.23**	**.17**	.09	.08	.02	.08$^-$	-.11	.04	.06	.07$^-$	**.16**	**.18**
local relevance	**.18**	**.14**	.08	.03	.01	.01$^-$	-.10	.02$^+$	.02	-.02	**.12**	**.13**
credibility	**.22**	.07	.06	.02$^-$	.05	-.01	**-.13**	.01$^+$	-.01	.00$^-$	.09	.08
emotional appeal	**.32**	**.22**	**.16**	**.12**$^+$	**.14**	.02$^-$	-.01	.10$^+$	-.01	.02	**.31**	**.25**
sufficiency	**.25**	**.18**	.06	.09$^-$	.00	.04$^-$	-.10	.03$^+$	.07	.06$^-$	**.15**	**.19**$^+$
IBM-AQR												
quality (WA)		**.08**		**.06**		**.01**		.00		**-.02**		**.08**$^-$
quality (MACE-P)		**.08**		**.05**		.01		.00		-.01		**.07**$^-$
stance		**.07**		.01		**-.03**		**.01**		**-.03**$^+$		.04
CORPS												
applause		**.02**		**.04**		**.07**		**.05**		**.01**		**.10**
laughter		**-.07**		**-.05**		**-.05**		**-.03**		**-.02**		**-.11**

Table 4: Spearman ρ between human annotations (HU) and multi-label BERT predictions (BM), respectively, and quality, stance and audience reactions. Bold values are statistically significant ($p < 0.05$). $^+$/$^-$: The correlation to the SBERT-Wiki predictions was considerably higher / lower (by at least 0.05).

data are as expected: a positive correlation for *applause* and a negative one for *laughter*, but again the effect is very weak.

Correlation with topic   To control for topic effects, we computed the correlation between topic and argument quality and between topic and MF in the IBM-AQR. While we found no correlation between topic and argument quality, there was a weak correlation between some topics and specific MFs (see Table 5).

Topic	Moral Foundation	Spearman's ρ
The vow of celibacy should be abandoned	*Purity-Degradation*	.326
We should prohibit school prayer	*Purity-Degradation*	.298
We should ban targeted killing	*Care-Harm*	.237

Table 5: Topics with correlations to MFs greater than .2 according to multilabel-BERT predictions.

5   Discussion

A crucial issue for using moral values for argumentation analysis concerns the reliability of the (manual and automatic) annotations. Before we can reliably use moral values for the analysis of arguments, we need to ensure the quality of the annotations, as the low inter-annotator agreement for MF annotation casts doubt on the validity of the findings. While we expect that more extensive training and more detailed guidelines will increase IAA for human annotation at least slightly, we still think that due to the fuzziness of the concept of morality, high agreement scores are not very probable. Thus, we would like to propose a different approach to the annotation of moral foundations where we ground the annotations in lexical semantics. This approach has already been shown to improve IAA for a similarly difficult annotation task, namely the annotation of causal language (Dunietz et al., 2015). The authors created a lexical resource for terms that can trigger causality in text and instructed annotators to disambiguate instances of those terms in context, showing that their modularized, dictionary-based approach yields substantially increased IAA scores.

Inspired by their work, we propose to anchor MF annotations in lexical semantics, using an expanded version of the MFD as seed terms. The annotators will then be presented with instances of these terms and instructed to disambiguate them in context, and also to annotate a small, predefined set of semantic roles, such as *Betrayer, Harm_doer, Victim*, and so on. Setting up the annotation of moral values as a frame semantic annotation task has several advantages. First, the addition of semantic roles would make the annotations more informative by encoding the core participants of moral arguments, i.e., the target of the moral evaluation and the affected party. Second, anchoring the annotations in lexical semantics would make it easier to provide the annotators with precise guidelines. This might not only increase the consistency of the annotations but might also help to control for annotator bias. An open question, however, concerns coverage as it is not yet clear whether this approach would miss too many relevant expressions of moral values, given that it only captures explicitly stated moral evaluation but not implicit judgments. Whether the merits of our proposal outweigh its drawbacks needs to be explored in future work.

Being able to predict moral values in text reliably can open up new research avenues in argumentation. E.g., recent work in psychology has shown that moral values play an important role in debates on political and social issues (Feinberg and Willer, 2013; Voelkel and Feinberg, 2018; Feinberg and Willer, 2019). For example, Feinberg and Willer (2013) have shown that debates on environmental issues are often framed in terms of moral values such as *Care-Harm*, a moral foundation that is at the core of liberal belief systems, while conservatives, in contrast, seem to value all five MFs more similarly (Graham et al., 2009). This often results in highly polarized discussions, and Feinberg and Willer (2013) argue that reframing such issues in terms of moral values that explicitly address the opponents' belief system might have the potential to depolarize controversial debates and improve understanding between the camps by addressing the "moral empathy gap" (see Feinberg and Willer (2019) and references therein).

6 Conclusion and Future Work

In the paper, we evaluated different models for predicting moral sentiment in debates, based on Moral Foundations Theory. We then used our models to predict moral values in three argumentation datasets. We investigated whether we could find a correlation between morality and (i) argument quality, (ii) stance, and (iii) audience reactions for political speeches.

We found weak but significant correlations between general morality and argument quality in the ArgQuality data and a consistent positive correlation between moral sentiment and audience approval in CORPS as well as a negative correlation for moral sentiment and laughter. However, our study has several limitations that need to be addressed. First, the annotation experiment has been conducted by two annotators only, not allowing us to retrieve more reliable labels using the wisdom of the crowd. Also, the size of the test set is rather small, thus questioning the reliability of the results. Another problem is the low accuracy of the classifiers for the prediction of moral values. While results were substantially higher than the random baseline and an MFD-based baseline, we still expect a considerable amount of noise in the classifiers' predictions, which might impact the results of the correlation study. It is conceivable that cleaner predictions might increase the effect size of the observed correlations, which would be consistent with the slightly larger correlation coefficients found for the human annotations (HU). This, however, still needs to be confirmed.

The next steps should include the creation of larger test sets where the annotations have been validated by more than two annotators as well as the evaluation of semantically grounded approaches to coding moral values, to assess their reliability and validity. Another important task is the development of more accurate and robust classifiers for the prediction of moral sentiment.

Acknowledgements

This work has been funded by the Deutsche Forschungsgemeinschaft (DFG) within the project ExpLAIN, Grant Number STU 266/14-1, as part of the Priority Program "Robust Argumentation Machines (RATIO)" (SPP-1999), as well as within the SFB 884 on the Political Economy of Reforms at the University of Mannheim (projects B6 and C4).

References

Stephen H. Bach, Bert Huang, Ben London, and Lise Getoor. 2013. Hinge-loss Markov random fields: Convex inference for structured prediction. In *Conference on Uncertainty in Artificial Intelligence*.

Thomas Davidson, Dana Warmsley, Michael Macy, and Ingmar Weber. 2017. Automated hate speech detection and the problem of offensive language. *arXiv preprint arXiv:1703.04009*.

Jesse Dunietz, Lori Levin, and Jaime Carbonell. 2015. Annotating causal language using corpus lexicography of constructions. In *Proceedings of The 9th Linguistic Annotation Workshop*, pages 188–196, Denver, Colorado, USA, June. Association for Computational Linguistics.

Matthew Feinberg and Robb Willer. 2013. The moral roots of environmental attitudes. *Psychological Science*, 24(1):56–62. PMID: 23228937.

Matthew Feinberg and Robb Willer. 2019. Moral reframing: A technique for effective and persuasive communication across political divides. *Social Psychology and Personality Compass*, pages 56–62.

Christiane Fellbaum. 2010. Princeton university: About wordnet.

Jeremy A. Frimer, Reihane Boghrati, Jonathan Haidt, Jesse Graham, and Morteza Dehgani. 2019. Moral Foundations Dictionary for Linguistic Analyses 2.0. Unpublished manuscript. Available from `https://osf.io/xakyw/`.

Dean Fulgoni, Jordan Carpenter, Lyle Ungar, and Daniel Preoţiuc-Pietro. 2016. An Empirical Exploration of Moral Foundations Theory in Partisan News Sources. In Nicoletta Calzolari (Conference Chair), Khalid Choukri, Thierry Declerck, Sara Goggi, Marko Grobelnik, Bente Maegaard, Joseph Mariani, Helene Mazo, Asuncion Moreno, Jan Odijk, and Stelios Piperidis, editors, *The 10th International Conference on Language Resources and Evaluation*, LREC'16, pages 3730–3736, Paris, France, may. European Language Resources Association (ELRA).

Justin Garten, Reihane Boghrati, Joe Hoover, Kate M. Johnson, and Morteza Dehghani. 2016. Morality between the lines: Detecting moral sentiment in text. In *Proceedings of IJCAI 2016 Workshop on Computational Modeling of Attitudes*.

Joseph Graham, Jonathan Haidt, and B. A. Nosek. 2009. Liberals and conservatives rely on different sets of moral foundations. *Journal of personality and social psychology*, 96(5:1029).

Jesse Graham, Jonathan Haidt, Sena Koleva, Matt Motyl, Ravi Iyer, Sean P. Wojcik, and Peter H. Ditto. 2013. Chapter Two - Moral Foundations Theory: The Pragmatic Validity of Moral Pluralism. *Advances in Experimental Social Psychology*, 47:55 – 130.

Shai Gretz, Roni Friedman, Edo Cohen-Karlik, Assaf Toledo, Dan Lahav, Ranit Aharonov, and Noam Slonim. 2019. A large-scale dataset for argument quality ranking: Construction and analysis. *arXiv preprint arXiv:1911.11408*.

Marco Guerini, Danilo Giampiccolo, Giovanni Moretti, Rachele Sprugnoli, and Carlo Strapparava. 2013. The New Release of CORPS: A Corpus of Political Speeches Annotated with Audience Reactions. In Isabella Poggi, Francesca D'Errico, Laura Vincze, and Alessandro Vinciarelli, editors, *Multimodal Communication in Political Speech. Shaping Minds and Social Action*, pages 86–98, Berlin, Heidelberg. Springer Berlin Heidelberg.

Ivan Habernal and Iryna Gurevych. 2016. What makes a convincing argument? empirical analysis and detecting attributes of convincingness in Web argumentation. In *Proceedings of the 2016 Conference on Empirical Methods in Natural Language Processing*, pages 1214–1223, Austin, Texas, November. Association for Computational Linguistics.

Jonathan Haidt and Craig Joseph. 2004. Intuitive ethics: How innately prepared intuitions generate culturally variable virtues. *Daedalus*, 133(4):55–66.

Taher H. Haveliwala. 2003. Topic-sensitive pagerank: A context-sensitive ranking algorithm for web search. *IEEE transactions on knowledge and data engineering*, 15(4):784–796.

Joe Hoover, Gwenyth Portillo-Wightman, Leigh Yeh, Shreya Havaldar, Aida Mostafazadeh Davani, Ying Lin, Brendan Kennedy, Mohammad Atari, Zahra Kamel, Madelyn Mendlen, Gabriela Moreno, Christina Park, Tingyee E. Chang, Jenna Chin, Christian Leong, Jun Yen Leung, Arineh Mirinjian, and Morteza Dehghani. 2020. Moral Foundations Twitter Corpus: A Collection of 35k Tweets Annotated for Moral Sentiment. *Social Psychological and Personality Science*, 0(0):0.

Kristen Johnson and Dan Goldwasser. 2018. Classification of Moral Foundations in Microblog Political Discourse. In *The 56th Annual Meeting of the Association for Computational Linguistics*, ACL'18, pages 720–730, July.

George Lakoff. 1997. *Moral Politics: What Conservatives Know That Liberals Don't.* University of Chicago Press.

Paul G. Lewis. 2019. Moral Foundations in the 2015-16 U.S. Presidential Primary Debates: The Positive and Negative Moral Vocabulary of Partisan Elites. *Social Sciences*, 8(233).

Ying Lin, Joe Hoover, Gwenyth Portillo-Wightman, Christina Park, Morteza Dehghani, and Heng Ji. 2018. Acquiring Background Knowledge to Improve Moral Value Prediction. In *2018 IEEE/ACM International Conference on Advances in Social Networks Analysis and Mining (ASONAM)*, pages 552–559.

Akiko Matsuo, Kazutoshi Sasahara, Yasuhiro Taguchi, and Minoru Karasawa. 2018. Development of the Japanese Moral Foundations Dictionary: Procedures and Applications. *CoRR*, abs/1804.00871.

Jeffrey Pennington, Richard Socher, and Christopher D. Manning. 2014. Glove: Global vectors for word representation. In *Proceedings of the 2014 conference on empirical methods in natural language processing (EMNLP)*, pages 1532–1543.

Nils Reimers and Iryna Gurevych. 2019. Sentence-BERT: Sentence Embeddings using Siamese BERT-Networks. In *Proceedings of the 2019 Conference on Empirical Methods in Natural Language Processing and the 9th International Joint Conference on Natural Language Processing (EMNLP-IJCNLP)*, pages 3982–3992, Hong Kong, China, November. Association for Computational Linguistics.

Rezvaneh Rezapour, Saumil H. Shah, and Jana Diesner. 2019. Enhancing the Measurement of Social Effects by Capturing Morality. In *Proceedings of the Tenth Workshop on Computational Approaches to Subjectivity, Sentiment and Social Media Analysis*, pages 35–45, Minneapolis, USA, June. Association for Computational Linguistics.

Conny Roggeband and Rens Vliegenthart. 2007. Divergent framing: The public debate on migration in the Dutch parliament and media, 1995–2004. *West European Politics*, 3(30):524–548.

Hendrik Schuff, Jeremy Barnes, Julian Mohme, Sebastian Padó, and Roman Klinger. 2017. Annotation, Modelling and Analysis of Fine-Grained Emotions on a Stance and Sentiment Detection Corpus. In *Proceedings of the 8th Workshop on Computational Approaches to Subjectivity, Sentiment and Social Media Analysis*, pages 13–23, Copenhagen, Denmark, September. Association for Computational Linguistics.

Julius Sim and Chris C. Wright. 2005. The Kappa Statistic in Reliability Studies: Use, Interpretation, and Sample Size Requirements. *Physical Therapy*, 85(3):257–268, 03.

Manfred Stede. 2020. Automatic argumentation mining and the role of stance and sentiment. *Journal of Argumentation in Context*, 9(1):19–41.

Hiroki Takikawa and Takuto Sakamoto. 2017. Moral Foundations of Political Discourse: Comparative Analysis of the Speech Records of the US Congress and the Japanese Diet. *CoRR*, abs/1704.06903.

Liling Tan. 2014. Pywsd: Python Implementations of Word Sense Disambiguation (WSD) Technologies [software]. https://github.com/alvations/pywsd.

Jan G. Voelkel and Matthew Feinberg. 2018. Morally reframed arguments can affect support for political candidates. *Social Psychological and Personality Science*, 9(8):917–924. PMID: 30595808.

Henning Wachsmuth, Nona Naderi, Yufang Hou, Yonatan Bilu, Vinodkumar Prabhakaran, Tim Alberdingk Thijm, Graeme Hirst, and Benno Stein. 2017. Computational Argumentation Quality Assessment in Natural Language. In *Proceedings of the 15th Conference of the European Chapter of the Association for Computational Linguistics: Volume 1, Long Papers*, pages 176–187. Association for Computational Linguistics.

Ian Wood, John P. McCrae, Vladimir Andryushechkin, and Paul Buitelaar. 2018. A Comparison Of Emotion Annotation Schemes And A New Annotated Data Set. In *Proceedings of the Eleventh International Conference on Language Resources and Evaluation (LREC 2018)*, Miyazaki, Japan, May. European Language Resources Association (ELRA).

Jing Yi Xie, Renato Ferreira Pinto Junior, Graeme Hirst, and Yang Xu. 2019. Text-based inference of moral sentiment change. In *Proceedings of the 2019 Conference on Empirical Methods in Natural Language Processing and the 9th International Joint Conference on Natural Language Processing (EMNLP-IJCNLP)*, pages 4654–4663, Hong Kong, China, November. Association for Computational Linguistics.

Aspect-Based Argument Mining

Dietrich Trautmann
Center for Information and Language Processing
Ludwig Maximilian University of Munich, Germany
dietrich@trautmann.me

Abstract

Computational Argumentation in general and Argument Mining in particular are important research fields. In previous works, many of the challenges to automatically extract and to some degree reason over natural language arguments were addressed. The tools to extract argument units are increasingly available and further open problems can be addressed. In this work, we are presenting the task of Aspect-Based Argument Mining (ABAM), with the essential subtasks of Aspect Term Extraction (ATE) and Nested Segmentation (NS). At the first instance, we create and release an annotated corpus with aspect information on the token-level. We consider aspects as the main point(s) argument units are addressing. This information is important for further downstream tasks such as argument ranking, argument summarization and generation, as well as the search for counter-arguments on the aspect-level. We present several experiments using state-of-the-art supervised architectures and demonstrate their performance for both of the subtasks. The annotated benchmark is available at https://github.com/trtm/ABAM.

1 Introduction

The field of computational argumentation (Slonim et al., 2016) gained a lot of interest in the last couple of years. This is noticeable from both the number of the submitted publications related to this field and also from the high volume of emerging datasets (Aharoni et al., 2014; Levy et al., 2017; Habernal et al., 2018; Stab et al., 2018; Trautmann et al., 2020a), specific task formulations (Wachsmuth et al., 2017; Al-Khatib et al., 2020) and models (Kuribayashi et al., 2019; Chakrabarty et al., 2019).

Similar to aspect-based sentiment analysis (Pontiki et al., 2014), we also see the possibility of breaking down arguments into smaller attributes or meaningful components in the argument mining domain. We consider these components as *aspects* of the arguments. Previous works already utilized aspect-information for several subtasks within the argument mining domain (Fujii and Ishikawa, 2006; Misra et al., 2015; Gemechu and Reed, 2019). However, these works vary significantly in the definition of aspects and do not focus on the aspect-based argument mining explicitly, e.g., employ aspects as a source of side or additional information.

For instance, Fujii and Ishikawa (2006) are mainly focusing on the summarization of opinions, visualizing pro and contra arguments for a given topic. Thereby, the authors are extracting aspects, calling them *points at issue*, and ranking the arguments according to them. However, their approach relies on rule-based extraction solely. In Misra et al. (2015), the authors are proposing summarization methods to recognize specific arguments and counter-arguments in social media texts, to further group them across discussions into *facets* (i.e., aspects) on which that issue is argued. Still, this work is limited to a couple of topics and samples. Finally, Gemechu and Reed (2019) also mention aspects as part of four functional components, where the authors interchangeably label aspects and concepts for the specific words. However, to the best of our knowledge, the authors did not publish their labeled data, making a comparative evaluation of aspect extraction methods impossible. We, in contrast, specifically address the aspect term

Proceedings of the 7th Workshop on Argument Mining, pages 41–52
Barcelona, Spain (Online), December 13, 2020.

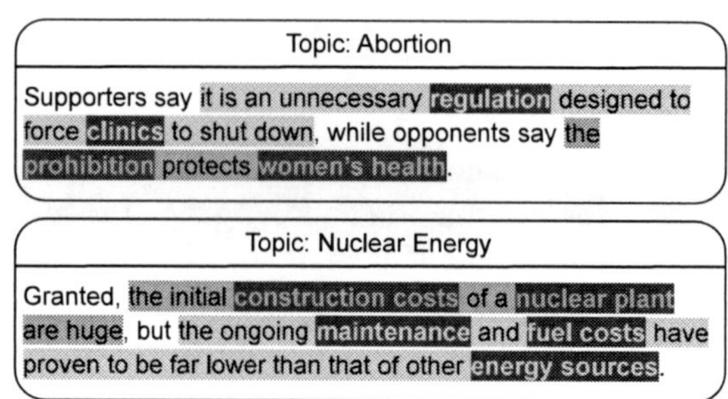

Figure 1: Example annotation of argumentative spans, the corresponding stances (green: supporting/pro; red: opposing/contra) and the aspects (underlined) for the topics *abortion* and *nuclear energy*.

extraction, concentrate on the proper definition of aspects and therefore directly emphasize and present the task of Aspect-Based Argument Mining (ABAM) in this work.

One of the potential applications for the ABAM is the ability to search for specific subtopics within a larger controversial area. For instance, for the topic *abortion*, one can particularly be interested in *regulation* or *health*-related aspects (first example in Figure 1). Whereas for the topic of *nuclear energy*, one can care for solely *enviromental*, *cost-* or *safety*-related aspects (second example in Figure 1). By searching or filtering for the particular aspects, one has the possibility to select for specific information and, therefore, to get more fine-grained results. Another benefit is the ability to compare opposing arguments on the aspect-level.

In this regard, necessary subtasks within the ABAM include the explicit *Aspect Term Extraction* (ATE) on token-level and the *Nested Segmentation* (NS) of argumentative parts along with their aspects within a given sentence. Our work is based on Trautmann et al. (2020a), where the authors already addressed the task of argument unit segmentation. We extend their benchmark with aspect term extraction on these argument units. The ABAM task can be performed in two ways: first, as a two-step pipeline approach with argument unit recognition and classification (AURC) followed by aspect term extraction, or as an end-to-end approach in the form of the nested segmentation task. Since the argument units are already provided by Trautmann et al. (2020a), we can use them directly for the second step in the pipeline, namely the ATE task. Whereas in the end-to-end scenario we adress both tasks (i.e., AURC and ATE) simultaneously for argumentative sentences.

One of the main challenges we faced during this work was the absence of publicly available benchmarks containing the aspect terms. Existing argument mining datasets do not contain the required information and therefore could not be directly applied for *Aspect-Based* Argument Mining. We address this challenge by extending an existing fine-grained argument corpus (Trautmann et al., 2020a) with crowd-sourced token-level aspect information. This is our focused main contribution. While annotating the corpus, we were faced multiple difficulties, including the proper definition of aspects and the creation of rules required for the aspect extraction. It is important to note, that within this work, we refer to aspects as the main point(s) arguments are addressing.

Last but not least, since we are extending the existing corpus, we do not explicitly concentrate on the stance definition and its annotation. Furthermore, as stated in Trautmann et al. (2020a), there are two main argument mining directions: *closed domain discourse-level* and the argument mining from the *information seeking* perspective. The authors of the underlying corpora follow the latter and provide the reasons for that in their work. We, therefore, adopt their vision on that point.

Summarizing the abovementioned points, our contribution within this work is as follows:

- We are emphasizing and presenting the task of Aspect-Based Argument Mining on its own.
- We are extending an existing corpus with token-level aspect terms, making a comparative evaluation of ABAM methods possible.
- We are presenting a number of strong baselines with a corresponding error analysis.

2 Problem Statement

We define the ABAM task as following: Given a list of several topic related texts (documents or para-graphs), we segment the texts into N sentences

$$sentence_i = [t_1, t_2, t_3, \ldots, t_n] \tag{1}$$

The problem is to select, if available, one (or several) span(s)

$$span_j = [t_k, \ldots, t_l] \tag{2}$$

inside each $sentence_i$, with $k >= 1$, $l <= n$, $l - k >= SEG_{min}$ and $l - k <= SEG_{max}$ (with $SEG_{min} = 3$ tokens and $SEG_{max} = n$ tokens in a segment), and a corresponding stance

$$stance_j \in [PRO, CON] \tag{3}$$

Tokens outside of argumentative spans are assigned the NON stance label. Furthermore, regularly there is at least one aspect in every selected span with

$$aspect_j = [t_p, \ldots, t_q] \tag{4}$$

where $p >= k$, $q <= l$, $q - p >= ASP_{min}$ and $q - p <= ASP_{max}$ (with $ASP_{min} = 1$ token and $ASP_{max} = 5$ tokens per aspect).

3 Related Work

Regarding the abovementioned problem definition (§2), we selected three research areas as thematically closed to our task.

Sentiment Analysis: The SemEval workshop organized the task of aspect-based sentiment analysis (Pontiki et al., 2014; Pontiki et al., 2015; Pontiki et al., 2016). Its subtasks also involved the aspect term extraction, which mainly inspired our approach and definition of the aspect term. Recent works applied adversarial training of pretrained language models (Karimi et al., 2020) and a combination of contextualized embeddings and hierarchical attention (Trusca et al., 2020) for new state-of-the-art results on this tasks.

Argument Mining: In our work we adopt the definition of argument facets from the previous work and adjust it for our task. For instance, Misra et al. (2015) used the information on argument facets for the summarization of arguments in social media. Furthermore, the authors used argument facets for the argument similarity task (Misra et al., 2016). The abovementioned works were a first approach in the area of argument facet extraction and were limited to solely a couple of topics and samples. Recent work extended this approach to 28 topics and used the aspect information for the argument similarity task and argument clustering (Reimers et al., 2019). However, the focus of Reimers et al. (2019) was on the pairwise classification of argumentative sentences and not on the aspect term extraction task itself. Lastly, the work by Bar-Haim et al. (2020) defined argument key-points to create concise summaries from a large set of arguments.

Nested Named Entity Recognition: The task of nested-NER is similar to the nested segmentation task (§5.1.2) that we propose. Early work (Finkel and Manning, 2009) presented newspaper and biomedical corpora, and modeled the data by manual feature extraction. Recent works proposed recurrent neural networks (Katiyar and Cardie, 2018) and sequence-to-sequence (Straková et al., 2019) approaches. The latter modeled nested labels as multilabels, a method that we also adopted for our task with overlapping stance and aspect labels.

NN	NNS JJ NNS	JJ HYPH NN NN
NNS	NN POS NN	JJ HYPH NN NNS
NN NN	NN POS NNS	JJ HYPH JJ NN
NN NNS	NNS POS NN	JJ HYPH JJ NNS
JJ NN	NNS POS NNS	JJ JJ NN NN
JJ NNS	IN NN NN	JJ JJ NN NNS
NN NN NN	IN NN NNS	JJ NN HYPH NN
NN NN NNS	JJ NN NN	JJ NN HYPH NNS
NN IN NN	JJ NN NNS	JJ NN JJ NN
NN IN NNS	JJ JJ NN	JJ NN JJ NNS
NN HYPH NN	JJ JJ NNS	JJ NN NN NN
NN HYPH NNS	NN HYPH NN NN	JJ NN NN NNS
NN JJ NN	NN HYPH NN NNS	JJ HYPH NN NN NN
NN JJ NNS	NN POS JJ NN	JJ HYPH NN NN NNS
NNS JJ NN	NN POS JJ NNS	

Table 1: The final set of the 44 Part-of-Speech patterns.

4 Corpus Creation

The creation of the ABAM benchmark is based on the argument units from the AURC corpus (Trautmann et al., 2020a) and is divided into two main parts. The first part addresses two studies for the annotation task formulation, whereas the second part describes the final corpus creation. We outsourced the data annotation to independent (crowd-)annotators and based on their results we created the gold labels.

4.1 Expert Study

We conducted two expert studies on random samples of ten argument units per stance and topic, selected from the AURC corpus. The resulting sets contained 160 samples for each study.

4.1.1 Token-Level Annotation

The first expert study task was to select explicit aspect terms from a given argument unit on the token-level. Two graduate domain experts performed the annotation. Experts were free to select every input-token which fits the following task description: *"The aspects are defined as the most important point(s) the argument unit is addressing"*.

After the annotation step, the Inter-Annotator Agreement (IAA) for the 160 samples was computed. We decided for Cohen's κ (Cohen, 1960) as our agreement measure, that resulted in the initial score of 0.538. According to Viera et al. (2005), this score is in the *moderate agreement* range. Furthermore, the primary analysis of the selected aspect terms from both annotators yielded a list of especially *frequent part-of-speech* (PoS) patterns for the selected tokens. To further improve the annotation process, the PoS information was employed in the second expert study.

4.1.2 Candidates Selection

The aspect candidate selection step is crucial for the correct aspect term extraction task. To select the aspect candidates for the second study, we rely on the part-of-speech information. Specifically, the PoS patterns that occurred more than twice in the previous expert study (i.e., token-level annotation) where picked, and some additional PoS patterns were defined (e.g., the singular and plural form of nouns). The tag set is based on the Part-of-Speech tags used in the Penn Treebank Project[1] and the stanza NLP library[2]. The final PoS pattern list is comprehensive and representative (includes 44 patterns, see Table 1), and ensures linguistically and grammatically correct candidates, without affecting the actual discourse. These PoS patterns were applied on a different set of 160 random samples to create a list of aspect term candidates for every argument unit.

---

[1] https://www.ling.upenn.edu/courses/Fall_2003/ling001/penn_treebank_pos.html
[2] https://stanfordnlp.github.io/stanza/

#	topic	#sentences	#segments	#aspects (total)	#aspects (unique)
T1	abortion	415	435	910	484
T2	cloning	343	365	843	492
T3	marijuana legalization	626	676	1889	887
T4	minimum wage	624	689	1981	745
T5	nuclear energy	615	671	1992	980
T6	death penalty	588	637	1325	545
T7	gun control	480	519	1081	429
T8	school uniforms	705	800	2019	923
	total	4396	4792	12040	**4525**[†]

Table 2: Count of sentences, segments and (total & unique) aspects in the ABAM corpus. [†]Clarification: The total count of unique aspects for all topics is 4525, but the sum of all unique aspects per topic is 5485. This is due to some aspects appearing in several topics (c.f. Table 3).

The annotators were asked to solve the same task as before, but now by selecting one or several options from the aspect term candidates list. If none of the aspect term candidates were appropriate, the option *NONE* was selected. This simplification of the task, compared to the first study, led to a raised Cohen's κ of 0.790. This is considered as a *substantial agreement* (Viera et al., 2005) and we deem this as a viable approach for the aspect term extraction.

4.2 Corpus Annotation

Based on the insights from the first two studies, the annotation guidelines (§A) were extended with clearer task formulations and examples. Additionally, the final set of PoS patterns (full list in Table 1) was applied on all argument units from the AURC corpus. The AURC corpus was slightly preprocessed to account for duplicates on the sentence- and segment-level, as well as on some minor errors on span boundaries.

Two independent (crowd-)annotators with a linguistic background and a minimum professional working proficiency in English were recruited for the aspect term extraction task. The annotation procedure was the same as described in §4.1.2. The inter-annotator agreement score for the two expert annotators resulted in a Cohen's κ of 0.874 for all eight (8) topics. This is considered as an *almost perfect agreement* (Viera et al., 2005).

Annotation Merge For the gold standard we selected the annotations where both of the annotators agreed on the token-level. This ensured that we always had a selection of aspects if neither of the annotators selected the NONE option. Additionally, shorter aspect terms are favoured by this annotation merge.

Gold Standard The final descriptive statistics of the ABAM corpus are depicted in the Table 2. There are 12040 aspects in total and 4525 unique (lemmatized) aspects. The topic with the most segments (T8 in Table 2), also yielded the most total aspects (2019). Furthermore, there are 58.10% of the aspects with only one token, 32.12% with 2 tokens, 7.94% with 3 tokens, 1.73% with 4 tokens and only 0.12% with 5 tokens.

Common Aspects In further aspect analysis we aggregated the most common aspects for the eight topics. The top five aspects and the absolute occurence counts per topic, are shown in Table 3. Furthermore, three aspects (*life, problem, government*) appeared in all eight topics and the aspects *people, cost, society, risk, law* appeared in seven topics.

5 Experimental Setup

This section presents our experimental setup regarding the two tasks, the employed models and the data set splits.

topic	aspect (occurrences)
abortion	child (28), life (26), woman (24), unsafe abortion (22), death (16)
cloning	animal (24), child (20), clone (20), disease (16), scientist (16)
marijuana legalization	drug (51), marijuana (44), people (41), alcohol (37), medical marijuana (27)
minimum wage	worker (119), job (52), increase (46), employer (41), economy (39)
nuclear energy	energy (42), electricity (35), fossil fuel (34), environment (30), nuclear power plant (24)
death penalty	crime (62), deterrent (30), punishment (28), cost (27), criminal (27)
gun control	crime (56), gun (55), criminal (28), crime rate (25), gun control law (22)
school uniforms	student (140), parent (77), child (66), kid (60), school (57)
common aspects (in 8 of 8 topics)	life (91), problem (57), government (55)
common aspects (in 7 of 8 topics)	people (94), cost (78), society (51), risk (48), law (42)

Table 3: The top 5 most common aspects per topic and for aspects that appear in several topics.

5.1 Tasks

In this work we apply the two different, but related, sub-tasks for ABAM in the sequence labeling formulation, following Akhundov et al. (2018).

5.1.1 Aspect Term Extraction

In the first task (ATE), we employ only the aspect term information within the segments (argument untis). This sequence labeling task is a *binary* classification problem per token.

5.1.2 Nested Segmentation

In the second task (NS), we utilize full argumentative sentences (like the examples in Figure 1) with the *stance* (PRO, CON, NON) and *aspect* (O, ASP) information for every token as our input. We extend the stance labels with the aspect information for a total set of five possible combinations ([NON,O], [PRO,O], [PRO,ASP], [CON,O], [CON,ASP]).[3]

This is a *multiclass* sequence labeling problem, which solves both the argument unit segmentation and the aspect term extraction tasks.

5.2 Models

BERT   For the two subtasks, we decided for the BERT model (Devlin et al., 2019) as a recent state-of-the-art system on a number of natural language processing tasks. We utilize the base and large versions of BERT, as well as both versions of the models with an additional CRF-Layer (Sutton et al., 2012) as the final classification layer in the architecture. Further information about hyperparameter search and computing infrastructure are in §6.2, §B and §C.

PoS Patterns   Additionally, we applied the PoS-patterns from the aspect candidates creation step we used in §4. For the ATE task we labeled all tokens that match the PoS-patterns and report the results as the lower boundary of our approaches.

5.3 Evaluation

As the evaluation metric, we report the macro-F1 scores[4] for both of our tasks. Further information about accuracy, precision and recall can be found in §D.

---

[3] Tokens that are not part of argument units (spans) get the stance-label NON in this sequence labeling task and aspects are always within argumentative spans.

[4] https://github.com/chakki-works/seqeval

set \domain	INNER	CROSS
train	2447	2264
dev	333	516
test	693	1319

Table 4: Sample counts per set and domain for the aspect term extraction task.

set \domain	INNER	CROSS
train	2268	2097
dev	307	478
test	636	1185

Table 5: Sample counts per set and domain for the nested segmentation task.

5.4 Inner-Topic & Cross-Topic

For a better understanding of the model performance, we followed the two different dataset splits (domains) as they were defined for the AURC corpus (Trautmann et al., 2020a). In the inner-topic split we trained, evaluated and tested our models on the same set of topics (T1-T6, Table 2). In the cross-topic split we trained our model on T1-T5, selected the best hyperparameter from the evaluation on T6 and tested on T7 and T8. Detailed sample counts are shown in Table 4 and Table 5 for each task, domain and set.

6 Results

This section presents the results for our tasks as described in §5.1.

6.1 Tasks

6.1.1 Aspect Term Extraction

The best performing options are the $BERT_{LARGE}$ models (Table 6). Both of them perform similar, but the one with the CRF-layer is slightly better on the development set for inner-topic and the test set for the cross-topic. The inner-topic scores are higher compared to the more challenging cross-topic set-up, were we evaluate the models on unseen topics. All the models performed much better than the lower boundary from the PoS-Patterns Matches. However, this scores are still bellow the human performance of 0.895. The human performance on this task is based on the results from the second expert study (§4.1.2)

6.1.2 Nested Segmentation

The results for NS (Table 7), show that the $BERT_{LARGE}$ model outperforms the other listed approaches, except for the development set in the inner-topic set-up. Furthermore, the cross-topic set-up is also more challenging for this task, compared to the inner-topic setting.

domain	INNER		CROSS	
model \set	dev	test	dev	test
PoS-Patterns Matches	.600	.610	.518	.640
$BERT_{BASE}$	.819	.813	.673	.749
$BERT_{BASE}$+CRF	.823	.812	.669	.743
$BERT_{LARGE}$	.830	**.821**	**.683**	.754
$BERT_{LARGE}$+CRF	**.832**	.818	.681	**.756**
human performance			.895	

Table 6: F1 results on the dev and test sets for the inner-topic (INNER) and cross-topic (CROSS) set-ups for the aspect term extraction task.

domain	INNER		CROSS	
model \set	dev	test	dev	test
$BERT_{BASE}$	.507	.465	.278	.338
$BERT_{BASE}$+CRF	.521	.480	.270	.332
$BERT_{LARGE}$	.557	**.520**	**.315**	**.369**
$BERT_{LARGE}$+CRF	**.563**	.517	.293	.358

Table 7: F1 results on the dev and test sets for the inner-topic (INNER) and cross-topic (CROSS) set-ups for the nested segmentation task.

6.2 Hyperparameters

For our experimental setup with BERT, we fine-tuned the whole (standard) base and large models, as well as both models with an additional final CRF-Layer. We selected the hyperparameters on the development sets and in particular the learning rate (range: 0.00001 - 0.00009 in 0.00001 steps) and the dropout rate (range: 0 - 0.5 in 0.1 steps). We used grid search, to cover all possible combinations. The model parameters were optimized with AdamW (Loshchilov and Hutter, 2018). The training batch size was 32. Our reported results are the averages from three runs and one epoch took about 1 minute for the base models and less than 2 minutes for the large models on average. We fine-tuned for 10 epochs in the ATE task and for 20 epochs in the NS task. Detailed numbers of the final hyperparameters for each model and task can be found in the tables in the appendix §B.

7 Error Analysis

Recalling our definition of aspects: They are defined as the main point(s) argument units are addressing. Furthermore, considering our annotation guidelines in §A, the most important point is usually not equal to the given main topic. An overview of the main errors found during the evaluation of the development sets for the best performing models in the inner- and cross-topic set-ups, is given below.

Aspect Term Extraction   During the evaluation of ATE results, we observed a number of errors, which we grouped into the following categories:

- The models tend to favour NOUNS in general.
- Topic words, such as *abortion* or *marijuana legalization*, are often selected as aspects, which is in conflict with our guidelines.
- Phrase constructions like *thread of* ... are often selected as a whole aspect by the models. For the benchmark, we, in contrast, focus on the main representative word of such constructions (e.g., *suicide* vs. *thread of suicide*).
- In the case of ADJECTIVE+NOUN, we suggest to avoid general adjectives (e.g. *new* in *new treatments*), whereas focused adjectives that are part of the concept should be selected (e.g. *recreational* in *recreational marijuana*). Our observation is, that models in general could not sufficiently differentiate between such adjectives.
- Models lack the understanding of domain-specific phrasems like *in vitro fertilisation* or *life without parole* and tend to select only the nominalized part of them (e.g., *fertilisation*, *parole*).

Overall the inner-topic set-up achieved much better performace compared to the cross-topic set-up and both models showed significantly better results over the PoS-Patterns Matches baseline. However, in the cross-topic set-up we faced more repeated errors, such as the tendency to select topic words as aspects and not sufficient understanding of domain-specific phrasems.

Nested Segmentation   The typology of the main errors in the NS task is similar to the ATE task. Additionally, in the NS task, a number of errors occured due to the wrong assigment of the stance labels, especially in the cross-topic set-up. These results confirm the insight from Trautmann et al. (2020a), where most of the errors arose due to the wrong stance classification. Apparently, the BERT-based models tend to attach to sentiment words for the stance predictions, which is not always correlated.

8 Conclusion

ABAM is a challenging task that, to the best of our knowledge, was not directly addressed before. We made two important contributions: First, we created and released a publicly available benchmark for Aspect-Based Argument Mining. Second, we showcased several baselines for the two subtasks, namely the Aspect Term Extraction and the Nested Segmentation, and performed an elaborative error analysis. We believe that these findings as well as the benchmark are of high potential for further downstream tasks, such as argument ranking, argument summarization and the search for counter-arguments on the aspect-level.

For the future work, we foresee the investigation of unsupervised approaches for the Aspect Term Extraction task, since they showed promising results within the Aspect-Based Sentiment Analysis domain.

Furthermore, it would be of high interest to incorporate topic-specific knowledge (e.g., understanding of phrasems) into the models to address the discussed error types. In another line of work, one could also explore distant supervision (Rakhmetullina et al., 2018) or domain adaptation methods (März et al., 2019), as well as relational approaches (Trautmann et al., 2020b) for this task.

References

Ehud Aharoni, Anatoly Polnarov, Tamar Lavee, Daniel Hershcovich, Ran Levy, Ruty Rinott, Dan Gutfreund, and Noam Slonim. 2014. A benchmark dataset for automatic detection of claims and evidence in the context of controversial topics. In *Proceedings of the First Workshop on Argumentation Mining*, pages 64–68, Baltimore, Maryland, June. Association for Computational Linguistics.

Adnan Akhundov, Dietrich Trautmann, and Georg Groh. 2018. Sequence labeling: A practical approach. *arXiv preprint arXiv:1808.03926*.

Khalid Al-Khatib, Yufang Hou, Henning Wachsmuth, Charles Jochim, Francesca Bonin, and Benno Stein. 2020. End-to-end argumentation knowledge graph construction. In *Proceedings of the AAAI Conference on Artificial Intelligence*, volume 34, pages 7367–7374.

Roy Bar-Haim, Lilach Eden, Roni Friedman, Yoav Kantor, Dan Lahav, and Noam Slonim. 2020. From arguments to key points: Towards automatic argument summarization. *arXiv preprint arXiv:2005.01619*.

Tuhin Chakrabarty, Christopher Hidey, Smaranda Muresan, Kathy McKeown, and Alyssa Hwang. 2019. AM-PERSAND: Argument mining for PERSuAsive oNline discussions. In *Proceedings of the 2019 Conference on Empirical Methods in Natural Language Processing and the 9th International Joint Conference on Natural Language Processing (EMNLP-IJCNLP)*, pages 2933–2943, Hong Kong, China, November. Association for Computational Linguistics.

Jacob Cohen. 1960. A coefficient of agreement for nominal scales. *Educational and psychological measurement*, 20(1):37–46.

Jacob Devlin, Ming-Wei Chang, Kenton Lee, and Kristina Toutanova. 2019. BERT: Pre-training of deep bidirectional transformers for language understanding. In *Proceedings of the 2019 Conference of the North American Chapter of the Association for Computational Linguistics: Human Language Technologies, Volume 1 (Long and Short Papers)*, pages 4171–4186, Minneapolis, Minnesota, June. Association for Computational Linguistics.

Jenny Rose Finkel and Christopher D. Manning. 2009. Nested named entity recognition. In *Proceedings of the 2009 Conference on Empirical Methods in Natural Language Processing*, pages 141–150, Singapore, August. Association for Computational Linguistics.

Atsushi Fujii and Tetsuya Ishikawa. 2006. A system for summarizing and visualizing arguments in subjective documents: Toward supporting decision making. In *Proceedings of the Workshop on Sentiment and Subjectivity in Text*, pages 15–22.

Debela Gemechu and Chris Reed. 2019. Decompositional argument mining: A general purpose approach for argument graph construction. In *Proceedings of the 57th Annual Meeting of the Association for Computational Linguistics*, pages 516–526. Association for Computational Linguistics.

Ivan Habernal, Henning Wachsmuth, Iryna Gurevych, and Benno Stein. 2018. SemEval-2018 task 12: The argument reasoning comprehension task. In *Proceedings of The 12th International Workshop on Semantic Evaluation*, pages 763–772, New Orleans, Louisiana, June. Association for Computational Linguistics.

Akbar Karimi, Leonardo Rossi, Andrea Prati, and Katharina Full. 2020. Adversarial training for aspect-based sentiment analysis with bert. *arXiv preprint arXiv:2001.11316*.

Arzoo Katiyar and Claire Cardie. 2018. Nested named entity recognition revisited. In *Proceedings of the 2018 Conference of the North American Chapter of the Association for Computational Linguistics: Human Language Technologies, Volume 1 (Long Papers)*, pages 861–871, New Orleans, Louisiana, June. Association for Computational Linguistics.

Tatsuki Kuribayashi, Hiroki Ouchi, Naoya Inoue, Paul Reisert, Toshinori Miyoshi, Jun Suzuki, and Kentaro Inui. 2019. An empirical study of span representations in argumentation structure parsing. In *Proceedings of the 57th Annual Meeting of the Association for Computational Linguistics*, pages 4691–4698, Florence, Italy, July. Association for Computational Linguistics.

Ran Levy, Shai Gretz, Benjamin Sznajder, Shay Hummel, Ranit Aharonov, and Noam Slonim. 2017. Unsupervised corpus–wide claim detection. In *Proceedings of the 4th Workshop on Argument Mining*, pages 79–84, Copenhagen, Denmark, September. Association for Computational Linguistics.

Ilya Loshchilov and Frank Hutter. 2018. Decoupled weight decay regularization. In *International Conference on Learning Representations*.

Luisa März, Dietrich Trautmann, and Benjamin Roth. 2019. Domain adaptation for part-of-speech tagging of noisy user-generated text. In *Proceedings of the 2019 Conference of the North American Chapter of the Association for Computational Linguistics: Human Language Technologies, Volume 1 (Long and Short Papers)*, pages 3415–3420.

Amita Misra, Pranav Anand, Jean E. Fox Tree, and Marilyn Walker. 2015. Using summarization to discover argument facets in online idealogical dialog. In *Proceedings of the 2015 Conference of the North American Chapter of the Association for Computational Linguistics: Human Language Technologies*, pages 430–440, Denver, Colorado, May–June. Association for Computational Linguistics.

Amita Misra, Brian Ecker, and Marilyn Walker. 2016. Measuring the similarity of sentential arguments in dialogue. In *Proceedings of the 17th Annual Meeting of the Special Interest Group on Discourse and Dialogue*, pages 276–287, Los Angeles, September. Association for Computational Linguistics.

Maria Pontiki, Dimitris Galanis, John Pavlopoulos, Harris Papageorgiou, Ion Androutsopoulos, and Suresh Manandhar. 2014. SemEval-2014 task 4: Aspect based sentiment analysis. In *Proceedings of the 8th International Workshop on Semantic Evaluation (SemEval 2014)*, pages 27–35, Dublin, Ireland, August. Association for Computational Linguistics.

Maria Pontiki, Dimitrios Galanis, Harris Papageorgiou, Suresh Manandhar, and Ion Androutsopoulos. 2015. Semeval-2015 task 12: Aspect based sentiment analysis. In *Proceedings of the 9th international workshop on semantic evaluation (SemEval 2015)*, pages 486–495.

Maria Pontiki, Dimitrios Galanis, Haris Papageorgiou, Ion Androutsopoulos, Suresh Manandhar, Mohammad Al-Smadi, Mahmoud Al-Ayyoub, Yanyan Zhao, Bing Qin, Orphée De Clercq, et al. 2016. Semeval-2016 task 5: Aspect based sentiment analysis. In *10th International Workshop on Semantic Evaluation (SemEval 2016)*.

Aisulu Rakhmetullina, Dietrich Trautmann, and Georg Groh. 2018. Distant supervision for emotion classification task using emoji2emotion. In *Proceedings of the 1st International Workshop on Emoji Understanding and Applications in Social Media (Emoji2018). Stanford, CA, USA. http://ceurws. org*, volume 2130.

Nils Reimers, Benjamin Schiller, Tilman Beck, Johannes Daxenberger, Christian Stab, and Iryna Gurevych. 2019. Classification and clustering of arguments with contextualized word embeddings. In *Proceedings of the 57th Annual Meeting of the Association for Computational Linguistics*, pages 567–578, Florence, Italy, July. Association for Computational Linguistics.

Noam Slonim, Iryna Gurevych, Chris Reed, and Benno Stein. 2016. Nlp approaches to computational argumentation. In *Proceedings of the 54th Annual Meeting of the Association for Computational Linguistics: Tutorial Abstracts*.

Christian Stab, Tristan Miller, Benjamin Schiller, Pranav Rai, and Iryna Gurevych. 2018. Cross-topic argument mining from heterogeneous sources. In *Proceedings of the 2018 Conference on Empirical Methods in Natural Language Processing*, pages 3664–3674. Association for Computational Linguistics.

Jana Straková, Milan Straka, and Jan Hajic. 2019. Neural architectures for nested NER through linearization. In *Proceedings of the 57th Annual Meeting of the Association for Computational Linguistics*, pages 5326–5331, Florence, Italy, July. Association for Computational Linguistics.

Charles Sutton, Andrew McCallum, et al. 2012. An introduction to conditional random fields. *Foundations and Trends® in Machine Learning*, 4(4):267–373.

Dietrich Trautmann, Johannes Daxenberger, Christian Stab, Hinrich Schütze, and Iryna Gurevych. 2020a. Fine-grained argument unit recognition and classification. In *The Thirty-Fourth AAAI Conf. on Artificial Intelligence, New York City, NY, USA, AAAI 2020*. AAAI Press, 2.

Dietrich Trautmann, Michael Fromm, Volker Tresp, Thomas Seidl, and Hinrich Schütze. 2020b. Relational and fine-grained argument mining. *Datenbank-Spektrum*.

Maria Mihaela Trusca, Daan Wassenberg, Flavius Frasincar, and Rommert Dekker. 2020. A hybrid approach for aspect-based sentiment analysis using deep contextual word embeddings and hierarchical attention. *arXiv preprint arXiv:2004.08673*.

Anthony J Viera, Joanne M Garrett, et al. 2005. Understanding interobserver agreement: the kappa statistic. *Fam med*, 37(5):360–363.

Henning Wachsmuth, Benno Stein, and Yamen Ajjour. 2017. "PageRank" for argument relevance. In *Proceedings of the 15th Conference of the European Chapter of the Association for Computational Linguistics: Volume 1, Long Papers*, pages 1117–1127, Valencia, Spain, April. Association for Computational Linguistics.

A Annotation Guidelines

Annotation guidelines defined for the Aspect Term Extraction task in Aspect-Based Argument Mining.

Task Description

- Given a main topic and an argumentative segment (unit), please select one or several options from the aspect candidates list.

- If no aspect candidate could be selected from the list, pick the option *None*.

While selecting the aspects, please consider the following rules:

- An aspect is defined as the most important/relevant point for the argument made.

- The most important point is usually not equal to the given main topic.

- In case of doubt, shorter aspects candidates (generic terms; e.g. "life span") are prefered over longer candidates (e.g. "prolonged life span").

General Hints

- The selected aspect(s) should be related to the topic in general.

- The presence of AND/OR (usually) denote multiple aspects:
  - If a sentence contains multiple phrases (e.g., "abortion causes breast cancer AND it kills unborn children.");
  - If there is an enumeration and objects connected by AND/OR (e.g. "abortion causes breast cancer, infertility and pain.");

- In the case of ADJECTIVE+NOUN, general adjectives should be avoided (e.g. "new" in "new treatments"), whereas focused adjectives that are part of the concept should be selected (e.g. "recreational" in "recreational marijuana").

- Please, use these test-questions for yourself while annotating:
  - Do you want this argument to be shown to someone, if they select this aspect(s) of the topic, or are other aspect terms in this argument more relevant for the point made?
  - Which words make you understand the argument most?
  - Which words are the most relevant and mainly form the meaning of the argument made?
  - If you would compress the argument into a few most relevant words, which words would that be?

B Hyperparameters

The dropout rate of 0.1 was always the best option. The learning rates for the different models are displayed in Table 8 for the ATE task and in Table 9 for the NS task.

domain	INNER	CROSS
BERT$_{\text{BASE}}$	$6e-5$	$8e-5$
BERT$_{\text{BASE}}$+CRF	$9e-5$	$9e-5$
BERT$_{\text{LARGE}}$	$9e-5$	$9e-5$
BERT$_{\text{LARGE}}$+CRF	$9e-5$	$8e-5$

Table 8: Hyperparameters (learning rate) for the ATE task.

domain	INNER	CROSS
BERT$_{\text{BASE}}$	$7e-5$	$5e-5$
BERT$_{\text{BASE}}$+CRF	$8e-5$	$6e-5$
BERT$_{\text{LARGE}}$	$5e-5$	$7e-5$
BERT$_{\text{LARGE}}$+CRF	$7e-5$	$8e-5$

Table 9: Hyperparameters (learning rate) for the NS task.

C Compute Resources

We used Kaggle's Kernels[5] for the processing of the data and Google's Colab[6] for the training (fine-tuning) of our models. The former service offers a single 12GB NVIDIA Tesla K80 GPU, while the latter a single 16GB NVIDIA Tesla P100 GPU.

D Additional Results

The additionally reported numbers for accuracy, precision and recall can be found in the Table 10 for the ATE task, in the Table 11 for the NS task. The numbers are the average from three runs.

domain	INNER						CROSS					
set	dev			test			dev			test		
model \metric	acc.	pre.	rec.	acc.	pre.	rec.	acc.	pre.	rec.	acc.	pre.	rec.
PoS-Patterns Matches	.850	.490	.773	.853	.502	.779	.825	.404	.724	.870	.530	.809
BERT$_{\text{BASE}}$	.943	.784	.858	.942	.786	.842	.878	.580	.804	.912	.682	.830
BERT$_{\text{BASE}}$+CRF	.945	.789	.860	.942	.789	.836	.877	.575	.800	.911	.678	.822
BERT$_{\text{LARGE}}$	.946	.799	.864	.945	.803	.840	.881	.582	.827	.914	.686	.835
BERT$_{\text{LARGE}}$+CRF	.948	.798	.869	.943	.802	.835	.880	.585	.817	.914	.690	.837

Table 10: Accuracy (acc.), precision (pre.) and recall (rec.) results on the dev and test sets for the inner-topic (INNER) and cross-topic (CROSS) set-ups for the aspect term extraction task. These are the average scores from three runs.

domain	INNER						CROSS					
set	dev			test			dev			test		
model \metric	acc.	pre.	rec.	acc.	pre.	rec.	acc.	pre.	rec.	acc.	pre.	rec.
BERT$_{\text{BASE}}$	.704	.468	.552	.672	.434	.501	.560	.234	.343	.574	.296	.395
BERT$_{\text{BASE}}$+CRF	.710	.482	.568	.683	.450	.515	.553	.231	.324	.571	.298	.376
BERT$_{\text{LARGE}}$	.748	.512	.610	.709	.491	.552	.597	.266	.385	.607	.327	.423
BERT$_{\text{LARGE}}$+CRF	.749	.524	.608	.702	.491	.547	.575	.248	.358	.594	.320	.407

Table 11: Accuracy (acc.), precision (pre.) and recall (rec.) results on the dev and test sets for the inner-topic (INNER) and cross-topic (CROSS) set-ups for the nested segmentation task (args). These are the average scores from three runs.

---

[5] https://www.kaggle.com/kernels
[6] https://colab.research.google.com/signup

Annotation and Detection of Arguments in Tweets

Robin Schaefer
Applied Computational Linguistics
University of Potsdam
Potsdam, Germany
`robin.schaefer@uni-potsdam.de`

Manfred Stede
Applied Computational Linguistics
University of Potsdam
Potsdam, Germany
`stede@uni-potsdam.de`

Abstract

Notwithstanding the increasing role Twitter plays in modern political and social discourse, resources built for conducting argument mining on tweets remain limited. In this paper, we present a new corpus of German tweets annotated for argument components. To the best of our knowledge, this is the first corpus containing not only annotated full tweets but also argumentative spans within tweets. We further report first promising results using supervised classification (F1: 0.82) and sequence labeling (F1: 0.72) approaches.

1   Introduction

In recent years the field of argument mining, which focuses on the automatic identification of argument components and their relations in text, has developed substantially (Stede and Schneider, 2018). However, while the majority of research concentrates on well-structured documents (Moens et al., 2007; Stab and Gurevych, 2014), less work has been done on user-generated web content (Park and Cardie, 2014; Habernal and Gurevych, 2015). This shortcoming poses a problem as systems trained on formal and edited texts tend to be inapt of extracting patterns from the more informal user-generated content (Šnajder, 2016).

In this paper we focus on tweets, which are of great interest for the argument mining community due to the increasing use of the microblogging service Twitter[1] in political online discourse. While some first work on argument mining in tweets exists (Addawood and Bashir, 2016; Dusmanu et al., 2017), only a small number of available annotated corpora have been created that can be utilized for training tweet-specific argument mining systems (Bosc et al., 2016).

To improve on this point, we present a new corpus of German tweets annotated for claim and evidence[2]. To the best of our knowledge, this is the first argument tweet corpus not exclusively annotated with the full tweet as the unit of annotation. Instead, argumentative spans within tweets, henceforth called *argumentative discourse units* (ADU) (Peldszus and Stede, 2013), have been annotated as well. They render the corpus suitable not only for supervised classification but also for sequence labeling approaches. We also present first promising experimental results using this corpus.

This paper is structured as follows: Section 2 gives a short overview of the relevant social media and Twitter-related literature on argument mining. Section 3 describes the corpus, the annotation scheme and the annotation procedure. In Section 4 we present first classification and sequence labeling results using the annotated data. Section 5 discusses our results and gives a brief outlook.

2   Related Work

Related work on tweet-based argument mining has focused on separating argumentative tweets from non-argumentative ones and on defining new Twitter-specific tasks.

[1] `https://twitter.com/`

[2] We follow Aharoni et al. (2014) and others by using the term *evidence* instead of *premise*.

Proceedings of the 7th Workshop on Argument Mining, pages 53–58
Barcelona, Spain (Online), December 13, 2020.

Addawood and Bashir (2016) present a corpus of English tweets annotated for arguments and evidence types like news media accounts or expert opinions. First, arguments are identified on the full tweet level, followed by the subsequent annotation of evidence types. Annotators achieved Cohen's Kappa scores of 0.67 and 0.79, respectively. An SVM trained on linguistic and Twitter-related features yielded an F1 score of 0.89 on the binary classification task (non-argumentative vs argumentative).

Bosc et al. (2016) describe DART, a Twitter argument corpus annotated for arguments and their relations. In contrast to our work, they do not distinguish claim from evidence but join them in the category *argumentative*. Again, annotations are conducted on the full tweet level and result in a Krippendorff alpha score of 0.81. This corpus is used by Dusmanu et al. (2017) for argument classification. Using a set of lexical, Twitter-specific, semantic and sentiment features, they achieved an F1 score of 0.78 on the binary classification task (non-argumentative vs argumentative). They further investigated approaches to perform fact recognition and source identification.

Wojatzki and Zesch (2016) propose an alternative approach to argument mining in tweets. Specifically, they reconsider the challenging problem of implicit claim detection as a stance classification problem by reformulating implicit claims as implicit stances. This procedure is based on the assumption that an implicit stance can be more easily inferred from the respective tweet. They present the Atheism Stance Corpus, which contains tweets annotated for implicit stances. An SVM trained on token and character n-grams yielded an F1 score of 0.66. Schaefer and Stede (2019) improve on these results using different word and sentence embeddings (F1: 0.78).

Goudas et al. (2014) offer early results for argument mining not specifically on Twitter but on social media. They apply classification to separate non-argumentative from argumentative texts. In a subsequent step, sequence labeling is used to extract ADUs from the latter. This two-step approach makes their work comparable to ours. They report F1 scores of 0.77 and 0.42 for the two tasks, respectively.

3 Corpus Annotation

Our complete initial corpus consists of 77,100 tweets collected in 2019 via the Twitter API using the Python library Tweepy[3]. All tweets contain the keyword *klima* ("climate") and mainly concentrate on the topic of climate change, which was intensely discussed by German media and politics during that time. We conducted the following preprocessing steps.

First, we removed all retweets and excluded non-German tweets using the language identification tool langid (Lui and Baldwin, 2012). These steps led to a subset of 29,525 tweets. In the following, we grouped the tweets into pairs, consisting of a tweet, henceforth called *context tweet*, and the tweet to be annotated, which is a reply to the context tweet and, for this reason, is called *reply tweet*. This approach is motivated by the assumption that tweets in a reply relation are more likely to contain argumentation (Dykes et al., 2020). Moreover, given the short nature of tweets, providing a context is supposed to help interpreting the reply tweet's content. All tweets that were no replies were removed and missing context tweets were collected in an additional step. Finally, we removed all @-mentions at the beginning of a tweet, as these mainly point to the tweet's recipients. The final corpus consists of 12,296 context and reply tweet pairs. For the present study, a subset of 300 tweet pairs was annotated.[4]

3.1 Annotation Scheme

We focus on the two main components of argumentation: claim and evidence. We define a claim as a standpoint towards the topic being discussed (i.e. climate change). In contrast, an evidence unit is a statement used to support or attack such a standpoint. Hence, the crucial difference between claim and evidence is the characteristic of evidence units being always related to another statement while claims can be independent units. We distinguish further between evidence 1) *relating to a claim in the reply tweet*, 2) *relating to a claim in the context tweet* and 3) *relating to claims in both tweets*. Importantly, we do not define an ADU syntactically, e.g. by focusing exclusively on the clause or sentence level.

---

[3] https://www.tweepy.org/

[4] Corpus repository: https://github.com/RobinSchaefer/climate-tweet-corpus.

Due to the informal language used in the tweets we consider it appropriate to allow the annotators some flexibility to decide on the actual ADU span.

As distinguishing between claim and evidence can be a quite subjective task, especially on Twitter, annotators were advised to follow our component definitions as close as possible. Statements that function independently of other statements shall be annotated as claims. However, if a statement refers to another proposition either by supporting or attacking it or by giving additional information it shall be annotated as evidence, despite its potential usability as a claim. Therefore, annotators were further instructed to focus on possible causal relationships (in a wide sense) between two statements. If a statement directly follows from another it is likely to be a claim (e.g. [We have to limit $CO2$ emissions]$_{claim}$, [as too much $CO2$ has been shown to increase the greenhouse effect.]$_{evidence}$). We found that using this strategy to decide on the direction of the argumentation, i.e. which ADU is evidence and which ADU is the claim, facilitated the annotation procedure notably. For our purposes, we do not differentiate between correct and incorrect statements. We also do not explicitly annotate relations between two components.

3.2 Annotation Procedure and Results

Two annotators, one of which is a co-author of this paper, were trained in an iterative two-step procedure. First, both annotators individually labelled a subset of 20 tweet pairs according to the annotation scheme. They compared their results, discussed different interpretations and tried to consolidate them. This procedure was repeated until both annotators felt comfortable in completing the task.

For the actual annotation study we again used a two-step approach. Annotators first had to answer two multiple choice questions asking if a claim or evidence can be identified in the reply tweet. Only if one of the two components was found the annotator would continue to the ADU annotation step. No restrictions on the allowed maximal number of components per tweet were made, as this could potentially have led to differing choices in longer tweets. While annotations themselves only were created for ADU spans, we also derived separate tweet-level annotation sets for claim, evidence and argument (claim or evidence) annotations. Also, we experimented with analysing annotations both on the tweet and the ADU level.

First, we present mean percentages of the ADU annotation frequencies. Of the 300 tweets 14% were annotated as non-argumentative. 27% of the tweets contained exactly one ADU (25%: claim; 2%: evidence). 59% of the tweets were annotated for multiple ADUs (27%: 1 claim & 1 evidence unit; 2% 1 claim & >1 evidence units; 15%: >1 claims & 1 evidence unit) which demonstrates the need for ADU-level annotation even in short texts like tweets.

Metric	Claim	Evidence
Cohen's Kappa	0.55	0.37

Table 1: Inter Annotator Agreement (Questions)

Metric	Multi (s)	Argumentative (s)	Argumentative (t)	Claim (t)	Evidence (t)
Cohen's Kappa	0.38	0.45	0.53	0.55	0.44

Table 2: Inter Annotator Agreement (s = ADU span, t = full tweet)

We calculated Cohen's Kappa scores to measure Inter Annotator Agreement (IAA) (Artstein and Poesio, 2008). As shown in Table 1, results for the claim and evidence questions were 0.55 and 0.37, respectively, which indicates that deciding on the presence of evidence is more subjective. This pattern returns in the scores based on the annotations on the tweet level (Table 2). Whereas results for argument and claim annotations are somewhat similar, the kappa for evidence annotation is reduced. Further, the results show that the multi class annotation (claim vs evidence vs non-argumentative) is particularly difficult. As this task is somewhat subjective in nature, a drop of performance is expected. Although we are aware that the IAA results are relatively low, we consider them acceptable due to the subtlety of the task. This is in line with the interpretation of annotation results by Aharoni et al. (2014), who report 0.39 and 0.4 for claim and evidence annotation tasks, respectively.

4 Experiments and Results

In this section, we present first experimental results based on the annotated corpus. We apply two different approaches: For the tweet-level annotations we trained supervised classification models. This is comparable to the prior studies of Addawood and Bashir (2016) and Dusmanu et al. (2017). In addition, we use the ADU-level annotations for running a sequence labeling approach similar to Goudas et al. (2014). We experimented with different combinations of feature sets, preprocessing steps and models. However, we only present the best results here.

Features	Target	Preproc	F1 (w)	Precision (w)	Recall (w)
Bigrams	Argument	l,p,s	0.8	0.75	0.86
Pretrained BERT Embeddings	Argument	p	**0.82**	0.8	0.86
Uni- & Bigrams	Claim	l,p	0.79	0.78	0.82
Pretrained BERT Embeddings	Claim	p	**0.82**	0.8	0.85
Uni- & Bigrams	Evidence	l,p	**0.67**	0.68	0.68
Pretrained BERT Embeddings	Evidence	p,s	0.59	0.59	0.62

Table 3: Classification Results (l = lowercase, p = punctuation, s = stopword, w = weighted)

Tweet level. Classification models were trained on different combinations of n-grams and on pretrained BERT-based document embeddings (Devlin et al., 2019). The latter were created using FLAIR, an NLP framework that contains a unified interface for employing different types of text embeddings (Akbik et al., 2019). All shown classification results are yielded using eXtreme Gradient Boosting (XGBoost) (Chen and Guestrin, 2016), which is a variant of the Gradient Boosting approach introduced by Friedman (2000). We implemented three different classification tasks based on the respective binary target sets: *argumentative* vs *non-argumentative*, *claim* vs *no claim* or *evidence* vs *no evidence*. All results are 10-fold cross-validated.

Table 3 shows macro F1, precision and recall scores, which are weighted for the unbalanced distribution of classes. Pretrained BERT embeddings yield better F1 scores for argument (0.82 vs 0.8) and claim (0.82 vs 0.79) classifications. Interestingly, a model trained on uni- and bigrams performs better on the evidence task than the BERT-based model (0.67 vs 0.59). Importantly, scores for the argument and claim tasks are substantially higher than for the evidence task.

Features	Target	F1 (w)	Precision (w)	Recall (w)
Unigrams	Argument	0.69	0.69	0.72
Linguistic & Twitter Features	Argument	0.7	0.7	0.74
Pretrained BERT Embeddings	Argument	**0.72**	0.73	0.72
Unigrams	Claim	0.53	0.55	0.53
Linguistic & Twitter Features	Claim	0.56	0.58	0.56
Pretrained BERT Embeddings	Claim	**0.59**	0.6	0.59
Unigrams	Evidence	0.73	0.68	0.8
Linguistic & Twitter Features	Evidence	0.73	0.71	0.78
Pretrained BERT Embeddings	Evidence	**0.75**	0.76	0.76

Table 4: Sequence Labeling Results (w = weighted)

ADU level. Sequence labeling models were trained on the following features: 1) unigrams, 2) a combination of linguistic (e.g., n-grams, POS Tags) and Twitter-related (e.g., hashtags, @-mentions) features, 3) pretrained BERT-based word embeddings, which were again created using FLAIR. We chose a Conditional Random Fields approach (Lafferty et al., 2001), using the sklearn-crfsuite[5]. Again, all results

---

[5] sklearn-crfsuite (`https://sklearn-crfsuite.readthedocs.io`) is a scikit-learn wrapper based on CRFsuite (`http://www.chokkan.org/software/crfsuite/`).

are from 10-fold cross-validation.

In the sequence labeling approach BERT-based models perform best for all three labeling tasks. Using a set of linguistic and Twitter-related features improves the F1 scores compared to the simple unigram models in the argument (0.7 vs 0.69) and claim (0.56 vs 0.53) tasks. However, no improvement is achieved in the evidence task. Interestingly, scores are highest for the evidence task whereas the results for the claim task are considerably lower. This pattern contrasts with the tweet-level classification results.

5　Discussion and Outlook

In this paper we presented a new corpus of German tweets annotated for claim and evidence. While a few previous studies on tweet corpus creation for argument mining exist (Bosc et al., 2016), to the best of our knowledge our corpus is the first tweet dataset with ADU annotations. It is also the first German tweet dataset generally annotated for argumentation.

Although we showed that due to the subtlety of the task relatively low IAA scores were achieved, classification and sequence labeling results based on the dataset are promising. Classifying argument and claim components led to robust F1 scores around 0.8. Solely evidence units posed somewhat of a challenge for the classifier. However, sequence labeling models performed best for evidence units. With both approaches we surpassed the results presented by Goudas et al. (2014).

Given that the IAA scores for evidence annotations were reduced as well, we conclude that evidence units pose an especially hard problem to solve. Recalling our definitions of claim and evidence, this seems intuitive. As evidence units are only defined with respect to claims, a decision has to be made about the exact boundary between both components. Moreover, since tweets tend to contain a high degree of implicitness, it can be demanding to judge if a sequence in fact is relating to a claim. We plan to take this issue into account by refining our annotation scheme further.

Another interesting path of future work will be the continuing development of the argument detector. Following Goudas et al. (2014), one possible way of enhancing results could be building a pipeline based on both classification and sequence labeling approaches. More specifically, a classifier customized for identifying argumentative tweets could function as a filter, thereby allowing to train a sequence labeling model on a purely argumentative tweet set. This could increase the model's precision. To this end, we intend to enlarge the number of annotated data.

Acknowledgements

We would like to thank Polina Krasilnikova for assisting in annotating our data and Crowdee (`https://www.crowdee.com/`) for support with their annotation environment. We further thank the anonymous reviewers for their helpful comments.

References

Aseel Addawood and Masooda Bashir. 2016. "what is your evidence?" a study of controversial topics on social media. In *Proceedings of the Third Workshop on Argument Mining (ArgMining2016)*, pages 1–11, Berlin, Germany, August. Association for Computational Linguistics.

Ehud Aharoni, Anatoly Polnarov, Tamar Lavee, Daniel Hershcovich, Ran Levy, Ruty Rinott, Dan Gutfreund, and Noam Slonim. 2014. A benchmark dataset for automatic detection of claims and evidence in the context of controversial topics. In *Proceedings of the First Workshop on Argumentation Mining*, pages 64–68, Baltimore, Maryland, June. Association for Computational Linguistics.

Alan Akbik, Tanja Bergmann, Duncan Blythe, Kashif Rasul, Stefan Schweter, and Roland Vollgraf. 2019. FLAIR: An easy-to-use framework for state-of-the-art NLP. In *Proceedings of the 2019 Conference of the North American Chapter of the Association for Computational Linguistics (Demonstrations)*, pages 54–59, Minneapolis, Minnesota, June. Association for Computational Linguistics.

Ron Artstein and Massimo Poesio. 2008. Inter-coder agreement for computational linguistics. *Comput. Linguist.*, 34(4):555–596, December.

Tom Bosc, Elena Cabrio, and Serena Villata. 2016. DART: a dataset of arguments and their relations on twitter. In *Proceedings of the Tenth International Conference on Language Resources and Evaluation (LREC'16)*, pages 1258–1263, Portorož, Slovenia, May. European Language Resources Association (ELRA).

Tianqi Chen and Carlos Guestrin. 2016. XGBoost: A scalable tree boosting system. In *Proceedings of the 22nd ACM SIGKDD International Conference on Knowledge Discovery and Data Mining*, KDD '16, pages 785–794, New York, NY, USA. Association for Computing Machinery.

Jacob Devlin, Ming-Wei Chang, Kenton Lee, and Kristina Toutanova. 2019. BERT: Pre-training of deep bidirectional transformers for language understanding. In *Proceedings of the 2019 Conference of the North American Chapter of the Association for Computational Linguistics: Human Language Technologies, Volume 1 (Long and Short Papers)*, pages 4171–4186, Minneapolis, Minnesota, June. Association for Computational Linguistics.

Mihai Dusmanu, Elena Cabrio, and Serena Villata. 2017. Argument mining on twitter: Arguments, facts and sources. In *Proceedings of the 2017 Conference on Empirical Methods in Natural Language Processing*, pages 2317–2322, Copenhagen, Denmark, September. Association for Computational Linguistics.

Natalie Dykes, Stefan Evert, Merlin Göttlinger, Philipp Heinrich, and Lutz Schröder. 2020. Reconstructing arguments from noisy text. *Datenbank-Spektrum*, 20(2):123–129.

Jerome H. Friedman. 2000. Greedy function approximation: A gradient boosting machine. *Annals of Statistics*, 29:1189–1232.

Theodosis Goudas, Christos Louizos, Georgios Petasis, and Vangelis Karkaletsis. 2014. Argument extraction from news, blogs, and social media. In Aristidis Likas, Konstantinos Blekas, and Dimitris Kalles, editors, *Artificial Intelligence: Methods and Applications*, pages 287–299, Cham. Springer International Publishing.

Ivan Habernal and Iryna Gurevych. 2015. Exploiting debate portals for semi-supervised argumentation mining in user-generated web discourse. In *Proceedings of the 2015 Conference on Empirical Methods in Natural Language Processing*, pages 2127–2137, Lisbon, Portugal, September. Association for Computational Linguistics.

John D. Lafferty, Andrew McCallum, and Fernando C. N. Pereira. 2001. Conditional random fields: Probabilistic models for segmenting and labeling sequence data. In *Proceedings of the Eighteenth International Conference on Machine Learning*, ICML '01, page 282–289, San Francisco, CA, USA. Morgan Kaufmann Publishers Inc.

Marco Lui and Timothy Baldwin. 2012. langid.py: An off-the-shelf language identification tool. In *Proceedings of the ACL 2012 System Demonstrations*, pages 25–30, Jeju Island, Korea, July. Association for Computational Linguistics.

Marie-Francine Moens, Erik Boiy, Raquel Mochales Palau, and Chris Reed. 2007. Automatic detection of arguments in legal texts. In *Proceedings of the 11th International Conference on Artificial Intelligence and Law*, ICAIL '07, page 225–230, New York, NY, USA. Association for Computing Machinery.

Joonsuk Park and Claire Cardie. 2014. Identifying appropriate support for propositions in online user comments. In *Proceedings of the First Workshop on Argumentation Mining*, pages 29–38, Baltimore, Maryland, June. Association for Computational Linguistics.

Andreas Peldszus and Manfred Stede. 2013. From argument diagrams to argumentation mining in texts: A survey. *Int. J. Cogn. Inform. Nat. Intell.*, 7(1):1–31, January.

Robin Schaefer and Manfred Stede. 2019. Improving implicit stance classification in tweets using word and sentence embeddings. In Christoph Benzmüller and Heiner Stuckenschmidt, editors, *KI 2019: Advances in Artificial Intelligence*, pages 299–307, Cham. Springer International Publishing.

Christian Stab and Iryna Gurevych. 2014. Identifying argumentative discourse structures in persuasive essays. In *Proceedings of the 2014 Conference on Empirical Methods in Natural Language Processing (EMNLP)*, pages 46–56, Doha, Qatar, October. Association for Computational Linguistics.

Manfred Stede and Jodi Schneider. 2018. *Argumentation Mining*, volume 40 of *Synthesis Lectures in Human Language Technology*. Morgan Claypool.

Michael Wojatzki and Torsten Zesch. 2016. Stance-based Argument Mining – Modeling Implicit Argumentation Using Stance. In *Proceedings of the KONVENS*, pages 313–322.

Jan Šnajder. 2016. Social media argumentation mining: The quest for deliberateness in raucousness.

News Aggregation with Diverse Viewpoint Identification Using Neural Embeddings and Semantic Understanding Models

Mark Carlebach[1]*, Ria Cheruvu[1]*, Brandon Walker[1]*,
Cesar Ilharco[2], Sylvain Jaume[1]†
[1] Harvard University, [2] Google Research

Abstract

Today's news volume makes it impractical for readers to get a diverse and comprehensive view of published articles written from opposing viewpoints. We introduce a transformer-based news aggregation system, composed of topic modeling, semantic clustering, claim extraction, and textual entailment that identifies viewpoints presented in articles within a semantic cluster and classifies them into positive, neutral and negative entailments. Our novel embedded topic model using BERT-based embeddings outperforms baseline topic modeling algorithms by an 11% relative improvement. We compare recent semantic similarity models in the context of news aggregation, evaluate transformer-based models for claim extraction on news data, and demonstrate the use of textual entailment models for diverse viewpoint identification.

1 Introduction

The advent of news aggregators has ushered in a new age of information, exposing readers to continuous streams of articles from diverse outlets. However, the proliferation of data makes finding viewpoints presented in different articles challenging. We introduce a novel transformer-based news aggregation system that identifies diverse viewpoints, depicted in Figure 1. Rather than use preset criteria or learned behavior, our system provides a list of viewpoints covered in news articles and allows users to decide which viewpoints to explore. Our system consists of the following components, illustrated in Figure 2: (i) *Topic Modeling* organizes articles from multiple news sources into clusters, (ii) *Hypothesis Extraction* extracts an opinionated summary sentence (i.e., hypothesis) from each article, (iii) *Semantic Similarity* identifies differing viewpoints (i.e., sub-clusters) within each topic based on the hypotheses, (iv) *Premise Extraction* extracts a summary sentence (i.e., premise) from a group of articles associated with a viewpoint, (v) *Textual Entailment* evaluates the entailment between the hypothesis of each article and the premise of its subcluster. As part of this work, we define hypothesis extraction and premise extraction as subsets of claim extraction, where a claim is defined as a sentence expressing viewpoints associated with a news article. We define a hypothesis as a single summary sentence that represents an article's viewpoint, and use the terms hypothesis extraction and single-document subjectivity analysis interchangeably. We define a premise as a single summary sentence that represents viewpoints shared by multiple articles, and use the terms premise extraction and multi-document subjectivity analysis interchangeably.

2 Related Work

News Aggregation: Thorne et al. propose a system involving Document Retrieval, Sentence Selection, and Recognizing Textual Entailment (RTE) for fact extraction and verification (Thorne et al., 2018). Their system expects a claim as input to identify relevant documents, select sentences as evidence from the document, and finally classify the claim. Other authors evaluate the performance of transformer-based models against baseline models for debate data (Chen et al., 2019a; Chen et al., 2019b; Gretz et

---

*The first three authors contributed equally. Their listing order is random.

†Corresponding author. Email: sylvain@csail.mit.edu

Proceedings of the 7th Workshop on Argument Mining, pages 59–66
Barcelona, Spain (Online), December 13, 2020.

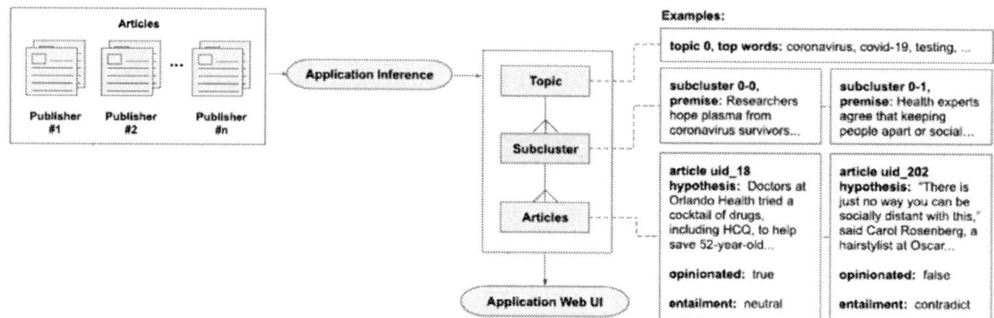

Figure 1: Architecture of our transformer-based system showing inference examples

al., 2020; Ein-Dor et al., 2020), which has applications for news data but is structured slightly differently. A single news article can be clustered under multiple topics and report multiple opinions within the same article. In contrast, debate data often directly align with one particular pre-defined topic and involve separate opinions. Our system differs from an argument search engine with indexing and retrieval (Stab et al., 2018; Wachsmuth et al., 2017). To adjust to the dynamic incoming stream and multiple sources of news data, we explore the generalization capability of language models to automate the news aggregation and viewpoint discovery problem. We have chosen to develop our own labeled article data set targeted specifically for news applications.

Topic modeling: A common approach to clustering documents based on textual content is Multinomial Latent Dirichlet Allocation (LDA) (Blei et al., 2003). Many alternatives have been investigated to improve semantic coherence by representing words with word2vec embeddings (Mikolov et al., 2013a). One such approach is the Embedded Topic Model (ETM) (Dieng et al., 2020), which uniquely represents each document as latent topics, where each topic is an embedding in the semantic space of the words. In this paper, we use ETM for our topic modeling and investigate using transformer-based embeddings in lieu of word2vec embeddings to improve quality of clustering.

Semantic Similarity: Semantic Textual Similarity (STS) refers to the goal of quantifying the degree of similarity between two bodies of text by capturing the degree to which the meanings of the two inputs overlap (Cer et al., 2017). Until recently, state-of-the-art STS systems have relied heavily on word embedding approaches (Mikolov et al., 2013b), which lack the capability to fully capture semantic context. Methods such as InferSent were developed as a solution to embed multiples words, phrases, or sentences into a single representation (Conneau et al., 2017). The Universal Sentence Encoder (USE) models (Cer et al., 2018), BERT (Devlin et al., 2019), and other models such as RoBERTa (Liu et al., 2019) and GPT-3 (Brown et al., 2020) have since made significant improvements on InferSent.

Claim Extraction: A key component of opinion-oriented information extraction from articles is identifying sentence(s) expressing viewpoints associated with articles (Wilson et al., 2005b; Chen et al., 2019b). Early attempts towards solving the problem of single-document subjectivity analysis involved the use of Naïve Bayes classifiers, AdaBoost, and rule-based classifiers trained on the Multi-Perspective Question Answering (MPQA) Opinion Corpus (Wilson et al., 2005b) for identifying subjective expressions and similar tasks (Wilson et al., 2005a; Somasundaran and Wiebe, 2010). Recent work (Xu et al., 2019; Hoang et al., 2019; Han and Kando, 2019) has shown fine-tuned BERT models and BERT-based models (Cer et al., 2018) perform well against baseline models for sentiment analysis and opinion mining tasks. BERT has been applied to multiple passages/documents for question and answering tasks (Wang et al., 2019). However, few transformer-based models were applied for multi-document subjectivity analysis (Liu and Lapata, 2019). In this work, we implement hypothesis extraction as a sentence-classification task and consider BERT-based models against a Naïve Bayes classifier to determine if transformer-based models perform well for hypothesis extraction. We propose abstractive summarization models, such as BART (Lewis et al., 2019) and T5 (Raffel et al., 2019), for premise extraction.

Textual Entailment: Recognizing textual entailment (RTE) involves identifying whether a hypothesis statement supports, contradicts, or is indifferent to a premise statement, regardless of whether the

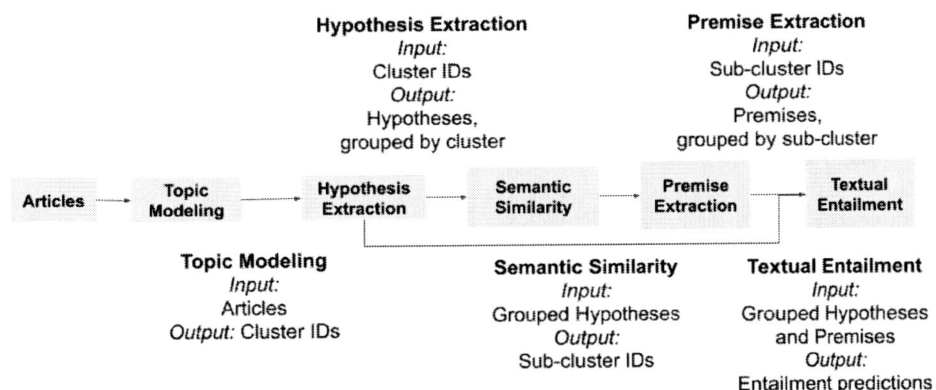

Figure 2: Our system processes news articles in five steps and generates entailment predictions.

premise and hypothesis lexically match (Sammons et al., 2012). Chen et al. leverage textual entailment to find evidence paragraphs in support of viewpoints (Chen et al., 2019b). Attempts towards RTE include Named Entity Recognition (NER) (Sammons et al., 2012), LSTMs with word embeddings, and transformer-based models, such as BART and RoBERTa, which deliver high performance for these tasks.

3 Methods

A demo of our system is available at https://harvard-almit.github.io/newsaggregator/. We tested this system on a dataset of over 1,000 scraped articles from various news outlets, such as Yahoo News and The Post and Courier. Figure 2 illustrates how news articles are processed across the components in our system: (i) *Topic Modeling* generates cluster IDs for the articles, (ii) *Hypothesis Extraction* generates hypotheses for the clustered articles, (iii) *Semantic Similarity* generates subcluster IDs using hypotheses, (iv) *Premise Extraction* generates premises for articles in each subcluster, and (v) *Textual Entailment*, consuming outputs of Hypothesis Extraction and Premise Extraction, generates entailment predictions and provides the results of our news aggregation system.

We perform topic modeling with three approaches using *20 Newsgroups* data (Lang, 1995) and Adjusted Rand Index Scoring (Hubert and Arabie, 1985): (i) Latent Dirichlet Allocation (LDA) using the *gensim* package (Řehůřek and Sojka, 2011), (ii) ETM with word2vec embeddings, and (iii) ETM with centroids of BERT based embeddings (Blei et al., 2003; Mikolov et al., 2013a; Dieng et al., 2020), where we select a value for *num_bert_centroids* as the number of embeddings ETM will use, and use k-means clustering (k=*num_bert_centroids*) from *FAISS* package (Johnson et al., 2019). For training hypothesis extraction models on the clustered articles, we use a modified version of the MPQA Opinion Corpus v3.0 consisting of expressive subjective elements (Deng and Wiebe, 2015). We train a multinomial Naïve Bayes classifier and fine-tune BERT, XLNet (Yang et al., 2019), and ALBERT (Lan et al., 2020) models using HuggingFace's *transformers* library (Wolf et al., 2020) on pre-processed MPQA data for sentence-level subjectivity analysis (i.e., binary opinion classification of sentences).

The semantic similarity module then clusters generated hypotheses of documents within a topic into clusters of semantically related articles, in which each article is associated with a single, more specific topic. We considered BERT, RoBERTa, and DistilBERT (Sanh et al., 2019) in a siamese network structure (Reimers and Gurevych, 2019), in addition to USE using the Pearson correlation coefficient, for the semantic similarity module. The models were fine-tuned on the Argument Facet Similarity Corpus by (Misra et al., 2016) and the STS-Benchmark dataset provided by the *SentEval* (Conneau and Kiela, 2018) package. For premise extraction, we fine-tuned a large BART model (406M parameters) (Lewis et al., 2019) and a small T5 model (60M parameters) (Raffel et al., 2019) using the *transformers* library on data taken from IBM's Project Debater Claim Stance Dataset (Bar-Haim et al., 2017). We reformatted this dataset into a summarization dataset for fine-tuning. We chose not to utilize the claims provided in the dataset, since the hypothesis extraction module already accomplishes this purpose, and used topics (statements that represent a group of articles) from the dataset instead. The final output of the system is provided by the textual entailment module. For each article in a semantic similarity sub-cluster, premises and hypotheses generated from the claim extraction module are input to the textual entailment module to predict whether the hypothesis contradicts, entails, or is unrelated to the premise. We evaluated Fairseq's pre-trained RoBERTa and BART models fine-tuned for MNLI (Ott et al., 2019) using the transformers library for textual entailment on the claim stance dataset presented by (Bar-Haim et al., 2017), given that BART reportedly performs similar to RoBERTa on the MNLI task (Lewis et al., 2019).

4   Results

Our results for topic modeling show ETM with word2vec embeddings outperforming LDA by 32% on unseen data, and ETM with BERT based embeddings outperforms ETM with word2vec embeddings based on the number of BERT centroids. When predicting on unseen data, ETM trained with 100K BERT centroids outperforms ETM with 25,535 word2vec embeddings by 11%, suggesting the benefits of long sequence contextualized embeddings. We found when predicting on unseen data, the improvements of ETM trained with BERT embeddings do not continue beyond a certain number of centroids due to overfitting. However, when predicting on seen data, ETM trained with BERT embeddings's outperformance increases as the number of BERT centroids increases to 1 million centroids. When predicting on seen data, ETM trained with 1 million BERT centroids outperforms ETM with word2vec embeddings by 17%. For hypothesis extraction, on a held-out dataset of the MPQA data, we found XLNet outperforms the Naïve Bayes classifier baseline by 23%, and provides better performance compared to BERT and ALBERT on the F1 score while ALBERT achieved a higher Matthews correlation coefficient score (see Table 1). We found the BERT-based model is capable of extracting distinct hypotheses from different entities for a particular article.

MODEL	F1	MCC
NAÏVE-BAYES BASELINE	0.740	0.302
BERT	0.878	0.722
XLNET	**0.911**	0.736
ALBERT	0.893	**0.757**

Table 1: XLNet outperforms other models on F1 using held-out MPQA data.

MODEL	STS-B	AFS
USE	0.78413	0.44501
SBERT	0.84195	0.75800
SROBERTA	0.84266	0.75502
SDISTILBERT	0.84135	0.73400

Table 2: Siamese BERT-based models outperform USE on STS-B and AFS by 6%.

In Table 2, for the semantic similarity task, we found the BERT-based models in a siamese network outperformed USE, making them well-suited for our use-case. The results presented are the Pearson correlation of the cosine distance between the embedding vectors and the human-labeled similarity score. The results indicate that we have fairly high correlation ($r \approx 0.84$) recognizing semantically similar sentences and moderate correlation ($r \approx 0.75$) recognizing argument facets. This gives us an average r value across the two tasks of approximately 0.80. Additionally, we note that the smaller DistilBERT yields results similar to its larger counterparts. For premise extraction, we achieved a loss of 1.260 with T5 and a loss of 6.192 with BART on the validation dataset. The T5 model typically outputs 3 sentences. The output is further processed to include the longer sentence to prevent run-off sentences from occurring in the predicted premises. We found BART's predictions were limited to topics in the training data contra T5's predictions that were directly related to article content. Sample predictions from T5 include "The house would be a great place to promote the liberal arts movement" and "The study believes that warm climates would limit the spread of the virus if people are immune from it". For textual entailment, BART has slightly higher accuracy (67%) compared to RoBERTa (65%) on the claim stance dataset. However, for our datasets, RoBERTa outputted predictions with higher probability compared to BART. Given these results, we implemented XLNet for hypothesis extraction, SBERT for semantic similarity, T5 for premise extraction, and RoBERTA for textual entailment. As for ETM, since it proves to be highly resource-intensive, we opted for LDA instead. The following examples show two groups of premise, hypothesis and predicted entailment generated by our system.

Premise	Health experts agree that keeping people apart, or "social distancing," during the coronavirus pandemic is essential for bringing the outbreak under control.
Hypothesis	"There is just no way you can be socially distant with this," said Carol Rosenberg
Entailment	Contradiction

Premise	Word that money would soon land in bank accounts across the country has led to a surge of scam phone calls, with fraudsters falsely claiming people had to provide personal information to collect government money.
Hypothesis	Clicking a link takes them to what looks like an official website asking for personal information with instructions that the step is "necessary" to process their check
Entailment	Neutral

5   Discussion

We found topics generated by ETM for our dataset were more coherent compared to LDA for topic modeling. ETM with BERT based embeddings outperforms ETM with word2vec embeddings when ETM is trained with a number of BERT centroids greater than the number of word2vec embeddings associated with the corpus. Training ETM with BERT centroids involves significantly more computational work than training ETM with word2vec embeddings. On the other hand, in settings where both model creation and predictions are based on the same, full dataset, ETM with BERT-based embeddings does perform better and could be incorporated. We demonstrate that hypothesis extraction can be phrased as subjectivity analysis, and we found XLNET and ALBERT can deliver high performance for this task. A novel aspect of our methodology is that we employ the generated hypotheses as input to the semantic similarity module. Current state-of-the-art models treat semantic similarity as a pair-wise regression problem, making them computationally inefficient for clustering for news aggregation. We found that transformer-based models increased the quality of the clustering compared to USE. The results here show that we can efficiently find semantic clusters with standard clustering methods, e.g., k-Means++ (Arthur and Vassilvitskii, 2007), or density based clustering, e.g., DBSCAN (Ester et al., 1996), to present users with a diverse set of articles on a specific topic.

We show that premise extraction is closely related to the task of abstractive summarization, as premises must be constructed to enable a group of articles to agree or disagree with statements. We observed the small T5 model was able to significantly outperform the larger BART model. We demonstrate that multi-document and single-document claim extractions can be informative premises and hypotheses that are inputs to a textual entailment module. From the second premise-hypothesis pair in Section 4, we see there is a small contradiction that the model does not detect, but could potentially predict if a different premise-hypothesis pair was chosen, or if predictions were validated using phrases from the hypothesis (e.g., the model based its prediction on the phrase "what looks like an official website asking for personal information"). Consequentially, we found that different premise-hypothesis pairs within an article can lead to different predictions from the textual entailment module for the same article, due to opposing viewpoints described in the article and distinct word phrasing between sentences.

6   Conclusion

We have introduced a transformer-based news aggregation system, consisting of topic modeling, hypothesis extraction, semantic clustering, premise extraction, and textual entailment that allows readers to view articles from diverse viewpoints. Our results show relative improvements over baseline models in the range of 10-23% using Embedded Topic Modeling, semantic similarity through fine-tuned BERT models with a siamese network structure, and hypothesis extraction using large pre-trained language models for sentence-level subjectivity analysis. Our results also show a five-fold loss decrease when using a small T5 model, compared to a large BART model, for premise extraction. The system we have developed demonstrates that pre-trained BERT-based models of textual entailment can be used to identify diverse viewpoints.

References

David Arthur and Sergei Vassilvitskii. 2007. k-means++: the advantages of careful seeding. In *Proceedings of the Eighteenth Annual ACM-SIAM Symposium on Discrete Algorithms*, pages 1027–1035. Society for Industrial and Applied Mathematics.

Roy Bar-Haim, Indrajit Bhattacharya, Francesco Dinuzzo, Amrita Saha, and Noam Slonim. 2017. Stance classification of context-dependent claims. In *Proceedings of the 15th Conference of the European Chapter of the Association for Computational Linguistics (EACL)*, volume 1, pages 251–261, Valencia, Spain, April 3-7.

David M Blei, Andrew Y Ng, and Michael I Jordan. 2003. Latent dirichlet allocation. *Journal of Machine Learning Research*, 3:993–1022, January.

T. Brown, B. Mann, Nick Ryder, Melanie Subbiah, J. Kaplan, Prafulla Dhariwal, Arvind Neelakantan, Pranav Shyam, Girish Sastry, Amanda Askell, Sandhini Agarwal, Ariel Herbert-Voss, G. Krüger, Tom Henighan, R. Child, Aditya Ramesh, D. Ziegler, Jeffrey Wu, Clemens Winter, Christopher Hesse, Mark Chen, E. Sigler, Mateusz Litwin, Scott Gray, Benjamin Chess, J. Clark, Christopher Berner, Sam McCandlish, A. Radford, Ilya Sutskever, and Dario Amodei. 2020. Language models are few-shot learners. *ArXiv*, abs/2005.14165.

Daniel Cer, Mona Diab, Eneko Agirre, Iñigo Lopez-Gazpio, and Lucia Specia. 2017. SemEval-2017 task 1: Semantic textual similarity multilingual and crosslingual focused evaluation. In *Proceedings of the 11th International Workshop on Semantic Evaluation (SemEval-2017)*, pages 1–14, Vancouver, Canada, August. Association for Computational Linguistics.

Daniel Cer, Yinfei Yang, Sheng-yi Kong, Nan Hua, Nicole Limtiaco, Rhomni St. John, Noah Constant, Mario Guajardo-Cespedes, Steve Yuan, Chris Tar, Yun-Hsuan Sung, Brian Strope, and Ray Kurzweil. 2018. Universal sentence encoder. *CoRR*, abs/1803.11175.

Sihao Chen, Daniel Khashabi, Chris Callison-Burch, and Dan Roth. 2019a. Perspectroscope: A window to the world of diverse perspectives. *ACL system demonstration track*, abs/1906.04761.

Sihao Chen, Daniel Khashabi, Wenpeng Yin, Chris Callison-Burch, and Dan Roth. 2019b. Seeing things from a different angle: Discovering diverse perspectives about claims. In *Proceedings of the 2019 Conference of the North American Chapter of the Association for Computational Linguistics: Human Language Technologies, Volume 1 (Long and Short Papers)*, pages 542–557, Minneapolis, Minnesota, June. Association for Computational Linguistics.

Alexis Conneau and Douwe Kiela. 2018. SentEval: An evaluation toolkit for universal sentence representations. In *Proceedings of the Eleventh International Conference on Language Resources and Evaluation (LREC 2018)*, Miyazaki, Japan, May. European Language Resources Association (ELRA).

Alexis Conneau, Douwe Kiela, Holger Schwenk, Loïc Barrault, and Antoine Bordes. 2017. Supervised learning of universal sentence representations from natural language inference data. In *Proceedings of the 2017 Conference on Empirical Methods in Natural Language Processing*, pages 670–680, Copenhagen, Denmark, September. Association for Computational Linguistics.

Lingjia Deng and Janyce Wiebe. 2015. Mpqa 3.0: An entity/event-level sentiment corpus. In *Proceedings of the North American Chapter of the Association for Computational Linguistics: Human Language Technologies*, pages 1323–1328, Denver, Colorado, May 31 – June 5.

Jacob Devlin, Ming-Wei Chang, Kenton Lee, and Kristina Toutanova. 2019. Bert: Pre-training of deep bidirectional transformers for language understanding. In *Proceedings of North American Association for Computational Linguistics: Human Language Translation (NAACL-HLT) 2019*, pages 4171–4186, Minneapolis, Minnesota, June 2-7.

Adji B Dieng, Francisco JR Ruiz, and David M Blei. 2020. Topic modeling in embedding spaces. In *Transactions of the Association for Computational Linguistics*, volume 8, pages 439–453.

Liat Ein-Dor, Eyal Shnarch, Lena Dankin, Alon Halfon, Benjamin Sznajder, Ariel Gera, Carlos Alzate, Martin Gleize, Leshem Choshen, Yufang Hou, Yonatan Bilu, Ranit Aharonov, and Noam Slonim. 2020. Corpus wide argument mining - a working solution. In *Thirty-Fourth AAAI Conference on Artificial Intelligence*.

Martin Ester, Hans-Peter Kriegel, Jörg Sander, and Xiaowei Xu. 1996. A density-based algorithm for discovering clusters in large spatial databases with noise. In Evangelos Simoudis, Jiawei Han, and Usama M. Fayyad, editors, *Proceedings of the Second International Conference on Knowledge Discovery and Data Mining (KDD-96)*, pages 226–231. AAAI Press.

Shai Gretz, Roni Friedman, Edo Cohen-Karlik, Assaf Toledo, Dan Lahav, Ranit Aharonov, and Noam Slonim. 2020. A large-scale dataset for argument quality ranking: Construction and analysis. In *Thirty-Fourth AAAI Conference on Artificial Intelligence*.

Wen-Bin Han and Noriko Kando. 2019. Opinion mining with deep contextualized embeddings. In *Proceedings of the 2019 Conference of the North American Chapter of the Association for Computational Linguistics: Student Research Workshop*, pages 35–42.

Mickel Hoang, Oskar Alija Bihorac, and Jacobo Rouces. 2019. Aspect-based sentiment analysis using bert. In *NEAL Proceedings of the 22nd Nordic Conference on Computational Linguistics (NoDaLiDa), September 30-October 2, Turku, Finland*, 167, pages 187–196. Linköping University Electronic Press.

Lawrence Hubert and Phipps Arabie. 1985. Comparing clusterings. *Journal of Classification*, 2:193–218.

J. Johnson, M. Douze, and H. Jégou. 2019. Billion-scale similarity search with gpus. *IEEE Transactions on Big Data*, pages 1–1.

Zhenzhong Lan, Mingda Chen, Sebastian Goodman, Kevin Gimpel, Piyush Sharma, and Radu Soricut. 2020. Albert: A lite bert for self-supervised learning of language representations. In *International Conference on Learning Representations*.

Ken Lang. 1995. Newsweeder: Learning to filter netnews. In *Proceedings of the Twelfth International Conference on Machine Learning*, pages 331–339.

Mike Lewis, Yinhan Liu, Naman Goyal, Marjan Ghazvininejad, Abdelrahman Mohamed, Omer Levy, Ves Stoyanov, and Luke Zettlemoyer. 2019. Bart: Denoising sequence-to-sequence pre-training for natural language generation, translation, and comprehension. *ArXiv*, abs/1910.13461.

Yang Liu and Mirella Lapata. 2019. Hierarchical transformers for multi-document summarization. *ArXiv*, abs/1905.13164.

Yinhan Liu, Myle Ott, Naman Goyal, Jingfei Du, Mandar Joshi, Danqi Chen, Omer Levy, Mike Lewis, Luke Zettlemoyer, and Veselin Stoyanov. 2019. Roberta: A robustly optimized bert pretraining approach. *arXiv preprint arXiv:1907.11692*.

Tomas Mikolov, Kai Chen, Greg Corrado, and Jeffrey Dean. 2013a. Efficient estimation of word representations in vector space. *arXiv preprint arXiv:1301.3781*.

Tomas Mikolov, Ilya Sutskever, Kai Chen, Greg S Corrado, and Jeff Dean. 2013b. Distributed representations of words and phrases and their compositionality. In C. J. C. Burges, L. Bottou, M. Welling, Z. Ghahramani, and K. Q. Weinberger, editors, *Advances in Neural Information Processing Systems 26*, pages 3111–3119. Curran Associates, Inc.

Amita Misra, Brian Ecker, and Marilyn Walker. 2016. Measuring the similarity of sentential arguments in dialogue. In *Proceedings of the 17th Annual Meeting of the Special Interest Group on Discourse and Dialogue*, pages 276–287, Los Angeles, September. Association for Computational Linguistics.

Myle Ott, Sergey Edunov, Alexei Baevski, Angela Fan, Sam Gross, Nathan Ng, David Grangier, and Michael Auli. 2019. fairseq: A fast, extensible toolkit for sequence modeling. In *NAACL-HLT*.

Colin Raffel, Noam Shazeer, Adam Roberts, Katherine Lee, Sharan Narang, Michael Matena, Yanqi Zhou, Wei Li, and Peter J. Liu. 2019. Exploring the limits of transfer learning with a unified text-to-text transformer. *ArXiv*, abs/1910.10683.

Radim Řehůřek and Petr Sojka. 2011. Gensim-statistical semantics in python. In *Proceedings of EuroScipy*.

Nils Reimers and Iryna Gurevych. 2019. Sentence-bert: Sentence embeddings using siamese bert-networks. In *Proceedings of the Conference on Empirical Methods in Natural Language Processing (EMNLP)*.

Mark Sammons, Vinod Vydiswaran, and Dan Roth. 2012. Recognizing textual entailment. *Multilingual Natural Language Applications: From Theory to Practice*, pages 209–258.

Victor Sanh, Lysandre Debut, Julien Chaumond, and Thomas Wolf. 2019. Distilbert, a distilled version of bert: smaller, faster, cheaper and lighter. In *EMC2: 5th Edition co-located with NeurIPS*.

Swapna Somasundaran and Janyce Wiebe. 2010. Recognizing stances in ideological on-line debates. In *Proceedings of the NAACL HLT 2010 Workshop on Computational Approaches to Analysis and Generation of Emotion in Text*, pages 116–124. Association for Computational Linguistics.

Christian Stab, Johannes Daxenberger, Chris Stahlhut, Tristan Miller, B. Schiller, Christopher Tauchmann, Steffen Eger, and Iryna Gurevych. 2018. Argumentext: Searching for arguments in heterogeneous sources. In *NAACL-HLT*.

James Thorne, Andreas Vlachos, Christos Christodoulopoulos, and Arpit Mittal. 2018. FEVER: a large-scale dataset for fact extraction and VERification. In *Proceedings of the 2018 Conference of the North American Chapter of the Association for Computational Linguistics: Human Language Technologies, Volume 1 (Long Papers)*, pages 809–819, New Orleans, Louisiana, June. Association for Computational Linguistics.

Henning Wachsmuth, Martin Potthast, Khalid Al Khatib, Yamen Ajjour, Jana Puschmann, Jiani Qu, Jonas Dorsch, Viorel Morari, Janek Bevendorff, and Benno Stein. 2017. Building an argument search engine for the web. In *ArgMining@EMNLP*.

Zhiguo Wang, Patrick Ng, Xiaofei Ma, Ramesh Nallapati, and Bing Xiang. 2019. Multi-passage bert: A globally normalized bert model for open-domain question answering. In *EMNLP/IJCNLP*.

Theresa Wilson, Paul Hoffmann, Swapna Somasundaran, Jason Kessler, Janyce Wiebe, Yejin Choi, Claire Cardie, Ellen Riloff, and Siddharth Patwardhan. 2005a. Opinionfinder: A system for subjectivity analysis. In *Proceedings of HLT/EMNLP 2005 Interactive Demonstrations*, pages 34–35.

Theresa Wilson, Janyce Wiebe, and Paul Hoffmann. 2005b. Recognizing contextual polarity in phrase-level sentiment analysis. In *Proceedings of Human Language Technology Conference and Conference on Empirical Methods in Natural Language Processing*.

Thomas Wolf, Lysandre Debut, Victor Sanh, Julien Chaumond, Clement Delangue, Anthony Moi, Pierric Cistac, Tim Rault, Rémi Louf, Morgan Funtowicz, Joe Davison, Sam Shleifer, Patrick von Platen, Clara Ma, Yacine Jernite, Julien Plu, Canwen Xu, Teven Le Scao, Sylvain Gugger, Mariama Drame, Quentin Lhoest, and Alexander M. Rush. 2020. Huggingface's transformers: State-of-the-art natural language processing. *ArXiv, abs/1910.03771*.

Hu Xu, Bing Liu, Lei Shu, and Philip S Yu. 2019. Bert post-training for review reading comprehension and aspect-based sentiment analysis. *Proceedings of North American Association for Computational Linguistic - Human Language Translation (NAACL-HLT) 2019*, pages 2324–2335, June.

Zhilin Yang, Zihang Dai, Yiming Yang, Jaime G. Carbonell, Ruslan Salakhutdinov, and Quoc V. Le. 2019. Xlnet: Generalized autoregressive pretraining for language understanding. In *33rd Conference on Neural Information Processing Systems (NeurIPS 2019)*, Vancouver, Canada.

ECHR: Legal Corpus for Argument Mining

Prakash Poudyal[1], Jaromír Šavelka[2], Aagje Ieven[3], Marie Francine Moens[4],
Teresa Gonçalves[5], Paulo Quaresma[6]

Department of Computer Science & Engineering, Kathmandu University, Nepal[1]
School of Computer Science, Carnegie Mellon University, USA[2]
Katholieke Universiteit Leuven, Faculty of Law, Leuven, Belgium[3],[4]
Department of Informatics, University of Evora, Portugal[5],[6]

prakash@ku.edu.np[1], jsavelka@andrew.cmu.edu[2], aagje.ieven@gmail.com[3],
sien.moens@cs.kuleuven.be[4], tcg@uevora.pt[5], pq@uevora.pt[6]

Abstract

In this paper, we publicly release an annotated corpus of 42 decisions of the European Court of Human Rights (ECHR). The corpus is annotated in terms of three types of clauses useful in argument mining: premise, conclusion, and non-argument parts of the text. Furthermore, relationships among the premises and conclusions are mapped. We present baselines for three tasks that lead from unstructured texts to structured arguments. The tasks are argument clause recognition, clause relation prediction, and premise/conclusion recognition. Despite a straightforward application of the bidirectional encoders from Transformers (BERT), we obtained very promising results (F_1 0.765 on argument recognition, 0.511 on relation prediction, and 0.859/0.628 on premise/conclusion recognition). The results suggest the usefulness of pre-trained language models based on deep neural network architectures in argument mining. Because of the simplicity of the baselines, there is ample space for improvement in future work based on the released corpus.

Keyword: European Court of Human Rights (ECHR), argumentation, argument mining, bidirectional encoders from transformers (BERT)

1 Introduction

Texts can be categorized into subjects such as law, philosophy, computing, science, etc., and annotated with information appropriate for the purpose of the research (e.g. argument mining, named entity recognition, etc.). This information is collectively called a corpus and forms a critical component of this research. The corpora are a source of knowledge for creating certain rules and regulations (i.e. a model) which are used in statistical and hypothetical tests. Although influenced by many other factors, the performance of statistical approaches still depends primarily on the quality and size of the corpus. Therefore during the process of creating a corpus, annotators need to prioritize their ability to maintain quality and quantity via inter-annotator agreement (Artstein, 2017). While creating corpora, it is desirable to ensure that a system will achieve the highest possible accuracy. Nevertheless, creating and constructing corpora is labor-intensive, as it is complex, time-consuming and requires experts who need to be well versed in the corresponding corpus field. For example, in the case of legal corpora, the annotating experts must be lawyers and should also be familiar with the legal arguments. With these constraints, there are a limited number of corpora available in the respective fields.

Proceedings of the 7th Workshop on Argument Mining, pages 67–75
Barcelona, Spain (Online), December 13, 2020.

In this paper a corpus of ECHR decisions is released to the public with a well-structured electronic format[1]. The corpus is annotated with a compact argumentation type system (3 types). Pointers to the work where the corpus has been already used prior to its release here are provided. The annotation process and the tools used are explained in detail. The resulting corpus is described and several tasks where it can be employed are proposed.

The rest of the paper is organized as follows: Section 2 presents the related work focusing on various corpora that are publicly available. Section 3 introduces the ECHR's Case Law. Section 4 describes the annotation types, the annotation process, and the tools that were used for annotation. Section 5 presents the summary statistics related to the resulting corpus. Section 6 presents the baselines for three fundamental argument mining tasks.

2   Related Work

A corpus is typically a representation of text, language, image, video, audio, and subject that is annotated with certain signs for a specific purpose. The performance of a predictive system based upon a corpus also depends on its quality and size. Depending on the goal, corpora are collected from different domains, such as Newspaper, Legal, Political, Scientific and Persuasive essays and also in various languages like English, Portuguese, German, Greek.

Lippi and Torroni (2016) mention that annotating corpora is complex, expensive and requires experts who are well versed in the corresponding field to ensure that annotations are correct. Further, the paper also describes the corpora of various domains concerning the argument mining area. Palau and Ieven (2009) deal with the theoretical aspects of the structure present in legal corpora; they highlight the different critical points humans need to encounter when applying theory to real argumentation and emphasize the association between real arguments and the theories that describe those arguments.

Several research centers in the world are devoted to developing corpora. One such center that plays an important role in many aspects of argumentation, from theoretical to practical, is Arg-tech Centre[2]. Its one of the goals is to develop freely available software tools to aid the researcher in the argumentation field. There are more than 50 corpora from different sectors offered in AIFdb (Bex et al., 2013). These corpora are available in different formats, such as SVG, PNG, DOT, JSON, LKIF, RTNL, RDF, PL. A popular corpus named Araucaria (Reed et al., 2008) was developed in the Arg-tech Centre. The granularity of the corpus was 'claim'and 'premise'. The corpus was collected from 19 newspapers (from the UK, US, India, Australia, South Africa, Germany, China, Russia and Israel), 4 parliamentary records (in the UK, US and India), 5 court reports (from the UK, US and Canada), 6 magazines (UK, US and India), and 14 other online discussion boards and *cause* sources such as the Human Rights Watch (HuRW) and the GlobalWarming.org.

Another research lab, Ubiquitous Knowledge Processing (UKP) Lab [3], TU Darmstadt, Germany, is dedicated to developing natural language and machine learning tools and techniques. One of their activities is to develop corpora for argument mining in English and German. Habernal and Gurevych (2017) created the *Argument Annotated User-Generated Web Discourse* consisting of 90,000 tokens from 340 documents with the datasets prepared using Toulmin argument classification (Backing, Claim, Premise, Rebuttal, Refutation). Habernal and Gurevych also created the *UKPConvArg1 Corpus*, a user-generated Web content corpus that consists of 11,650 argument pairs (Habernal and Gurevych, 2016b) and a new crowd-sourced benchmark data-set that contains 9,111 argument pairs labeled with 17 categories (Habernal and Gurevych, 2016a).

Kwon et al., (2006) developed the corpus based on public comments on the Environmental Protection Agency (EPA) standards rules on hazardous pollutants. Two annotators were involved in categorizing 630 documents in terms of 9 categories achieving an agreement of 0.60 on Cohen's Kappa coefficient. Rosenthal and McKeown (2012) created a corpus from two datasets: 285 LiveJournal[4] blog spots and 51

---

[1] http://www.di.uevora.pt/~pq/echr/
[2] http://www.arg-tech.org/
[3] https://www.ukp.tu-darmstadt.de/ukp-home/
[4] https://www.livejournal.com/

Wikipedia discussion forums; the datasets were annotated for the purpose of identifying claims (the ratio of claim vs. not claim is 60:40 in LiveJournal and 64:36 in Wikipedia). Aharoni et al., (2014) present an argumentative structure dataset consisting of 33 controversial topics; the corpus is derived from 586 Wikipedia articles and the authors state that the corpus was constructed (manual annotation) with great attention to detail.

Goudas et al., (2014) annotated 204 documents in Greek related to renewable energy. The documents contain 16,000 sentences and were collected from social media, news, blogs, and microblogs. 760 sentences were annotated with premise and claim at the clause-level. Similarly, Sardianos et al., (2015) choose 300 news items (sports, politics, economics, and culture, etc.) in the Greek language to annotate; two post-graduate students were assigned to annotate the corpus and since they were only moderately experienced, guidelines were provided to describe the identification of arguments focusing on discourse markers such as *because*, *in order to* and *but*. Each annotator was assigned to annotate 150 documents with argument components, and the final version of the corpus contained 1191 argument components.

3 ECHR's Case Law

Case-law documents are written using detailed information from the stakeholders of the court, factual information from the defendant, allegations made by the plaintiff, arguments from both parties, and a decision made by the judge. After collecting all information, it needs to be structured to be useful. To structure the data, and also to know the location of the components of the arguments, it is necessary to analyze and determine the content of each section available via case-law. From the website[5], it is known that case-law is divided into seven categories: Judgment, Decision, Communicated Case, Legal Summary, Advisory Opinion, Report and Resolution. Of these seven categories, two categories (Judgment and Decision) are found in the ECHR Corpus.

In the ECHR Corpus, there are 20 Decisions and 22 Judgments[6] issued by a chamber of seven judges ruling on the admissibility and merits of the cases. Both categories represent similar information, however, the 'Decision category' presents the information briefly (the average word length is 3500 words) in the corpus whereas, in the case of Judgments, more detailed information is available (an average word length of 10000 words). The Decision case-law documents are divided into six sections: i) Introduction, ii) The Facts, iii) Complaints, iv) Proceedings before the Commission, v) The Laws and vi) For the Reason. Judgment case-law documents are divided into eight sections: i) Introduction, ii) Procedure, iii) As the Facts, iv) The Circumstances of the Case, v) Proceedings before the Commission, vi) Final Submissions to the Court, vii) As to the Law, and viii) For the Reason.

The case-law documents begin with introducing the stakeholders of the courts (President, Judge, Registrar and Deputy Registrar, Lawyers, Plaintiff, Defendants, and their agents), with their designations, plaintiff, defendant and other members involved in the case. After this, procedure and facts regarding the plaintiff are described. The facts describe an overview of the case that includes information from previous cases, the reason for making an allegation and the chronological sequence of events. The structure of the case-law varies depending upon the exact laws. This information is included as necessary, meaning that the case will vary in length depending upon the case-law and any other essential information that is included. After providing facts of the plaintiff and defendant, the case-law includes the discussions held in the court based upon the allegation made by the plaintiff are presented. Likewise, the defendant provides the reason and claim from their perspective and returns a response to the claim made by the plaintiff. After several discussions and arguments presented by both parties, the Judge renders his decision. Detail information about ECHR case law documents can be found in (Mochales and Moens, 2008).

4 Annotation

The Language Intelligence and Information Retrieval Research Lab at the KU Leuven hired two lawyers to annotate the ECHR case-law documents (Palau and Ieven, 2009) . The annotators were given an

---

[5]https://hudoc.echr.coe.int/eng
[6]Released before 20 October 1999 by the European Commission on Human Rights.

argumentation scheme formalism and guidelines that describe the arguments.

Once the annotation was completed, they were compared and the Kappa inter-rater agreement tally was found to be 0.58. A third lawyer was selected to analyze the annotations and found that the main reason for the discrepancies was due to a different demarcation of argument boundaries or, put another way, to the ambiguity that is found in argumentative structure. Subsequently, a fourth annotator was selected and was given new guidelines, new sets of comments and recommendations. His annotation achieved 80% agreement which is quite a significant gain. Additional information regarding the evaluation of the corpus annotation process can be found in (Palau and Ieven, 2009), (Mochales and Moens, 2008).

The corpus is composed of 42 decisions. There are 1951 premises and 743 conclusions (note some argument constituents are premises/conclusions for more than one argument, and some constituents are both premises of one argument and conclusion for another).

- Premise – one or more premises are bound to exactly one conclusion.

- Conclusion

- Non-argument

The documents were annotated in the Gloss annotation environment developed at the University of Pittsburgh. Gloss is a lightweight tool focused on semantic annotation of textual documents. Through a small number of individual components it supports the whole annotation process, including corpus assembly, type system definition, document annotation, as well as quality control. The system is equipped with simple identity and role management that facilitates basic security as well as the ability of multiple users performing various roles within a project. Gloss was already used in multiple research projects, e.g. in Savelka and Ashley (2018; 2017).

The first step typically involves uploading the plain text documents; these can be organized in one or more collections. Next, the type system needs to be created. Gloss is very flexible with respect to type systems. It offers three built-in types (Annotation, Object, and ValueSet) that function as building blocks from which a type system of arbitrary complexity may be assembled. Types may be defined with an arbitrary number of attributes. Inheritance and composition of types are supported as well. Finally, a task may be created using one or more document collections and one or more type systems. Multiple users may be involved in a task either as annotators or editors (quality control).

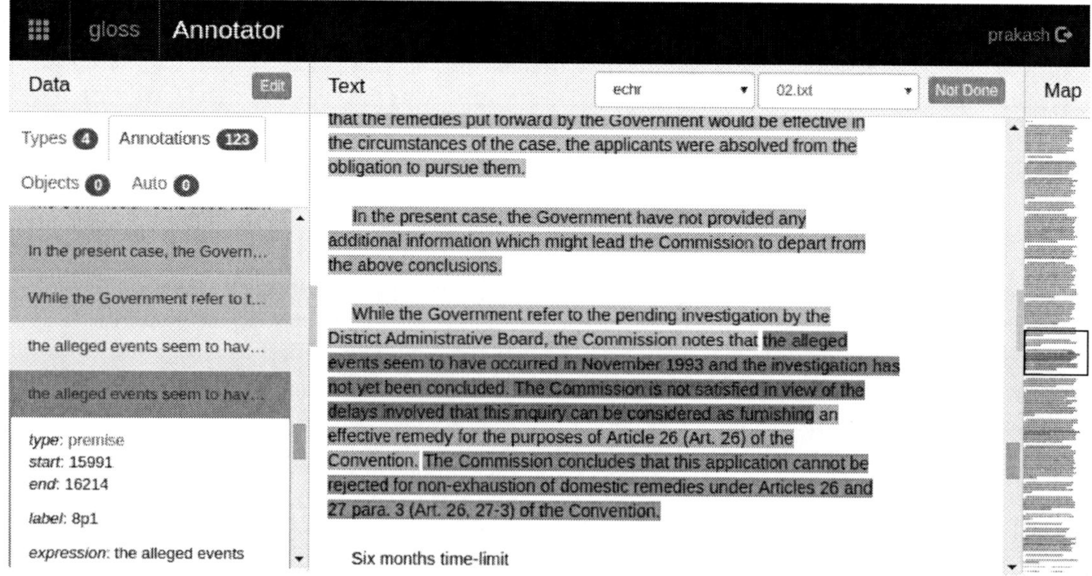

Figure 1: Annotation interface (Gloss) used in this work.

For the annotation itself, a user is presented with a list of documents from which he can select the one to work on. The available types are listed in the left pane. As the user creates annotations, an interactive list is being populated. The annotations may be easily edited or deleted after being created. The annotation is created through highlighting the respective span of text and picking the respective type from the pop-up menu. The annotation user interface is shown in Figure 1.

5 Resulting Corpus

Summary statistics about the resulting corpus are reported in Table 1; the data structure of the published corpus is sketched in Figure 2.

	Premises	Conclusions
Minimum	8	4
Mean	47.74	18.29
Maximum	147	50
Total	1951	743

Table 1: Summary dataset statistics at document level.

```
[
    {
        "name": "Case Name",
        "text": "Lorem ipsum dolor sit amet, consectetur adipiscing elit.",
        "clauses": [
            {
                "id": "5d3878c43e582511aa1cbdee",
                "type": "non-argument/argument",
                "start": 5,
                "end": 15
            }
            ...
        ],
        "arguments": [
            {
                "premises": [
                    "5d3878c43e582511aa1cbdee", ...
                ],
                "conclusion": "5d3878c43e582511aa1cbdee"
            }
            ...
        ]
    }
    ...
]
```

Figure 2: The data structure for storing the dataset.

The published JSON file is a list of the 42 cases. Each case is an object with the following fields:

- *name* – Stores the name of the file

- *text* – Stores the full-text of the case

- *clauses* – Lists the clauses annotated within the corresponding case

- *arguments* – Lists the argument structure of the clause

Each clause is an object with the following fields:

- *id* – Unique identifier

- *type* – A binary indicator of argument membership.

- *start* – Character offset where the clause starts in the *text*

- *end* – Character offset where the clause ends in the *text*

Each argument is an object with the following fields:

- *premises* – Lists the unique identifiers (*id*) of the clauses that are the premises of the argument

- *conclusion* – The unique identifier (*id*) of the clause which is the conclusion of the argument

Note that the information about the clause type is not provided directly in the clause objects. This decision is due to the fact that a clause can be of multiple types via its membership in different arguments. Therefore, the types of the clauses are encoded in the argument structures themselves: a clause which is not a part of any argument structure is of the *Non-argument* type; a clause which is listed as a premise in one or more argument structures is of the *Premise* type; the clause which is a conclusion of any argument structure is of the *Conclusion* type.

6 Baselines

In this section we present the baselines on the three tasks defined in the past that lead from unstructured texts to structured arguments. The tasks are argument clause recognition, clause relation prediction, and premise/conclusion recognition. As a basis for the classification algorithms we employ the RoBERTa pre-trained language model (Liu et al., 2019) which is a variation on the original BERT model (Devlin et al., 2018) with improved pre-training phase. A small layer is placed on top of the model to handle the classification. We work with the base version of RoBERTa to make sure the baselines are simple and easily reproducible. The base RoBERTa model runs perfectly fine on the GPUs one can access for free on Google Colaboratory.[7]

In all the experiments 5-fold cross-validation was used. The models were fine-tuned on each of the specific tasks for 15 epochs for each of the folds. In each of the iterations 20% of the data set was used for testing. Of the remaining 80% documents 20% were used for validation. After the end of each epoch we saved the current version of the model and recorded its performance on the validation set. For the evaluation on the test set we used the version of the model with the best F_1 score as evaluated on the validation set.

6.1 Argument Clause Recognition

In this task, the goal is to predict if a clause belongs to an argument or not. Specifically, this means recognizing if the clause is annotated with any of the two argument types, i.e. the premise or the conclusion, or with the non-argument type. The prior work understood this task as a binary classification problem and employed traditional ML methods, such as Random Forest or Support Vector Machines (SVM). Poudyal et al. (2016) achieved the best results ($F_1 = 0.705$) with the system based on SVM using a combination of low-level linguistic (word n-gram, POS n-grams) and hand-crafted features (e.g., the section of the document the clause comes from). Mochales and Moens (2011) use a Maximum Entropy classifier and report accuracy of 80%.

Here, we understand the task as binary classification as well. As a basis for the classification algorithms we employ the RoBERTa pre-trained language model as explained above. A small layer is placed on top of the model to handle the classification. Unlike in the case of SVM or Random Forest, one cannot provide the model with hand-crafted features. However, it is an apparent feature of this data set that an overwhelming majority (over 99%) of argument clauses is present in "AS TO THE LAW"/"THE LAW" section of the case texts. Since the ECHR cases have a uniform structure and the section can be reliably detected using text matching we leveraged the heuristic. We automatically predict every single clause outside of "AS TO THE LAW"/"THE LAW" section as being non-argument. The model is then trained

---

[7]`https://colab.research.google.com/`

Task	Precision	Recall	F-measure
Argument clause recognition	0.697	0.848	0.765
Argument relations mining	0.502	0.521	0.511
Premise recognition	0.832	0.887	0.859
Conclusion recognition	0.589	0.672	0.628

Table 2: The performance of the simple baseline systems modeling the three fundamental steps in argumentation mining as understood in this work.

on the clauses coming from "AS TO THE LAW"/"THE LAW" section only. In the evaluation phase, we simply considered the argument clauses outside of the section as false negatives.

The results of the experiment are reported in Table 2 (first row). The F_1 score on the positive class of 0.765 appears promising. However, we would like to emphasize that it is not our primary goal to achieve maximum performance. The main purpose of the system is to provide a straightforward, yet competitive, baseline. It is our assumption that significantly outperforming this baseline would require a system that would become a valuable contribution to the field of argument mining, especially argument mining from legal texts. Second, maximum caution is required when comparing to prior work in this case. Some small alterations of the corpus might have occurred (e.g., correction of obvious mistakes). Hence, the comparison is almost certainly not 1-to-1.

6.2 Argument Relation Mining

This task assumes that we have successfully identified the argument clauses. The ultimate goal is to assign the clauses into groups (i.e., arguments). The situation is somewhat complicated by the fact that a single clause may be a member of multiple arguments, e.g., it is a premise in one argument and conclusion in the other. Poudyal et al. (2019) use the Fuzzy c-means clustering algorithm (Bezdek et al., 1984) to perform this task. They report a macro F_1 (on a document level) of 0.50 and cluster purity of 0.50. Mochales and Moens (2011) approached the task differently. They used a manually created context-free grammar to produce full argument parses. They report an accuracy of around 60%.

As shown by the prior work this problem is very difficult. It is probably the crucial bottleneck in mining arguments as understood in this work. Hence, we propose a baseline that transforms the problem into a simpler one with very well defined and intuitive evaluation metrics. We understand the task as a sentence pair classification. Specifically, given a pair of argument clauses coming from the same document we want to predict if they are members of the same argument. Thus, we effectively cast the task into a binary classification while allowing for the membership of individual clauses in multiple arguments. Of course, the drawback of this approach is that one does not receive a final grouping. An additional phase would be required to turn the output into the arguments. This is left for future work.

As a basis for the classification algorithms we again employ the RoBERTa model with a small classification layer on top of it. Note that using every possible pairing of argument clauses retrieved from a document would not be a sound strategy. This would lead to a highly unbalanced data set where only a very small number of examples would be positive. Instead one can leverage the fact that argument clauses typically cluster in small proximity to each other. For training we only consider the pairs of arguments that are no more than five sentences apart. The window of five was set heuristically as it appeared neither too small nor too large. Any too argument clauses that are further apart than the set threshold are automatically predicted as not being in the argument relation. The actual relations that exist but are missed using this strategy are considered as false negatives for the purpose of the evaluation.

The results of the experiment are reported in Table 2 (middle row). They confirm what has been shown earlier, i.e., this part of the task is very challenging.

6.3 Premise/Conclusion Recognition

This task also assumes that we have successfully identified the argument clauses. The goal is to decide which of the clauses are conclusions and which of them are premises. Note that it is possible for a single clause to be a premise in one argument and a conclusion in another one. Mochales and Moens (2011) appear to train two SVM models, one to recognize premises and one to recognize conclusions. Notably, they appear to use highly sophisticated hand-crafted features, e.g., a category of the preceding sentence, discursive cues, or type of main verb. They report F_1 score of 0.681 for premises and 0.741 for conclusions.

We follow the example set in Mochales and Moens (2011) and approach this task by training two separate binary classifiers, one for each clause type. An alternative would be to understand this task as a multi-label classification. For each classifier the task is to decide if the clause is a premise/conclusion or not. As a basis for the classification algorithms we again employ the pre-trained RoBERTa model with a small classification layer on top of it.

The results of the experiment are reported in Table 2 (third and fourth row). Interestingly, in Mochales and Moens (2011) it was reported that recognizing premises is more difficult than conclusions. Our experiments show the exact opposite. This is most certainly due to the fact that the hand-crafted features used in Mochales and Moens (2011) were much more suitable for recognizing conclusions than premises.

7 Conclusions

In this paper, the ECHR Corpus is described in detail. The procedure undertaken for annotating the components of the arguments in the case-law is described, and an analysis of the quality of the corpus, including its statistical nature and structure is offered.

It is a characteristic of legal corpora that many, if not all, case law documents are interconnected to each other through citations. For that, as a future work it is necessary to annotate the related content/information provided by the citation link. For example, in the ECHR corpus excerpt

> "**The notion of security of person has not been given an independent interpretation** *(see in this respect Selçuk and Asker v. Turkey, nos. 23184/94 and 23185/94, Commission's report of 28 November 1996, §§ 185-187).*"

the first phrase in bold is the conclusion, and the text in italics is the premise. In future work, the annotator would check the report mentioned and annotate that sentence as a premise. This work might help in achieving higher classification performances.

Acknowledgements

The authors would like to thank Raquel Mochaleus Palau for her enormous contribution in the process of developing this corpus. Thanks also goes to Rama Nepal who assisted Prakash Poudyal while annotating the corpus. Finally, authors would like to extend sincere thanks to the reviewers for their constructive comments and suggestions.

References

Ehud Aharoni, Anatoly Polnarov, Tamar Lavee, Daniel Hershcovich, Ran Levy, Ruty Rinott, Dan Gutfreund, and Noam Slonim. 2014. A benchmark dataset for automatic detection of claims and evidence in the context of controversial topics. In *ArgMining@ACL*, pages 64–68.

Ron Artstein, 2017. *Inter-annotator Agreement*, pages 297–313. Springer Netherlands, Dordrecht.

Floris Bex, John Lawrence, Mark Snaith, and Chris Reed. 2013. Implementing the argument web. *Communications of the ACM*, 56(10):66–73.

James C. Bezdek, Robert Ehrlich, and William Full. 1984. Fcm: The fuzzy c-means clustering algorithm. *Computers and Geosciences*, 10(2):191 – 203.

Jacob Devlin, Ming-Wei Chang, Kenton Lee, and Kristina Toutanova. 2018. Bert: Pre-training of deep bidirectional transformers for language understanding. *arXiv preprint arXiv:1810.04805.*

Theodosis Goudas, Christos Louizos, Georgios Petasis, and Vangelis Karkaletsis. 2014. Argument extraction from news, blogs, and social media. In *Hellenic Conference on Artificial Intelligence*, pages 287–299. Springer.

Ivan Habernal and Iryna Gurevych. 2016a. What makes a convincing argument? empirical analysis and detecting attributes of convincingness in web argumentation. In *Proceedings of the 2016 Conference on Empirical Methods in Natural Language Processing*, pages 1214–1223.

Ivan Habernal and Iryna Gurevych. 2016b. Which argument is more convincing? analyzing and predicting convincingness of web arguments using bidirectional lstm. In *ACL (1)*.

Ivan Habernal and Iryna Gurevych. 2017. Argumentation mining in user-generated web discourse. *Computational Linguistics.*

Namhee Kwon, Stuart W Shulman, and Eduard Hovy. 2006. Multidimensional text analysis for erulemaking. In *Proceedings of the 2006 international conference on Digital government research*, pages 157–166.

Marco Lippi and Paolo Torroni. 2016. Argumentation mining: State of the art and emerging trends. *ACM Transactions on Internet Technology (TOIT)*, 16(2):10.

Yinhan Liu, Myle Ott, Naman Goyal, Jingfei Du, Mandar Joshi, Danqi Chen, Omer Levy, Mike Lewis, Luke Zettlemoyer, and Veselin Stoyanov. 2019. Roberta: A robustly optimized bert pretraining approach. *arXiv preprint arXiv:1907.11692.*

Raquel Mochales and Marie-Francine Moens. 2008. Study on the structure of argumentation in case law. In *Proceedings of the 2008 Conference on Legal Knowledge and Information Systems*, pages 11–20.

Raquel Mochales and Marie-Francine Moens. 2011. Argumentation mining. *Artificial Intelligence and Law*, 19(1):1–22.

Raquel Mochales Palau and Aagje Ieven. 2009. Creating an argumentation corpus: do theories apply to real arguments?: a case study on the legal argumentation of the echr. In *Proceedings of the 12th International Conference on Artificial Intelligence and Law*, pages 21–30. ACM.

Prakash Poudyal, Teresa Goncalves, and Paulo Quaresma. 2016. Experiments on identification of argumentative sentences. In *Proceeding of 9th International Conference on Software, Knowledge, Information Management and Applications (SKIMA) Chengdu, China*, Dec.

Prakash Poudyal, Teresa Gonçalves, and Paulo Quaresma. 2019. Using clustering techniques to identify arguments in legal documents. In *ASAIL@ ICAIL*.

Chris Reed, Raquel Mochales Palau, Glenn Rowe, and Marie-Francine Moens. 2008. Language resources for studying argument. In *Proceedings of the 6th conference on language resources and evaluation-LREC 2008*, pages 91–100.

Sara Rosenthal and Kathleen McKeown. 2012. Detecting opinionated claims in online discussions. In *Semantic Computing (ICSC), 2012 IEEE Sixth International Conference on*, pages 30–37. IEEE.

Christos Sardianos, Ioannis Manousos Katakis, Georgios Petasis, and Vangelis Karkaletsis. 2015. Argument extraction from news. In *ArgMining@ HLT-NAACL*, pages 56–66.

Jaromír Savelka and Kevin D Ashley. 2017. Detecting agent mentions in us court decisions. In *JURIX*, pages 39–48.

Jaromir Savelka and Kevin D Ashley. 2018. Segmenting us court decisions into functional and issue specific parts. In *JURIX*, pages 111–120.

Argument from Old Man's View: Assessing Social Bias in Argumentation

Maximilian Spliethöver
Department of Computer Science
Paderborn University
Paderborn, Germany
mspl@mail.upb.de

Henning Wachsmuth
Department of Computer Science
Paderborn University
Paderborn, Germany
henningw@upb.de

Abstract

Social bias in language — towards genders, ethnicities, ages, and other social groups — poses a problem with ethical impact for many NLP applications. Recent research has shown that machine learning models trained on respective data may not only adopt, but even amplify the bias. So far, however, little attention has been paid to bias in computational argumentation. In this paper, we study the existence of social biases in large English debate portals. In particular, we train word embedding models on portal-specific corpora and systematically evaluate their bias using WEAT, an existing metric to measure bias in word embeddings. In a word co-occurrence analysis, we then investigate causes of bias. The results suggest that all tested debate corpora contain unbalanced and biased data, mostly in favor of male people with European-American names. Our empirical insights contribute towards an understanding of bias in argumentative data sources.

1 Introduction

Social bias can be understood as implicit or explicit prejudices against, as well as unequal treatment or discrimination of, certain social groups in society (Sweeney and Najafian, 2019; Papakyriakopoulos et al., 2020). A social group might be described by physical attributes of its members, such as sex and skin color, but also by more abstract categories, such as culture, heritage, gender identity, and religion. A typical, probably in itself biased, example of social bias is the old man's belief in classic gender stereotypes. In most cases, social bias is deemed negative and undesirable.

Recent research shows that bias towards social groups is also present in Machine Learning and Natural Language Processing (NLP) models (Chang et al., 2019), manifesting in the encoded states of a language model (Brown et al., 2020) or simply causing worse performance for underrepresented classes (Sun et al., 2019). Such bias has been studied for different NLP contexts, including coreference resolution (Rudinger et al., 2018), machine translation (Vanmassenhove et al., 2018), and the training of word embedding models (Bolukbasi et al., 2016). In contrast, Computational Argumentation (CA) has, to our knowledge, not seen any research in this direction so far. Given that major envisioned applications of CA include the enhancement of human debating (Lawrence et al., 2017) and the support of self-determined opinion formation (Wachsmuth et al., 2017), we argue that studying social bias is particularly critical for CA.

In general, social bias may affect diverse stages of CA: In argument acquisition, for example, researchers may introduce social bias unintentionally, for instance, by collecting arguments from web sources that are only popular in a certain part of the world. This is known as *sample bias* (Chang et al., 2019). In argument quality assessment, a machine learning model may develop a *prejudicial bias* and judge arguments made by a certain social group better, for instance, because it considers features inadequate for the task, such as the gender (Jones, 2019). And in argument generation, a model might produce arguments that have an *implicit bias* towards a certain social group, for instance, because the features chosen are based on prior experience of the researchers and may not properly represent the whole population (Fiske, 2004). As the examples indicate, social bias can, among other reasons, be caused by the source data and how it is being processed. As a starting point, this paper therefore focuses on social bias in the source data underlying CA methods. In particular, we ask the following questions:

Proceedings of the 7th Workshop on Argument Mining, pages 76–87
Barcelona, Spain (Online), December 13, 2020.

1. What, if any, types of social bias are present in existing argument sources and how do different sources compare to each other in this regard?

2. How much do certain groups of users contribute to the overall social bias of a source?

3. What kinds of linguistic utterances contribute towards certain types of social bias?

Applications such as those outlined above usually rely on web arguments for scaling reasons. To study the questions, we hence resort to five English debate portals that give access to arguments on versatile topics: *4forums.com*, *convinceme.net*, *createdebate.com*, *debate.org*, and *ChangeMyView*. All five have been deployed in CA corpora (Abbott et al., 2016; Durmus and Cardie, 2019; Al Khatib et al., 2020).

First, we analyze the general presence of social bias in each of the five debate portals. To this end, we train three custom word embedding models, one for each available corpus. Next, we evaluate the models for social bias using a widely used bias metric, called WEAT (Caliskan et al., 2017), and compare the results. We then inspect the debate.org portal more closely with regard to specific social groups. In particular, we group the texts based on the provided user information and apply the same evaluation. Lastly, to gain a better understanding of what makes some texts more biased than others, we explore their language by analyzing word co-occurrences with group identity words in the texts.

Our findings suggest that all three corpora are generally biased towards male (compared to female) and European-American (compared to African-American) people. This bias is not only reflected in the WEAT results, but also in unbalanced occurrences of identity words for certain social groups. More generally, we observe that the use of names as identity terms for social groups has unpredictable effects. With those insights, we contribute an initial understanding of social bias in sources of dialectical argumentative texts.

2   Related Work

In recent years, research on different types of bias in natural language has received a considerable amount of attention. Media bias is one prominent example (Fan et al., 2019), particular the political bias of news articles (Chen et al., 2020). In various sub-fields of NLP, studies on media bias are concerned with analyzing techniques utilized by media outlets when reporting news. These include the framing of an event by phrasing the report with positive or negative terms, and selective reporting by including or omitting facts depending on the tone and (political) stance a media outlet wants to convey (Chen et al., 2018; Hamborg, 2020; Lim et al., 2020). We do not target media bias here but *social* bias.

Social bias can emerge from pre-existing stereotypes towards any social group (Sweeney and Najafian, 2019), often leading to prejudices and discrimination. Stereotypes are understood as "beliefs about the characteristics of group members" (Fiske, 2004). They may be so powerful that they do not only limit the freedom of individuals, but also cause hate, exclusion, and — in the worst case — extermination (Fiske, 1993). Even if stereotypes, and with that social biases, are individually controllable, they persist to this day; prominent examples of social groups that have historically been subject to bias are ethnicities, genders, and age groups (Fiske, 1998). A major factor in carrying and reinforcing those biases is language (Sap et al., 2020). In spoken and written argumentation and debates, biased language can be present if, for example, one sides argues in self-interest (Zenker, 2011) to favor a certain social group or uses unbalanced arguments (Kienpointner and Kindt, 1997).

As CA methods are receiving more and more attention (Stede and Schneider, 2018), it is important to understand how existing social biases influence them. One possible source is the human-generated data on which automated systems are trained and evaluated (Chang et al., 2019). In CA, one of the main sources of data are online debate portals, both for research and for applications (Ajjour et al., 2019).

Prior work has evaluated different properties of dialogical argumentation on debate portals. For example, Durmus and Cardie (2019) evaluated the success rate of users in debates on debate.org based on prior experience, the users' social network in the portal, and linguistic features of their arguments. The authors find that information on a user is more informative in predicting the success compared to linguistic features. Al Khatib et al. (2020) retrieved all debates and posts from *Reddit's* discussion forum ChangeMyView to analyze the characteristics of debaters there. With this information, they were able to enhance existing approaches to predict the persuasiveness of an argument and a debater's resistance to be persuaded.

While the evaluation of debates notably misses work on social biases, other forms of bias have been studied. Stab and Gurevych (2016), for example, attempted to build a classifier that predicts the presence or absence of myside bias in monological texts. In contrast, this work offers an initial evaluation of social bias in dialogical argumentation by analyzing the posts of debate portals.

More generally, many approaches have been proposed to identify different types of social bias in word embedding models. In one of the first studies, Bolukbasi et al. (2016) showed that pre-trained models contain gender bias. They found that it is revealed when generating analogies for a given set of words. This suggests that the distance between word vectors can act as a proxy to identify biases held by a model. Building on that notion, methods to automatically quantify the bias in a pre-trained word embedding model were presented. Caliskan et al. (2017) introduce a metric named the *Word Embedding Association Test* (WEAT) that adapts the idea of the *Implicit Association Test* (Greenwald et al., 1998). Other methods include the *Mean Average Cosine Similarity (MAC)* test (Manzini et al., 2019), the *Relational Inner Product Association (RIPA)* test (Ethayarajh et al., 2019), the *Embedding Coherence Test (ECT)*, and the *Embedding Quality Test (EQT)* (Dev and Phillips, 2019). For a more detailed literature review on detecting and mitigating biases in word embedding models, see Sun et al. (2019). Our approach builds on the WEAT metric to evaluate social biases in embedding models generated from debate portal texts.

Probably closest to our work is the study of Rios et al. (2020). Building on a method developed by Garg et al. (2018), the authors analyzed scientific abstracts of biomedical studies published in a time span of 60 years to quantify gender bias in the field and to track changes over time. For this purpose, they generated separate word embedding models for each decade in their data and evaluated them using the WEAT metric. Using the RIPA test in addition, the authors identified the "most biased words" (Rios et al., 2020) of each model. While we will apply a similar method to detect social bias in textual data, our study differs in two main regards: First, instead of biomedical abstracts, we evaluate dialogical argumentative structures extracted from online debate portals and compare them to each other. Second, we additionally conduct a word co-occurrence analysis of the textual data as an attempt to get more insights into the WEAT results; something that is notably missing in previous studies.

3 Data

To study social bias in argumentative language, we consider the dialogical argumentation found on online debate portals. As our analysis below is based on training word embedding models, which need sufficient data to find statistically meaningful co-occurrences, we resort to the three previously published corpora described below. The texts in these corpora have a similar argumentative structure, benefiting comparability:

IAC The *Internet Argument Corpus v2* (Abbott et al., 2016) contains around 16k debates from multiple debate portals, including *createdebate.com*, *convinceme.net*, and *4forums.com*. The debates tackle various topics that are led by users of the respective portals. As the number of arguments from the single portals are rather small compared to the other two corpora, we only consider this corpus as a whole.

CMV The *Webis-CMV-20* corpus (Al Khatib et al., 2020) covers posts and comments of roughly 65k debates from the internet platform *reddit.com*, specifically from its subreddit *ChangeMyView*. Each debate consists of multiple comments and arguments, including the opening post in which a user states an opinion and arguments on a given issue and prompts other users to provide opposing arguments. The most convincing counter arguments can then be awarded by the initiator of the debate.

debate.org The corpus of Durmus and Cardie (2019) is based on *debate.org*. It contains around 78k debates, each consisting of multiple arguments, written by over 45k users in total. In addition to the debates, the corpus has detailed self-provided user information, such as gender, ethnicity, and birth date. Adding information to one's profile is voluntary and, thus, neither available for all users in the corpus nor fully reliable. Still, we will use the available information to analyze arguments of certain user groups.

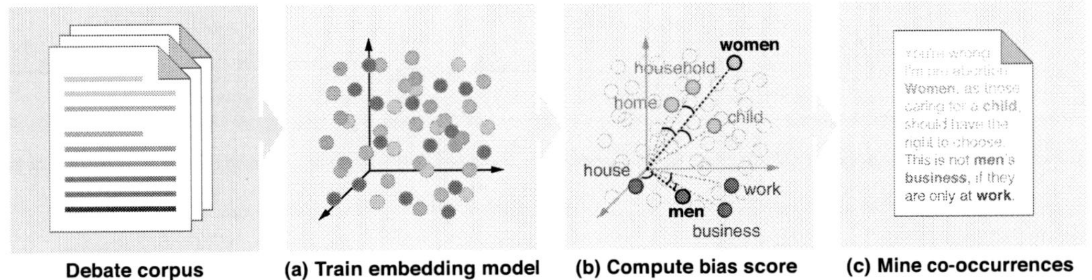

Debate corpus   **(a) Train embedding model**   **(b) Compute bias score**   **(c) Mine co-occurrences**

Figure 1: Overview of the methodology of our experiments: Given a debate corpus, (a) a custom embedding model is trained. (b) A bias score is computed using one of the WEAT tests. (c) Word co-occurrences that give hints about the bias are mined from the corpus (the shown example is made-up for emphasis).

4 Experiments

This section presents the experiments that we carried out on the given data in light of our three research questions, as well as the underlying methodology. We describe how we train embedding models, evaluate their bias, and analyze the word co-occurrences causing the observed bias. Figure 1 illustrates the process.[1]

4.1 Training of Word Embedding Models and Computation of Bias Scores

The Implicit Association Test (Greenwald et al., 1998) measures the response times of study participants for pairing concepts based on word lists and uses it as a proxy for bias (Caliskan et al., 2017). The test requires four lists of words: two target word lists, A and B, and two association word lists, X and Y. Target word lists implicitly describe a concept, such as a social group, while association word lists describe an association, such as being pleasant or unpleasant. The WEAT metric (Caliskan et al., 2017) aims to adapt this method to word embedding models. Under the assumption that word vectors with similar meaning are closer to each other, it computes the mean cosine distance between the four lists in a given model. The score represents the effect size of the difference in distances, which is formulated as follows:

$$\frac{\text{mean}_{x \in X} s(x, A, B) \; - \; \text{mean}_{y \in Y} s(y, A, B)}{\text{std\_dev}_{w \in X \cup Y} s(w, A, B)}$$

where $s(x, A, B)$ is the difference in cosine distances for each word in A to x and each word in B to x. The effect size then acts as a proxy to quantify bias.

Portal-specific Models   To apply the WEAT metric to the texts of debate portals, we first extract all posts from the corpora and train one separate custom word embedding model on each corpus using the GloVe algorithm (Pennington et al., 2014). Given the custom models, we then evaluate social bias in them, focusing on three of the most common bias types: towards *ethnicity*, *gender*, and *age* (Fiske, 2004). These types are roughly represented by seven of the originally proposed WEAT tests, found in Table 1. As a notion of stability of the results, we additionally create five embedding models that are trained on random splits of the evaluated corpora and calculate the standard deviation of their WEAT scores.

Baseline Models   To be able to assess the WEAT results obtained for the trained custom embedding models, we also evaluate two pre-trained models that have shown different levels of bias in previous work and use those in the sense of "baselines". They allow us to interpret the results in context. As our upper bias boundary, we choose the GloVe model pre-trained on CommonCrawl data (Pennington et al., 2014), as it has shown to comprise a high level of bias of different types (Caliskan et al., 2017; Sweeney and Najafian, 2019). Similarly, we use the pre-trained Numberbatch model 19.08 (Speer et al., 2017) as the lower boundary. Not only is this model claimed to be debiased in multiple ways (Speer, 2017), it has also been shown to be the least biased compared to other pre-trained models (Sweeney and Najafian, 2019).

---

[1] The code for reproducing the experiments can be found at `https://github.com/webis-de/argmining20-social-bias-argumentation`.

Type	Test	Target words		Association words	
		Compared concepts	**Examples**	**Compared concepts**	**Examples**
	WEAT-1	Flowers vs. insects	rose, spider	Pleasant vs. unpleasant	freedom, hatred
	WEAT-2	Instruments vs. weapons	guitar, gun	Pleasant vs. unpleasant	freedom, hatred
Ethnicity	WEAT-3	European- vs. African-Amer. names	Sara, Alonzo	Pleasant vs. unpleasant	freedom, hatred
	WEAT-4	European- vs. African-Amer. names	Brad, Darnell	Pleasant vs. unpleasant	freedom, hatred
	WEAT-5	European- vs. African-Amer. names	Brad, Darnell	Pleasant vs. unpleasant	joy, agony
Gender	WEAT-6	Male vs. female names	John, Amy	Career vs. family	executive, children
	WEAT-7	Math vs. arts	algebra, poetry	Male vs. female terms	man, woman
	WEAT-8	Science vs. arts	physics, symphony	Male vs. female terms	father, mother
	WEAT-9	Mental vs. physical disease	sad, cancer	Temporary vs. permanent	occasional, chronic
Age	WEAT-10	Young vs. old people's names	Tiffany, Bernice	Pleasant vs. unpleasant	joy, agony

Table 1: Overview of the 10 WEAT tests from Caliskan et al. (2017). As we focus on *ethnicity*, *gender*, and *age* type, we evaluate the given embedding models only on the tests printed in black. The given examples are drawn from the lists; equal words across tests indicate that the same list was used.

Group-specific Models As indicated in Section 3, the debate.org corpus comes with detailed meta-information about several users. To gain insights into the bias of different user groups, we therefore repeat the process outlined above for posts from self-identified "black" and "white" users,[2] female and male users, as well as users below the age of 23 and of 23+[3] in the debate.org dataset. While the age threshold may seem random, age data was sparse and, so, the boundaries were chosen to maximize balance, in order to allow for a rough evaluation of "younger" and "older" users. More or less, the three chosen pairs of user groups coincide with the evaluated social groups and, thus, may provide insightful comparisons.

4.2 Mining and Analysis of Word Co-occurrences

We further conduct a preliminary word co-occurrence analysis for each corpus with the aim to gain additional insights into the observed WEAT results. To achieve this, we first remove noise, such as stopwords, punctuation, and URLs from the corpora. Afterwards, we take as input all social group identity words of the WEAT tests, as exemplified in Table 1. For each list, we extract all words co-occurring with the words in the lists in a window size of 20 (ten words to the left and ten words to the right of the target word). Next, we count their total occurrences and manually evaluate the 100 most common words. As a by-product, we also retrieve the total number of occurrences of target words, which further contribute towards an understanding of the WEAT results.

As the WEAT evaluations only analyze the word embedding models, there is no notion of how often two target and association words are actually used in nearby context. Thus, to better understand such relations, we additionally evaluate the co-occurrences of words in the target and association lists on the sentence level. For each WEAT test, we first build all possible word pairs from the four lists in order to then filter the posts. If a post does not contain both words in a pair, it is discarded. The remaining posts are then split into sentences, allowing us to finally count the co-occurrences of each pair.

5 Results

Portal-specific and Baseline Models The WEAT results on the embedding models of the complete corpora in comparison to the baseline models can be seen in Table 2. Except for the WEAT-8 test, GloVe CommonCrawl yields the highest bias values (ranging from 1.0896 to 1.8734) and Numberbatch yields rather low bias values, respectively. Among the corpora, the Internet Argument Corpus v2 (IAC) shows

---

[2]In principle, we refrain from using those terms to refer to ethnicities, as they reduce groups to skin color, are thus stereotypes and not adequate to represent the groups (Bryc et al., 2015), promoting topological thinking (Jorde and Wooding, 2004). However, as they are present on debate.org, we use them here to refer to the respective user groups that self-identified as "black" or "white".

[3]The age of a user is the number of years from the specified birthday to 2017, the year of the data collection (Durmus and Cardie, 2019). In all our tests, we assumed those information to be true. As we identified some anomalies, e.g. more than 200 users are assigned an unlikely age of 118 years, we acknowledge that the results might not be particularly reliable.

Type	Embedding Model	(a) Ethnicity			(b) Gender			(c) Age
		WEAT-3	WEAT-4	WEAT-5	WEAT-6	WEAT-7	WEAT-8	WEAT-10
Pretrained	Numberbatch (debiased)	0.3203	*–0.0994*	0.5621	1.7527	*0.0153*	0.7429	0.8023
	GloVe CommonCrawl	**1.4367**	**1.5778**	**1.3803**	**1.8734**	**1.0896**	1.2780	**1.2527**
Custom	IAC	0.2933	0.3624	*0.1300*	–0.3396	0.4009	0.6265	*0.3208*
	CMV	*–0.0632*	0.4956	0.4175	1.3151	–0.3055	*0.4626*	0.7839
	debate.org: Full corpus	0.4125	0.5742	0.5811	1.2775	0.5833	**1.3053**	0.4018

Table 2: Bias values of the custom embedding models, trained on the three debate portal corpora, in comparison to the pretrained baseline models according to the WEAT metric. The higher the absolute value, the larger the bias. The highest value in each column is marked bold, the lowest italicized.

Embedding Model	(a) Ethnicity			(b) Gender			(c) Age
	WEAT-3	WEAT-4	WEAT-5	WEAT-6	WEAT-7	WEAT-8	WEAT-10
debate.org: ethnicity-black	0.2483	**1.1304**	**1.5238**	–0.2073	–0.0007	0.7710	n/a
debate.org: ethnicity-white	–0.1915	–0.4062	*0.2535*	0.5080	*0.0006*	**1.3182**	0.4592
debate.org: gender-female	0.3198	0.8689	1.3645	0.1251	**1.0460**	0.7991	0.9661
debate.org: gender-male	*0.0363*	*0.2730*	0.8751	**0.7665**	0.8377	1.3231	*0.2112*
debate.org: age-below-23	**–1.7250**	0.4406	–1.1198	–0.2220	0.5045	*0.5158*	n/a
debate.org: age-23-up	–0.9210	0.8369	0.5143	*0.0624*	0.1848	0.6525	**2.0051**

Table 3: Bias values for the group-specific embedding models of the debate.org corpus, according to WEAT. Higher absolute values mean larger bias, the highest in each column is marked bold, the lowest italicized. WEAT-10 has no result for *ethnicity-black* and *age-below-23* due to too many out-of-vocabulary tokens. The WEAT-10 value above 2 of the *age-23-up* corpus is probably caused by a floating point error.

the lowest values on average (e.g., 0.1300 for WEAT-5) and thus seems to be the least biased. In contrast, the debate.org corpus has higher values in almost all tests, with a noteworthy difference in the gender bias tests WEAT-6 and WEAT-8. In cases where it does not have the highest values (as for WEAT-6), it is surpassed by the CMV corpus. Compared to the WEAT scores of the baseline models, the results of all debate corpora are mostly closer to the debiased Numberbatch model than to GloVe CommonCrawl.

Regarding the general direction of the WEAT scores, we see in Table 2 that most of the observed effect sizes are positive, indicating a closer association of the first list of target words with the first list of association words (see Table 1 for the list ordering). This means that (a) European-American names are more associated with pleasant terms than African-American ones, (b) male names/terms are more closely associated with career, math, and science terms than female ones, and (c) young people's names are more associated with pleasant words that old people's names.

Group-specific Models A similar observation can be made for the debate.org sub-corpora in Table 3. Especially for the embedding models based on posts of female and black users, though, the standard deviation of the WEAT bias values is higher than for the whole corpus, suggesting less reliable results. For the respective user groups, the WEAT scores further seem to indicate a bias against the own social group. For example, the WEAT-3 and WEAT-4 test of the models for black and white users indicate closer associations to pleasant terms with the respective other social group (positive values for black, negative values for white). For female users, the analog notion applies to WEAT-6, WEAT-7 and WEAT-8. Another interesting observation can be made for the age groups: While the ethnicity WEAT tests indicate that older users are more biased towards European-American names, the exact opposite is true for younger users. In general, depending on the specific WEAT test, posts from all user groups seem to be biased in different regards. For example, while on average female users have the highest WEAT values, male users seem to be slightly more biased towards genders. Similarly, posts of younger users show the highest WEAT values in the ethnicity tests.

With some exceptions, the overall direction of the WEAT results in Tables 2 and 3 suggests that the three evaluated debate corpora are all biased towards men (compared to women) and the European-American

(a) Ethnicity	WEAT-3		WEAT-4		WEAT-5	
Corpus	European	African	European	African	European	African
IAC	1075:883	5:14	280:206	14:22	93:69	8:3
CMV	1503:1461	52:35	324:257	47:26	141:80	18:19
debate.org	1960:2009	23:26	530:429	45:73	180:108	32:19

(b) Gender	WEAT-6		WEAT-7		WEAT-8		(c) Age	WEAT-10	
Corpus	Male	Female	Male	Female	Male	Female	Corpus	Young	Old
IAC	313:712	35:74	1108:732	244:156	2648:682	278:133	IAC	36:19	1:2
CMV	865:1229	37:104	4586:3976	2006:1653	5840:4008	1396:1255	CMV	73:42	5:9
debate.org	456:844	31:101	3790:1957	572:438	5351:2011	446:405	debate.org	41:21	3:3

Table 4: Absolute co-occurrences per WEAT evaluation between social group identity words and association words. The number left to the colon denotes the count of words from the first association list (e.g. *pleasant*), the number right to the colon the count for the second association list (e.g., *unpleasant*). Note that for WEAT-7 and WEAT-8, the numbers denote the counts of the respective target word lists.

ethnicity group (compared to the African-American group). That said, when building future CA systems, the IAC corpus is probably the best choice to reduce social biases in general. It is important to note, though, that it is also the smallest corpus of the three and does not include user information. The CMV corpus seems like a good compromise between the two, as it received lower WEAT values than the debate.org corpus and offers more data at the same time.

Word Co-occurrences   The co-occurrence counts in Table 4 confirm the observed bias values in some cases. In the debate.org corpus, male identity words indeed occur more often with the math-related terms of the WEAT-7 test compared to female identity words. As a specific example, the word "he" co-occurs with math-related terms 1662 times, while the female counterpart "she" is only mentioned 178 times in a sentence with the same class of words. Similarly, in the CMV corpus, science-related terms of the WEAT-8 test appear 2006 times in the same sentence as the male identity word "his" while only sharing the same sentence 1396 times with all female identity words *combined*.

In most cases, however, words from both groups are only rarely mentioned in the same sentences, compared to the overall size of the corpora. For the tests that use names as social group identifiers, e.g. WEAT-6, this problem is even more noticeable, as indicated by the lower numbers presented in Table 4. In all three corpora, names generally co-occur less often with the association words in the same sentence compared to terms that describe a concept, as used, for example, in WEAT-7 and WEAT-8. This not only makes it harder to directly interpret the WEAT results. It also indicates that the cosine distance, on which the WEAT score is based, relies more on either a distant context, such as an entire post, or on common co-occurrences with potentially unrelated words. That said, the results presented above should be interpreted with care.

6   Discussion

To put the results into context, we will discuss two additional observations more closely in the following, namely the low number of occurrences of some identity words as well as the influence of using names for social group lexicons. We will then close this section with limitations observed during the analysis.

6.1   Low Occurrence of Identity Words

In some experiments, the number of occurrences of identity words should be considered when interpreting the results: In the WEAT-10 tests, the old people's names used for the social group of elderly people generally have a very low frequency. In the posts of black debate.org users, they sum up to only 18 occurrences in total. The same is true for users above the age of 22. Even though the overall number of occurrences seems sufficient to conduct the WEAT evaluation, this definitely calls the meaningfulness of the embedding model into question and, with that, the association tests for those groups.

Also, the occurrence *ratio* of identity words of two social groups being compared with WEAT deserves discussion. For all evaluated tests, at least twice as many identity words of one group are mentioned as for the other, in the highest case even 101 as many. The identity words of the European-American group utilized by WEAT-3, for example, occur on average 54.8 times as often as the African-American ones across the three debate corpora. While this ratio is not as high for the other tests, the general tendency is that European-American names are mentioned more often. The same is true for male names and terms, which are used more frequently than female ones, and young people's names that occur more often than old people's names across all corpora. Adding to this is the fact that the identity words are, compared to corpus sizes, only rarely used together in close context, say, in a sentence. The distance between two words in the vector space thus relies mostly on the co-occurrence with other, unrelated words.

On one hand, these observations make it less trivial to interpret WEAT results, as the different occurrences cause unequal probabilities for the two identity word lists to co-occur with the tested association words. On the other hand, they imply that the evaluated corpora are not very diverse and, so, provide imbalanced data with respect to the evaluated social groups. For debate.org, this imbalance can also be seen in the size of certain user groups, resulting in an unequal number of arguments from different groups.

Another potential confounding factor is the number of out-of-vocabulary (OOV) words. When the total number of identity words is low, many OOV words may make results even more unreliable. Among others, this is the case for the female user posts of the debate.org corpus. African-American names from the WEAT-3 test make up 41 of the 49 OOV words, leaving only 9 of the initial 50 names for the association test. A similar case is WEAT-10 for users above 22. From the eight old people's names, only one appears in the sub-corpus. An immediate effect of the missing words is, however, not visible from the results.

One practical consequence of the discussed unequal distribution is that automated systems, trained and evaluated on these corpora, may favor arguments of the majority group. The underlying discrimination against minority groups may lead to unfair behavior in all stages of CA, e.g., to a better ranking of arguments from majority groups in quality assessments or to generated arguments that reflect the opinion of the majority group mainly. These examples stress the need for more diverse debate corpora representing different social groups in a more balanced way. Creating such corpora will not be easy, though, since detailed user information is not often available on debate portals and other argument sources.

6.2 Using Names as Social Groups

A general issue underlying the results is that a list of names does not describe the concept of a social group to a level required by co-occurrence methods such as WEAT. For example, the token "palin" often co-occurs with the female list word "sarah" used in WEAT-6, referring to the politician *Sarah Palin*. Consequently, in the debate.org corpus, some other highly ranked terms relate to politics, such as "president", "conservative", and "supporter". While we did not observe this for all three corpora, it demonstrates that using names as identity words can cause public persons to somewhat act as representatives. Texts about them thus also influence the associations of the tests, independent of whether they are part of the group or their behavior is representative of it. This discrepancy leads to associations authors of evaluated texts have with the public persons rather than the social group and may ultimately influence the bias evaluation.

Another issues lies in the overall occurrence of names. Male and female *names*, for instance, appear less often in the debate texts than male and female *terms*. As already discussed above, a smaller number of occurrences of identity words may make the results more prone to distortions, due to small fluctuations in co-occurrences, and thus less reliable in general.

Together, these issues suggest that names might not be appropriate to represent a social group and to analyze bias for the evaluated corpora. Also, it seems questionable whether they are generally statistically representative of the target social groups. Partially, however, the lists of names also led to expected associations, as is the case for the WEAT-3, WEAT-4 and WEAT-5 test on the CMV corpus. The terms co-occurring with the African-American names suggest that they were at least to a small degree able to capture the associations, since some of the most co-occurring terms included "African" and "black".[4]

---

[4]We do not suggest that these terms adequately represent and describe the African-American social group, but simply state that the association between the social group and the terms generally holds.

6.3 Limitations

One limitation of our methodology is that it relies on the chosen embedding model to accurately model distances and associations between words. This makes it less applicable to smaller datasets, let alone single texts. Additionally, the influence of multiple factors on WEAT results is unclear. For example, choosing an alternative algorithm to generate an embedding model may yield different results, e.g., word2vec (Mikolov et al., 2013) or FastText (Bojanowski et al., 2017). Future work should explore more sophisticated methods to analyze social bias that do not depend on embedding models, as they are a point of uncertainty that might never be fully explainable due to the nature of generating the models.

Further, the results presented in this work are limited to the accuracy of WEAT. This dependence is problematic for three main reasons: First, it assumes that the calculation done by the test accurately models the associations between the lexicons. While Caliskan et al. (2017) show that they are able to reproduce results from previous psychology studies with humans, it remains open whether the notion generally applies. Second, it expects that the lexicons of the tests are representative of the social groups they ought to model. Especially with a list of names, however, this assumption can lead to unexpected results and might not hold, as shown above. The same is true for the co-occurrence analysis, which is also based on (and limited to) the social group lexicons of Caliskan et al. (2017). Lastly, the test assumes that all evaluated biases are quantifiable. While this allows for automation, this assumption is certainly questionable, among other reasons because every person might perceive bias differently.

Given those limitations, we would like to emphasize that the results presented in this work are meant as a first evaluation that needs to be further backed up and investigated with more tests in the future.

7 Conclusion

In this paper, we have analyzed social bias in three debate corpora commonly used in CA research. To this end, we have trained custom word embedding models and evaluated their associations for multiple social groups using WEAT. Further, we have analyzed co-occurrences of terms used to define the social groups. We have found all three corpora to show social bias, mostly towards women and African-American people. According to our evaluation, the smallest corpus, IAC (Abbott et al., 2016), carries the least social bias, whereas the debate.org corpus (Durmus and Cardie, 2019) shows mostly the highest. The CMV corpus (Al Khatib et al., 2020) seems like a middle ground, as it contains the most data and is less biased than the debate.org corpus. In all three corpora, we have found imbalances regarding the representation of the evaluated social groups.

Future work should investigate additional ways in which social bias may be present in CA methods, as the underlying data is not the only source. Other possible causes may be the features selected for a trained model or the way in which a model is applied to a real world problem. We believe that future CA corpora should be evaluated and mitigated for social bias. As data is underlying most CA methods, it is essential that it is as representative for as many social groups as possible in a balanced manner.

References

Rob Abbott, Brian Ecker, Pranav Anand, and Marilyn Walker. 2016. Internet Argument Corpus 2.0: An SQL schema for Dialogic Social Media and the Corpora to go with it. In *Proceedings of the Tenth International Conference on Language Resources and Evaluation (LREC 2016)*, pages 4445–4452, Portorož, Slovenia. European Language Resources Association (ELRA).

Yamen Ajjour, Henning Wachsmuth, Johannes Kiesel, Martin Potthast, Matthias Hagen, and Benno Stein. 2019. Data acquisition for argument search: The args.me corpus. In *KI 2019: Advances in Artificial Intelligence - 42nd German Conference on AI, Kassel, Germany, September 23-26, 2019, Proceedings*, pages 48–59.

Khalid Al Khatib, Michael Völske, Shahbaz Syed, Nikolay Kolyada, and Benno Stein. 2020. Exploiting Personal Characteristics of Debaters for Predicting Persuasiveness. In *Proceedings of the 58th Annual Meeting of the Association for Computational Linguistics*, pages 7067–7072, Online. Association for Computational Linguistics.

Piotr Bojanowski, Edouard Grave, Armand Joulin, and Tomas Mikolov. 2017. Enriching Word Vectors with Subword Information. *Transactions of the Association for Computational Linguistics*, 5:135–146. Publisher: MIT Press.

Tolga Bolukbasi, Kai-Wei Chang, James Y Zou, Venkatesh Saligrama, and Adam T Kalai. 2016. Man is to Computer Programmer as Woman is to Homemaker? Debiasing Word Embeddings. In *Advances in Neural Information Processing Systems 29*, pages 4349–4357. Curran Associates, Inc.

Tom B. Brown, Benjamin Mann, Nick Ryder, Melanie Subbiah, Jared Kaplan, Prafulla Dhariwal, Arvind Neelakantan, Pranav Shyam, Girish Sastry, Amanda Askell, Sandhini Agarwal, Ariel Herbert-Voss, Gretchen Krueger, Tom Henighan, Rewon Child, Aditya Ramesh, Daniel M. Ziegler, Jeffrey Wu, Clemens Winter, Christopher Hesse, Mark Chen, Eric Sigler, Mateusz Litwin, Scott Gray, Benjamin Chess, Jack Clark, Christopher Berner, Sam McCandlish, Alec Radford, Ilya Sutskever, and Dario Amodei. 2020. Language Models are Few-Shot Learners. arXiv:2005.14165, Version: 3.

Katarzyna Bryc, Eric Y. Durand, J. Michael Macpherson, David Reich, and Joanna L. Mountain. 2015. The Genetic Ancestry of African Americans, Latinos, and European Americans across the United States. *The American Journal of Human Genetics*, 96(1):37–53.

Aylin Caliskan, Joanna J. Bryson, and Arvind Narayanan. 2017. Semantics derived automatically from language corpora contain human-like biases. *Science*, 356(6334):183–186.

Kai-Wei Chang, Vinod Prabhakaran, and Vicente Ordonez. 2019. Bias and Fairness in Natural Language Processing. In *Proceedings of the 2019 Conference on Empirical Methods in Natural Language Processing and the 9th International Joint Conference on Natural Language Processing (EMNLP-IJCNLP): Tutorial Abstracts*, Hong Kong, China. Association for Computational Linguistics.

Wei-Fan Chen, Henning Wachsmuth, Khalid Al-Khatib, and Benno Stein. 2018. Learning to Flip the Bias of News Headlines. In *Proceedings of the 11th International Conference on Natural Language Generation*, pages 79–88, Tilburg University, The Netherlands. Association for Computational Linguistics.

Wei-Fan Chen, Khalid Al Khatib, Henning Wachsmuth, and Benno Stein. 2020. Analyzing political bias and unfairness in news articles at different levels of granularity. In *Proceedings of the 4th Workshop on Natural Language Processing and Computational Social Science*. To appear.

Sunipa Dev and Jeff Phillips. 2019. Attenuating Bias in Word vectors. In *The 22nd International Conference on Artificial Intelligence and Statistics*, pages 879–887.

Esin Durmus and Claire Cardie. 2019. A Corpus for Modeling User and Language Effects in Argumentation on Online Debating. In *Proceedings of the 57th Annual Meeting of the Association for Computational Linguistics*, pages 602–607, Florence, Italy. Association for Computational Linguistics.

Kawin Ethayarajh, David Duvenaud, and Graeme Hirst. 2019. Understanding Undesirable Word Embedding Associations. In *Proceedings of the 57th Annual Meeting of the Association for Computational Linguistics*, pages 1696–1705, Florence, Italy. Association for Computational Linguistics.

Lisa Fan, Marshall White, Eva Sharma, Ruisi Su, Prafulla Kumar Choubey, Ruihong Huang, and Lu Wang. 2019. In plain sight: Media bias through the lens of factual reporting. In *Proceedings of the 2019 Conference on Empirical Methods in Natural Language Processing and the 9th International Joint Conference on Natural Language Processing (EMNLP-IJCNLP)*, pages 6343–6349. Association for Computational Linguistics.

Susan T. Fiske. 1993. Controlling other people: The impact of power on stereotyping. *American Psychologist*, 48(6):621–628.

Susan T. Fiske. 1998. Stereotyping, prejudice, and discrimination. In *The handbook of social psychology*, volume 1-2, pages 357–411. McGraw-Hill, New York, NY, US, 4th edition.

Susan T. Fiske. 2004. *Social Beings: A Core Motives Approach to Social Psychology*. J. Wiley.

Nikhil Garg, Londa Schiebinger, Dan Jurafsky, and James Zou. 2018. Word embeddings quantify 100 years of gender and ethnic stereotypes. *Proceedings of the National Academy of Sciences*, 115(16):E3635–E3644.

Anthony G. Greenwald, Debbie E. McGhee, and Jordan L. K. Schwartz. 1998. Measuring individual differences in implicit cognition: The implicit association test. *Journal of Personality and Social Psychology*, 74(6):1464–1480.

Felix Hamborg. 2020. Media Bias, the Social Sciences, and NLP: Automating Frame Analyses to Identify Bias by Word Choice and Labeling. In *Proceedings of the 58th Annual Meeting of the Association for Computational Linguistics: Student Research Workshop*, pages 79–87, Online. Association for Computational Linguistics.

M. Tim Jones. 2019. Machine learning and bias. `https://developer.ibm.com/technologies/machine-learning/articles/machine-learning-and-bias/`. Last accessed: 2020-09-07.

Lynn B. Jorde and Stephen P. Wooding. 2004. Genetic variation, classification and 'race'. *Nature Genetics*, 36(11):S28–S33.

Manfred Kienpointner and Walther Kindt. 1997. On the problem of bias in political argumentation: An investigation into discussions about political asylum in Germany and Austria. *Journal of Pragmatics*, 27(5):555–585.

John Lawrence, Mark Snaith, Barbara Konat, Katarzyna Budzynska, and Chris Reed. 2017. Debating Technology for Dialogical Argument: Sensemaking, Engagement, and Analytics. *ACM Transactions on Internet Technology*, 17(3):24:1–24:23.

Sora Lim, Adam Jatowt, Michael Färber, and Masatoshi Yoshikawa. 2020. Annotating and Analyzing Biased Sentences in News Articles using Crowdsourcing. In *Proceedings of the 12th Language Resources and Evaluation Conference*, pages 1478–1484, Marseille, France. European Language Resources Association.

Thomas Manzini, Lim Yao Chong, Alan W Black, and Yulia Tsvetkov. 2019. Black is to Criminal as Caucasian is to Police: Detecting and Removing Multiclass Bias in Word Embeddings. In *Proceedings of the 2019 Conference of the North American Chapter of the Association for Computational Linguistics: Human Language Technologies, Volume 1 (Long and Short Papers)*, pages 615–621. Association for Computational Linguistics.

Tomas Mikolov, Ilya Sutskever, Kai Chen, Greg S Corrado, and Jeff Dean. 2013. Distributed Representations of Words and Phrases and their Compositionality. In *Advances in Neural Information Processing Systems 26*, pages 3111–3119. Curran Associates, Inc.

Orestis Papakyriakopoulos, Simon Hegelich, Juan Carlos Medina Serrano, and Fabienne Marco. 2020. Bias in word embeddings. In *Proceedings of the 2020 Conference on Fairness, Accountability, and Transparency*, FAT* '20, pages 446–457, Barcelona, Spain. Association for Computing Machinery.

Jeffrey Pennington, Richard Socher, and Christopher Manning. 2014. GloVe: Global Vectors for Word Representation. In *Proceedings of the 2014 Conference on Empirical Methods in Natural Language Processing (EMNLP)*, pages 1532–1543, Doha, Qatar. Association for Computational Linguistics.

Anthony Rios, Reenam Joshi, and Hejin Shin. 2020. Quantifying 60 Years of Gender Bias in Biomedical Research with Word Embeddings. In *Proceedings of the 19th SIGBioMed Workshop on Biomedical Language Processing*, pages 1–13, Online. Association for Computational Linguistics.

Rachel Rudinger, Jason Naradowsky, Brian Leonard, and Benjamin Van Durme. 2018. Gender Bias in Coreference Resolution. In *Proceedings of the 2018 Conference of the North American Chapter of the Association for Computational Linguistics: Human Language Technologies, Volume 2 (Short Papers)*, pages 8–14, New Orleans, Louisiana. Association for Computational Linguistics.

Maarten Sap, Saadia Gabriel, Lianhui Qin, Dan Jurafsky, Noah A. Smith, and Yejin Choi. 2020. Social Bias Frames: Reasoning about Social and Power Implications of Language. In *Proceedings of the 58th Annual Meeting of the Association for Computational Linguistics*, pages 5477–5490, Online. Association for Computational Linguistics.

Robyn Speer, Joshua Chin, and Catherine Havasi. 2017. ConceptNet 5.5: An Open Multilingual Graph of General Knowledge. In *Thirty-First AAAI Conference on Artificial Intelligence*, San Francisco, California USA.

Robyn Speer. 2017. ConceptNet Numberbatch 17.04: Better, less-stereotyped word vectors. https://blog.conceptnet.io/posts/2017/conceptnet-numberbatch-17-04-better-less-stereotyped-word-vectors/. Last accessed: 2020-09-03.

Christian Stab and Iryna Gurevych. 2016. Recognizing the Absence of Opposing Arguments in Persuasive Essays. In *Proceedings of the Third Workshop on Argument Mining (ArgMining2016)*, pages 113–118, Berlin, Germany. Association for Computational Linguistics.

Manfred Stede and Jodi Schneider. 2018. *Argumentation Mining*. Number 40 in Synthesis Lectures on Human Language Technologies. Morgan & Claypool.

Tony Sun, Andrew Gaut, Shirlyn Tang, Yuxin Huang, Mai ElSherief, Jieyu Zhao, Diba Mirza, Elizabeth Belding, Kai-Wei Chang, and William Yang Wang. 2019. Mitigating Gender Bias in Natural Language Processing: Literature Review. In *Proceedings of the 57th Annual Meeting of the Association for Computational Linguistics*, pages 1630–1640, Florence, Italy. Association for Computational Linguistics.

Chris Sweeney and Maryam Najafian. 2019. A Transparent Framework for Evaluating Unintended Demographic Bias in Word Embeddings. In *Proceedings of the 57th Annual Meeting of the Association for Computational Linguistics*, pages 1662–1667, Florence, Italy. Association for Computational Linguistics.

Eva Vanmassenhove, Christian Hardmeier, and Andy Way. 2018. Getting Gender Right in Neural Machine Translation. In *Proceedings of the 2018 Conference on Empirical Methods in Natural Language Processing*, pages 3003–3008, Brussels, Belgium. Association for Computational Linguistics.

Henning Wachsmuth, Martin Potthast, Khalid Al-Khatib, Yamen Ajjour, Jana Puschmann, Jiani Qu, Jonas Dorsch, Viorel Morari, Janek Bevendorff, and Benno Stein. 2017. Building an argument search engine for the web. In *Proceedings of the 4th Workshop on Argument Mining*, pages 49–59. Association for Computational Linguistics.

Frank Zenker. 2011. Experts and Bias: When is the Interest-Based Objection to Expert Argumentation Sound? *Argumentation*, 25(3):355.

Use of Claim Graphing and Argumentation Schemes in Biomedical Literature: A Manual Approach to Analysis

Eli Moser
Department of Health Sciences
McMaster University
Hamilton, Ontario, Canada
mosere@mcmaster.ca

Robert E. Mercer
Department of Computer Science
The University of Western Ontario
London, Ontario, Canada
mercer@csd.uwo.ca

Abstract

Argumentation in an experimental life science paper consists of a main claim being supported with reasoned argumentative steps based on the data garnered from the experiments that were carried out. In this paper we report on an investigation of the large scale argumentation structure found when examining five biochemistry journal publications. One outcome of this investigation of biochemistry articles suggests that argumentation schemes originally designed for genetic research articles may transfer to experimental biomedical literature in general. Our use of these argumentation schemes shows that claims depend not only on experimental data but also on other claims. The tendency for claims to use other claims as their supporting evidence in addition to the experimental data led to two novel models that have provided a better understanding of the large scale argumentation structure of a complete biochemistry paper. First, the claim graph displays the claims within a paper, their interactions, and their evidence. Second, another aspect of this argumentation network is further illustrated by the Model of Informational Hierarchy (MIH) which visualizes at a meta-level the flow of reasoning provided by the authors of the paper and also connects the main claim to the paper's title. Together, these models, which have been produced by a manual examination of the biochemistry articles, would be likely candidates for a computational method that analyzes the large scale argumentation structure.

1 Introduction

The large and ever-growing quantity of biomedical literature is well known (Hunter and Cohen, 2006). Included in biomedicine are the foundational experimental life sciences, such as genetics and biochemistry. Despite the importance and abundance of this literature, few computational models have been proposed that address the argumentation that is used to support the claims made in the papers describing outcomes of experiments. Such models would allow the mechanization of argumentation analysis which could enable scientific claim validation, a task made difficult because of the huge number of claims being made. A claim is any statement made within a paper which presents a novel finding based on the conducted experiment (Leonelli, 2015). A claim requires evidence to verify it. The structure of individual claims and their evidence is well illustrated by the Toulmin model (Toulmin, 2003), and the logic underlying these relationships can be categorized with argumentation schemes and premise classes (Karbach, 1987; Green, 2014a; Al Qassas et al., 2015; Green, 2015; Mayer et al., 2018).

The Toulmin model of argumentation is adept at illustrating the components of an individual argument. When composing argumentation text, every claim that is made must be supported by evidence and a warrant connecting the claim and evidence (Karbach, 1987). In the experimental sciences, the warrant is very often implicit, given that the intended audience can easily fill that slot in the argument structure. These arguments with implicit premises (and sometimes conclusions) are called enthymemes. Although each individual argument can be modelled in this way, it fails to recognize the variations in how claims relate to their supporting evidence, and the means by which the warrant supports that relation. To account for this, the Toulmin model can be supplemented with argumentation schemes. Argumentation

Proceedings of the 7th Workshop on Argument Mining, pages 88–99
Barcelona, Spain (Online), December 13, 2020.

schemes vary by context, and none have been synthesized for biomedical literature specifically. In this research a set of 15 novel argumentation schemes developed for categorizing genetic research argumentation (Green, 2015) were used and were found to be fully transferable beyond genetics to biochemistry arguments. While categorizing all of the claims of a paper, it became evident that often the evidence for a claim was another claim, and that the majority of claims within the paper were interconnected in this way. As a result, it is possible to construct a visual representation of all of a paper's claims in a graph. This graph illustrates which claims are supported by what data and also which claims are the most representative of a paper's findings overall. The varying degrees of claim significance demonstrated by this graph can be organized into a hierarchical model, which accounts for all data within a paper while still allowing for nuance to be maintained. In addition, the analysis of individual claims is not lost, as each progression of information from one level of specificity to the next is facilitated by argumentation schemes and the Toulmin model structure.

The next step to understanding the argumentation set forth in a scientific paper is analyzing the complete argumentation structure of the full paper. We present here our preliminary work on the analysis of this larger scale argumentation structure of biochemistry papers. This study is done by examining the flow of the paper from its data used as premises to support certain claims, some of which are used as premises for other claims, ending finally with the main claim of the paper. This research follows a similar path to Lawrence and Reed (2017), who manually constructed large scale graphs, and adds to the argumentation structure research by examining complete biochemistry articles and linking the argument schemes. Two models of analysis will demonstrate the interactions of claims. The first model is a high-level argument diagram of the data and claims structure capturing the essence of Green (2014b) and in the spirit of other high-level diagramming models (Stab et al., 2014; Kirschner et al., 2015; Eger et al., 2017; Stab and Gurevych, 2017) and diagramming-assisting software (Janier et al., 2014). The network of data and claims allows one to investigate its properties. In particular, the data is found in figures, tables, and other comments by the paper's authors. This data initiates the argumentation flow which ends in the main claim of the paper. This investigation leads to the second model, the Model of Informational Hierarchy (MIH). It makes more precise the units of the argument structure and their position in that structure. This hierarchical description of data and claims differs from other argumentation structures such as online debates (Lawrence and Reed, 2017) and student essays (Eger et al., 2017). In addition to the main focus, our research also demonstrates the applicability of Green's (2014a; 2015) argumentation schemes not only to genetics, but also to other biomedical research, biochemistry, in particular. Also, as an application of these models, the MIH can be viewed as a precursor to biomedical literature summarization.

The paper is organized as follows: Some related work to provide context for the current work is presented next. This is followed by a short description of the the five biochemistry papers that were used in the study. Then, the two main contributions, the claim graph and the Model of Informational Hierarchy, are explained. We conclude with a summary and some proposed future research directions.

2 Related Work

Our interest in investigating the larger scale argumentation structure has a similar motivation to the works of Wachsmuth et al. (2017) and Lawrence and Reed (2017), who are interested in investigating various properties of large scale argument networks. This new dimension adds to the previous works they point to as examples that consider particular aspects of argument structure: distinguishing argumentative and non-argumentative sentences (Moens et al., 2007), classifying text spans as premises or conclusions (Mochales Palau and Moens, 2009), classifying relations between specific sets of premises and their conclusion (Feng and Hirst, 2011), or classifying the different types of premise that can support a given conclusion (Park and Cardie, 2014). In addition to these examples, various manual and computational studies have been done to analyze different argumentation aspects, including: the structure of valid arguments in legal documents using feature-based machine learning (Mochales Palau and Moens, 2011), opinion and didatic texts using Rhetorical Structure Theory (Saint-Dizier, 2012), debates using textual entailment (Cabrio and Villata, 2012), and deconstructing the argumentation into the premises (referred to as evidence in the evidence-based medical text genre) and conclusions (also referred to as claims) in scientific articles manually, with feature-based machine learning, or with neural end-to-end machine learning (Blake, 2010; Teufel, 2010; Green et al., 2011; Liakata et al., 2012; Sándor and de Waard, 2012; Longo et al., 2012; Longo and Hederman, 2013; Graves et al., 2014; Green, 2014a; Green, 2015; Kirschner et al., 2015; Mayer et al., 2018; Mayer et al., 2020). Lippi and Torroni (2015) provide an excellent survey of research done until 2015 which is further updated to 2018 by Stede and Schneider (2018). Corpus creation and analysis has also been another aspect of argumentation mining studies (Stab and Gurevych, 2017). More recently, neural net machine learning has provided a new machine learning paradigm for doing cross-domain claim analysis (Daxenberger et al., 2017). Eger et al. (2017) and Mayer et al. (2020) provide neural end-to-end models for computational argumentation mining. They label student essays and randomized control trials, respectively, with a BIO encoding to indicate argumentative and non-argumentative text spans, component type, and the stance between the components.

The rich history of work in argumentation mining has tended to focus on non-scientific text, however work in scientific text argumentation mining does have a following. The research done on various aspects of argumentation in scientific text begins with Argumentation Zoning (AZ) (Teufel et al., 1999; Teufel and Moens, 2002), also being some of the earliest work in argumentation mining. AZ is based on rhetorical moves, an important precursor for mapping out certain aspects of argument structure. Rhetorical moves, captured as AZ or more generally, have been investigated in a few science genres: computational linguistics (Teufel et al., 1999; Teufel and Moens, 2002), biochemistry (Kanoksilapatham, 2005), molecular biology (Mizuta et al., 2006), and chemistry (Teufel, 2010). Argumentation schemes (Walton et al., 2008) have been an important aspect of argumentation and argumentation mining. Green (2014a; 2015) has provided an important addition to these argumentation schemes for experimental scientific writing, specifically for genetics articles. While Green's argumentation schemes deal with aspects of the experiment, its outcomes, and the analysis of those outcomes, other work (Teufel, 2014) focusses on a different aspect of argumentation (via rhetorical moves): placing a research paper in its scientific context. Al Qassas et al. (2015) propose argumentation schemes for clinical discussions and use these schemes in an argument graph to analyze a discussion.

Argument diagramming is a technique that is commonly used to describe argumentation. While a manual operation, in the digital age, some computer-supported argument visualization tools have been developed. Araucaria (Reed and Rowe, 2004) and OVA+ (Janier et al., 2014) are two examples. The first provides support for mapping argumentation schemes. The second was developed for assisting with diagramming the larger scale argumentation structures. Lawrence and Reed (2017) provides an argument diagram for large scale online discussions. Eger et al. (2017) while mainly focussed on a neural end-to-end model for computational argumentation mining also provides an almost tree-like argumentation structure of complete student essays.

3 Dataset

Although there has been significant research on the deconstruction of individual claims and the methods of identifying claims within texts of various sorts (Mochales Palau and Moens, 2009; Blake, 2010; Feng and Hirst, 2011; Teufel, 2010; Green et al., 2011; Liakata et al., 2012; Sándor and de Waard, 2012; Longo et al., 2012; Longo and Hederman, 2013; Graves et al., 2014; Green, 2014a; Green, 2015; Kirschner et al., 2015; Mayer et al., 2018; Mayer et al., 2020), we are interested here in working with a new subset of scientific texts, biochemistry texts in particular, and linking claims into a larger argumentation structure. The dataset that we have used consists of five papers. Although the number of papers in the dataset used in this research is small, what sets it apart is that the annotation of the claims has been done by our domain expert, Dr. Derek McLachlin, one of the co-authors of the five papers. Our findings and the techniques and models presented are all based on the analysis of papers by our domain expert. The five papers all concern the dimerization interactions of the b-subunit of *Escherichia coli* ATP synthase. Having a co-author of the paper source the claims directly increased their reliability as representative of the papers' findings. Dr. McLachlin additionally provided detailed lists of claim interactions, indicating the direct source of evidence behind each claim.

Although the source material for the findings reported here is limited to one author, the literature used follows a structure ubiquitous to biomedical research, specifically, the progression of abstract, introduction, procedure/methods and materials, results, and discussion (Nair and Nair, 2014). This is standard for research of this nature and doesn't affect the applicability of the proposed models to other similar literature. Once a paper's claims and their sources have been determined it is possible to employ graphing techniques and information modeling.

4   Argumentation Structure

As stated earlier, the focus of this paper is the investigation of large scale argumentation structure in the spirit of Lawrence and Reed (2017) and Wachsmuth et al. (2017). The notion of large scale for our purposes is one complete biochemistry article. As discussed in Section 3, the claims and their spans have been provided by one of the co-authors of each paper. In addition, the interaction of the data and the claims has been provided by this co-author. Our research uses the Toulmin model (Toulmin, 2003). We have chosen the argumentation schemes provided by Green (2015) because they have an experimental science basis (cf. the clinical discussion schemes proposed by Al Qassas et al. (2015) and the randomized control trial evidence classes proposed by Mayer et al. (2018)). We refer to the model and scheme as the Toulmin-Green model. Green (2014a) has noted that many of the arguments in scientific writing are enthymemes, arguments that are missing premises or conclusions, and in most cases it is the warrants that are missing. What is missing from the information provided by our domain expert are the warrants. These have been provided by the first author of the current paper. An example of an argument:

> Premise (Claim 19) [grounds]: The highest level of disulfide formation was observed with the S60C + L65C and A61C + L65C combinations.
> Premise [missing warrant]: Proximity is necessary for disulfide binding between residues.
> Claim 21A (Green's Argumentation Scheme: Effect to Cause (5)): The result suggests that residue 65 of one subunit is close to residues 60 and 61 of the other

Given these elements, we are now able to analyze the argument structure of a biochemistry paper. We provide a categorization of the claims, a graphing technique that demonstrates the large scale argumentation structure, and an organization of the data and claims that we call the Informational Hierarchy.

4.1   Claim Categorization

In developing a claim based graphing technique the most fundamental component are the claims themselves. We were fortunate to have a co-author of the five biochemistry papers that we analyzed provide the claims and the reasons for making the claims. Having these claims and their support, they were individually categorized into three distinct groupings:

1. Figure-Claims (claims which were supported directly by experimental data)

2. Claim-Claims (claims supported by other claims, either claims based on figures or claims based on other claims)

3. Other (the majority of the claims in this category were experimental observations which could not fit into the displayed data)

In the five papers analysed over half of the claims fell into the "figure-claim" category, with a small minority falling into the "other" category.

The categorization step of claim analysis is important due to the informational distinction between claim-claims and figure-claims in the information hierarchy model, as well as their distinct visual treatment within the graph. Figure based claims are direct results of the data, while claim based claims encompass more findings and are generally more significant. See Figure 1 for an example of a claim graph for one of the analyzed papers. All claims used in the graph are represented by a number corresponding to the order in which they appear in the paper. Figure-claims and "other" claims are illustrated

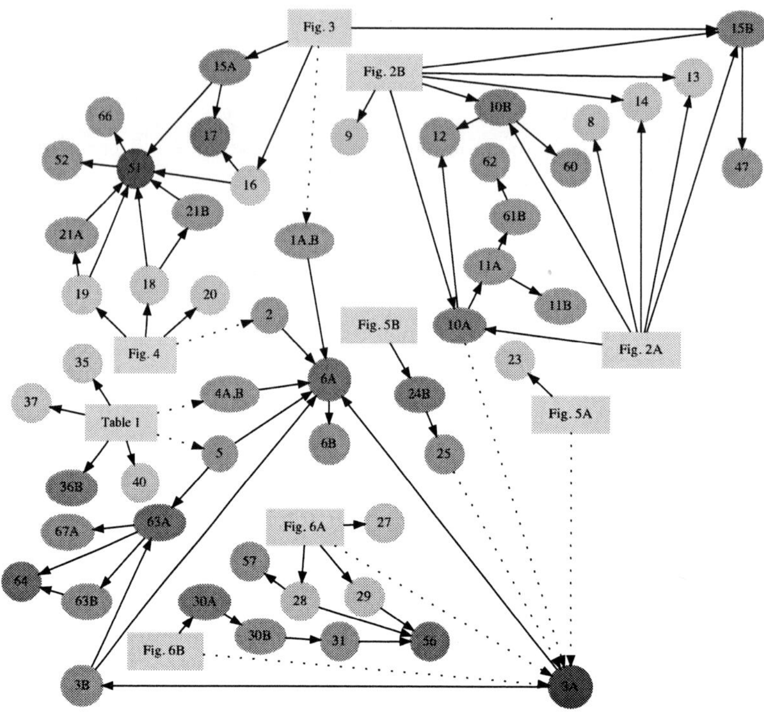

Figure 1: Claim graph for the paper "Dimerization Interactions of the *b* Subunit of the *Escherichia coli* F_1F_0-ATPase".

with a blue coloured circle labeled with their claim number. Claim-claims are illustrated with a red coloured circle labeled with their claim number. The intensity of the colour of a claim is dependent on the number of figures/claims which support it. As a result, the more intense the colour of the claim is, the more significant it is to the paper. This colour coding is done to make more central claims evident.

4.2 Claim Graphing

An example of a claim graph, created for the paper "Dimerization Interactions of the *b* Subunit of the *Escherichia coli* F_1F_0-ATPase" (McLachlin and Dunn, 1997) can be seen in Figure 1. The graph is composed of nodes representing the figures and tables of the paper, the grey rectangles labelled with their names in the paper; figure-claim nodes, the blue-toned nodes, which represent claims attributed to figures; and red-toned claim-claim nodes which represent claims that are supported by other claims and occasionally (but very rarely) supported by both another claim as well as a figure/table. Finally, colour intensity was adjusted to account for claim support, the more supporting figures/tables/claims a claim had, the darker the respective value. Directional edges indicate the premise-claim associations. The edges point from the support for a claim to the supported claim illustrating the directional flow of information. The dotted edges are meant to represent stylistic rather than argumentative moves. In the example given in Figure 1, nodes 1–5 are found in the abstract and are recapitulations of claims made in the discussion section of the paper (the nodes representing these discussion section claims are currently not shown in the graph). Nodes 6A and 6B assemble these claims ("Taken together the results are consistent with a model ..."). The graph is presented with as few intersecting edges as is possible (none in the example given in Figure 1).

4.3 Discussion of the Graphing Technique

Once a graph has been constructed it is possible to understand a paper's components, their interactions, and their varying significance. The graph visualises the interactions between figures, claims, and most importantly, which claims are the most illustrative of the paper's findings.

Claim significance is allocated based on the amount of support an individual claim receives, and not the amount of support it provides. This is because one of the future applications using the graph is to aid in the condensing or summarizing of a paper. As such, the concept of significance is dependent on how much information a claim encompasses. Figures and claims which have a noticeably high number of outgoing arrows are noteworthy on the grounds that they are important evidence. Their centrality is accounted for because figures and claims which provide a large amount of support are included in claims which receive a large amount of support. Significant claims represent a synthesis of smaller findings and data and provide a cumulative statement of the paper's results overall.

The density of support which classifies a claim as significant is relative to the total number of claims a paper makes. In applying this graphing technique universally the number of graphed claims will vary, and so will the density of support for individual claims. In a paper with twenty claims overall, the most densely supported claim may have only three supports while in a paper with sixty claims overall the main claim may be supported by eight. In general, a significant (secondary or main) claim will always have more than three supports and (in the papers that we analyzed) should be supported by 15% of all of a paper's claims. There is some variation in accordance with how many claims are not supported by results shown in the paper (the "other" category) however, it is usually unambiguous when looking at the graph which claims are the most supported.

Graphed claims can be separated into three categories according to the amount of support they have received, and the origin of that support. At this point in our research, this categorization is being subjectively determined by our sense of the claim's importance with respect to its role in summarizing the purpose of the paper. For this reason figure-based claims are never classified as main claims. They, like claim-based claims, have variation in the amount of support they receive, however since they are only statements about figures and not further analysis of figure statements, they do not have comparable summative value to claims based on claims based on figures. Regardless of how many figures a figure-claim has as direct supports, it is never a main claim, but will be accounted for as support for a claim-claim.

Within claim-claims there are additional levels of distinction, based on the number of support claims receive and the relevance of the claim content (i.e., what the claim is actually stating) to the paper itself. Relevance is also determined by how logically the claim content relates to the title of the paper, and therefore the thesis, of the paper. There are three levels of claim-claim relevance:

1. Tertiary Claim-Claims (1-2 supporting claims)

2. Secondary Claim-Claims (3 or more supporting claims, no direct relevance to the title/main concept)

3. Main Claims (3 or more supporting claims, direct relevance to the paper title/main concept)

When analysing the graph of a paper and the flow of information within it, there emerges a very clear progression of supports and detail. The importance of a claim is correlated to the amount of support it has, as is its summative ability. This makes sense, as the more information represented within a claim the more summative a claim will be. Once a main claim has been identified, it is possible to utilise it (in conjunction with the title) to summarize the entirety of the paper into a one or two sentence statement. Although convenient to distil information to that level, it is crucial to maintain the levels of complexity which precede it so that nuance can be sought at the observer's discretion. Luckily, this is preserved in the graph, as it is possible to trace the origins of the main claims content through the support arrows it is connected to, and the supports of those supports in turn. This progression from figure/table to main claim illustrated by the graphing process can itself be used as a means of understanding the inductive flow of information in research from the specifics of the data to the overall main claim, accounting for every component of the paper. The following is an example of this progression:

Premise (Figures 2A and 2B observations): The figures show results of SDS-PAGE (protein gel electrophoresis) and Western blotting. Band intensities show molecular masses of proteins with A128C, R138C, S139C, and S146C mutations. A128C and S139C have higher masses.
Premise [missing warrant]: band intensity indicates protein amount at a specific mass

Figure-Claims 10A and 10B (Green's Argumentation Scheme: Consistent with Predicted Effects (7)): The proteins containing the A128C and S139C mutations showed a strong tendency to dimerize, (Claim 10A) while cysteines at positions 138 and 146 did not tend to form disulphides under these conditions. (Claim 10B) [Claim 10A's slightly reworded restatement in the Discussion section is indicated by the dashed edge in the claim graph]

Premise (Figure 5B observation): The figures show results of SDS-PAGE (protein gel electrophoresis) and Western blotting. The band intensities indicate the molecular masses of the proteins containing the mutations at locations 124-132 and 138. The proteins with mutations at locations 124, 128, and 132 do not show dark bands at lower molecular masses.
Premise [missing warrant]: band intensity indicates protein amount at a specific mass
Figure-Claim 24B (Green's Argumentation Scheme: Effect to Cause (5)): ..., the most complete disulfide bond formation was observed at positions 124, 128, and 132

Premise: Claim 24B
Premise [missing warrant]: Disulfide binding follows 4-residue periodicity in an α-helical protein structure.
Claim 25 (Green's Argumentation Scheme: Effect to Cause (5)): The 4-residue periodicity of cross-linking ... suggests a parallel α-helical arrangement in this region. [Claim 25's reworded restatement in the Discussion section is indicated by the dashed edge in the claim graph]

Premise: the restated Claim 10A (indicated by the dashed edge)
Premise: the restated Claim 25 (indicated by the dashed edge)
Premise [missing warrant]: Proximity is necessary for disulfide binding
Premise [missing warrant]: Residues 128 and 128' and 139 and 139' are close together within the quaternary structure
[Information from Figs. 5A, 6A, and 6B (dashed edges) has not been included in this example.]
Claim 3A (Green's Argumentation Scheme: Effect to Cause (5)): Cysteines at positions 124, 128, 132, and 139 showed strong tendencies to form disulfides with their mates in the dimer, suggesting a parallel α-helical interaction between the subunits in this region.

4.4 The Model of Informational Hierarchy

The Model of Informational Hierarchy (MIH), shown in Figure 2, represents the development of information in experimental science literature by tracing the path of information through the graphing technique described above. The MIH is pyramidal in shape, in order to illustrate the inductive nature of the progression between levels. As the pyramid is traversed from the base to the top the specificity of the information decreases, and the summative ability of the information increases. The top levels of the MIH are built on those at the base, and thus account for the information contained within them. Unlike the graph, this model is able to account for levels of information even more specific than the data presented in figures and tables. Allocating data as the base of claim graphing is understandable as it is the results, and not the way that they were acquired, that are the main focus of claims made in scientific literature. In analysing the entirety of information in any given paper however, the raw data itself cannot be the base of the model. How the data was gathered informs the data, and even how the data can be interpreted. It is important to understand each level of the MIH and how it interacts with the levels surrounding it. The layers will be discussed in ascending order, beginning with the foundation.

Methods and Experimental Procedure Underlying the data of any scientific claim is the means by which that data was procured. Without an understanding of the methods used and the experimental procedure the veracity of the data presented is unknowable. The procedure informs how the data relates to the figure-claims. To know what a figure is showing, how it is showing it, and how that relates to figure-claims is all based on an understanding of the experimental methods and materials used, making the procedure the foundational level of the MIH.

Data (Figures and Tables) Following from the methods and experimental procedures of a biomedical paper comes the presentation of the experimental findings. The presentation of the data found in an experiment is as crucial as the means by which it was discovered, as it is the findings which the paper is written to communicate. The data (displayed in figures or tables) directly support figure-claims. There is no argumentation scheme which relates the experimental procedures/methods to the data of a paper, as the relationship between the two is evidentiary rather than based on a logical progression. However, a Toulmin-Green argumentation scheme relationship does exist between the data presented and figure-claims made. In these schemes the premise is derived from interpretation of the data informed by the methods/experimental procedure, resulting in the conclusion that is the figure-claim.

Figure-Claims and Experimental Observations The category of figure-claims represents claims based on experimental data presented directly by either a figure or a table. Claims which fall under the category of "Experimental Observations" are statements of outcomes noticed by the researchers that could not be easily included in the tables and figures used, but are still based directly on the findings.

Tertiary Claim-Claims Tertiary claim claims, as discussed in the discussion of the graphing technique, are claim-claims which are not deemed to be significant. They are based on figure-claims and experimental observations, but lack summative power (only 1-2 supports). They are an intermediate step between figure-claims and secondary claims.

Secondary Claim-Claims Secondary claims have enough support to be significant, however lack relevancy. They are not main claims due to their lack of direct relation to the paper's title (and thesis).

Main Claim The main claim is the most representative statement of the paper's findings, and the highest level of summarization. These claims are claim-claims with the greatest amount of support and will often be supported by other highly supported claims. In conjunction with the title, a main claim can be used to summarize the entirety of a paper's findings in a single sentence.

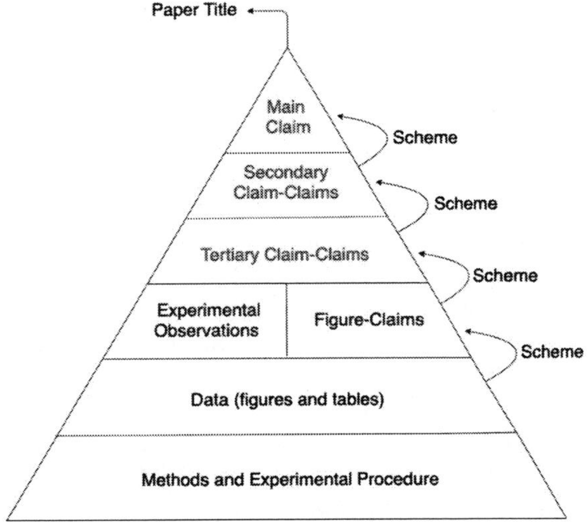

Figure 2: Model of Informational Hierarchy

4.5   Use of Argumentation Schemes

As seen in Figure 2, there are argumentation schemes included between each level of the information hierarchy. These schemes are from the Toulmin-Green model of claim argumentation and are what underlies all informational progression within the paper. In the claim graph as well, each arrow represents a logical progression which can be categorized with the Toulmin-Green model. For figure-claims the evidence comes from the data itself, the warrant is assumed knowledge or taken from the procedure. For claim-claims (at all levels of significance) the evidence comes from a previously made claim, and the warrant is often assumed knowledge. Although Dr. Green's argumentation schemes do not affect the progression of the information hierarchy, they are the connections which hold the graph and the information model together. Without them there would be no accountability for how statement significance progresses, and no legitimacy to the logic of those progressions.

5 Conclusions and Future Work

The purpose of analyzing the five papers with the Toulmin-Green model and subsequently generating the claim graph and the Model of Informational Hierarchy has been to illustrate a manual approach for generating a large scale argumentation structure for a complete biochemistry paper. The methods presented are novel for this science genre. One can compare this argumentation structure with those that have been established for debates (Lawrence and Reed, 2017), persuasive essays (Stab and Gurevych, 2017), and student essays (Eger et al., 2017). As is shown with the graph, claims in biochemistry articles are intrinsically interlinked, with claims using both other claims and data for their evidence. The MIH model lists argumentation schemes as intermediary steps between levels of information to illustrate the importance of claims relating to each other in a way that is categorizable and logically sound.

Beyond these results, there is potential for further research. The Toulmin-Green model, the claim graphing technique, and the MIH all have aspects which can be further developed.

Green's (Green, 2016; Green, 2018) innovative idea to use Prolog rules to generate argument schemes can be improved. As proposed, the body of each rule matches with the Prolog knowledge base extracted from the text. The body of each rule needs some discourse information to constrain what elements from these Prolog facts are allowed to be combined. We can use the information derived from the claim graph to add to these rule bodies, i.e., only those facts that are extracted from elements that are connected by an edge would be allowed to imply the argument scheme (the head of the rule). However, it still remains to be seen how to do this in an automatic way since the graphs have been constructed manually. Using discourse and rhetorical moves may be some directions to investigate. In addition to this, a method to produce implicit argument components for enthymemes is needed.

Biochemistry (and other experimental life sciences) papers are written following the IMRaD (Introduction, Methods, Results, and Discussion) structure. As indicated by dashed edges in the claim graph in Figure 1 and mentioned in the example in Section 4.3, the placement of a claim in this structure may have stylistic significance. This aspect of the writing style was not part of this initial study and needs to be further investigated and incorporated in the claim graph. Indeed, that a claim is restated and where this restatement is placed may provide further justification for the split into the three claim categories proposed in the MIH. As well, a characteristic of writing in the biochemistry genre is to explain the reasons for choosing the experiments discussed in the paper. This aspect is important to a full understanding of the argumentation structure. How to incorporate it in the claim graph needs to be investigated. Discussion of claims in the paper highlighted above commented on claims in previously published papers. This important inter-paper argumentation structure will be investigated.

An important next step is to produce the claim graph automatically. Methods to identify claims in biomedical text (albeit not always directly applicable to this type of experimental biochemistry article) ranging from rule-based (Blake, 2010) to neural end-to-end (Mayer et al., 2020) have been previously investigated and would comprise a first step toward this goal.

A future application of the Model of Informational Hierarchy could be summarization of the paper, a noted motivation for some of the earliest argumentation research (Teufel and Moens, 2002). Moving from the top of the hierarchy (the paper's title and main claim) downward would provide more and more detail which is not contained in an abstract. Real-time summarization at a user-specified level of detail seems possible. And a summarization focussed on a particular aspect of a paper's research claims combining the MIH and the claim graph could also be a possibility.

Acknowledgements

This research was funded by The Natural Sciences and Engineering Research Council of Canada (NSERC) through an Undergraduate Summer Research Award to Eli Moser and a Discovery Grant to Robert E. Mercer. We thank Dr. Derek McLachlin of the Department of Biochemistry, The University of Western Ontario for providing his analysis of the five papers used in this study. We also acknowledge the helpful comments provided by the reviewers.

References

Malik Al Qassas, Daniela Fogli, Massimiliano Giacomin, and Giovanni Guida. 2015. Analysis of clinical discussions based on argumentation schemes. *Proceedia Computer Science*, 64:282–289.

Catherine Blake. 2010. Beyond genes, proteins, and abstracts: Identifying scientific claims from full-text biomedical articles. *Journal of Biomedical Informatics*, 43:173–189.

Elena Cabrio and Serena Villata. 2012. Natural language arguments: A combined approach. In *Proceedings of the 20th European Conference on Artificial Intelligence (ECAI 2012)*, pages 205–210.

Johannes Daxenberger, Steffen Eger, Ivan Habernal, Christian Stab, and Iryna Gurevych. 2017. What is the essence of a claim? Cross-domain claim identification. In *Proceedings of the 2017 Conference on Empirical Methods in Natural Language Processing*, pages 2055–2066.

Steffen Eger, Johannes Daxenberger, and Iryna Gurevych. 2017. Neural end-to-end learning for computational argumentation mining. In *Proceedings of the 55th Annual Meeting of the Association for Computational Linguistics (Volume 1: Long Papers)*, pages 11–22.

Vanessa Wei Feng and Graeme Hirst. 2011. Classifying arguments by scheme. In *Proceedings of the 49th Annual Meeting of the Association for Computational Linguistics: Human Language Technologies*, pages 987–996.

Heather Graves, Roger Graves, Robert E. Mercer, and Mahzereen Akter. 2014. Titles that announce argumentative claims in biomedical research articles. In *Proceedings of the First Workshop on Argumentation Mining*, pages 98–99.

Nancy Green, Rachael Dwight, Kanyamas Navoraphan, and Brian Stadler. 2011. Natural language generation of biomedical argumentation for lay audiences. *Argument and Computation*, 2(1):23–50.

Nancy Green. 2014a. Towards creation of a corpus for argumentation mining the biomedical genetics research literature. In *Proceedings of the First Workshop on Argumentation Mining*, pages 11–18.

Nancy L. Green. 2014b. Argumentation for scientific claims in a biomedical research article. In *Proceedings of the Workshop on Frontiers and Connections between Argumentation Theory and Natural Language Processing (ArgNLP2014)*, volume 1341 of *CEUR Workshop Proceedings*.

Nancy Green. 2015. Identifying argumentation schemes in genetics research articles. In *Proceedings of the 2nd Workshop on Argumentation Mining*, pages 12–21.

Nancy L. Green. 2016. Implementing argumentation schemes as logic programs. In *Proceedings of the 16th Workshop on Computational Models of Natural Argument*, volume 1876 of *CEUR Workshop Proceedings*, pages 1–7.

Nancy L. Green. 2018. Towards mining scientific discourse using argumentation schemes. *Argument & Computation*, 9:121–135.

Lawrence Hunter and K. Bretonnel Cohen. 2006. Biomedical language processing: What's beyond PubMed? *Molecular Cell*, 21(5):589–594.

Mathilde Janier, John Lawrence, and Chris Reed. 2014. Ova+: an argument analysis interface. In *Proceedings of COMMA 2014*, pages 463–464.

Budsaba Kanoksilapatham. 2005. Rhetorical structure of biochemistry research articles. *English for Specific Purposes*, 24(3):269–292.

Joan Karbach. 1987. Using Toulmin's model of argumentation. *Journal of Teaching Writing*, 6(1):81–92.

Christian Kirschner, Judith Eckle-Kohler, and Iryna Gurevych. 2015. Linking the thoughts: Analysis of argumentation structures in scientific publications. In *Proceedings of the 2nd Workshop on Argumentation Mining*, pages 1–11.

John Lawrence and Chris Reed. 2017. Using complex argumentative interactions to reconstruct the argumentative structure of large-scale debates. In *Proceedings of the 4th Workshop on Argument Mining*, pages 108–117.

Sabina Leonelli. 2015. What counts as scientific data? A relational framework. *Philosophy of Science*, 82(5):810–821.

Maria Liakata, Shyamasree Saha, Simon Dobnik, Colin Batchelor, and Dietrich Rebholz-Schuhmann. 2012. Automatic recognition of conceptualization zones in scientific articles and two life science applications. *Bioinformatics*, 28(7):991–1000.

Marco Lippi and Paolo Torroni. 2015. Context-independent claim detection for argument mining. In *Proceedings of the Twenty-Fourth International Joint Conference on Artificial Intelligence (IJCAI 2015)*, pages 185–191.

Luca Longo and Lucy Hederman. 2013. Argumentation theory for decision support in health-care: A comparison with machine learning. In *Proceedings of the International Conference on Brain and Health Informatics*, pages 168–180.

Luca Longo, Bridget Kane, and Lucy Hederman. 2012. Argumentation theory in health-care. In *Proceedings of the 25th IEEE Symposium on Computer-Based Medical Systems*.

Tobias Mayer, Elena Cabrio, and Serena Villata. 2018. Evidence type classification in randomized controlled trials. In *Proceedings of the 5th Workshop on Argument Mining*, pages 29–34.

Tobias Mayer, Elena Cabrio, and Serena Villata. 2020. Transformer-based argument mining for healthcare applications. In *Proceedings of the 24th European Conference on Artificial Intelligence (ECAI 2020)*, pages 2108–2115.

Derek T. McLachlin and Stanley D. Dunn. 1997. Dimerization interactions of the *b* subunit of the *Escherichia coli* F_1F_0-ATPase. *Journal of Biological Chemistry*, 272(34):21233–21239.

Yoko Mizuta, Anna Korhonen, Tony Mullen, and Nigel Collier. 2006. Zone analysis in biology articles as a basis for information extraction. *International Journal of Medical Informatics*, 75(6):468–487.

Raquel Mochales Palau and Marie-Francine Moens. 2009. Argumentation mining: The detection, classification and structure of arguments in text. In *Proceedings of the 12th International Conference on Artificial Intelligence and Law*, page 98–107.

Raquel Mochales Palau and Marie-Francine Moens. 2011. Argumentation mining. *Artificial Intelligence and Law*, 19(1):1–22.

Marie-Francine Moens, Erik Boiy, Raquel Mochales Palau, and Chris Reed. 2007. Automatic detection of arguments in legal texts. In *Proceedings of the 11th International Conference on Artificial Intelligence and Law*, page 225–230.

P. K. Ramachandran Nair and Vimala D. Nair, 2014. *Organization of a Research Paper: The IMRAD Format*, chapter 2, pages 13–25. Springer.

Joonsuk Park and Claire Cardie. 2014. Identifying appropriate support for propositions in online user comments. In *Proceedings of the First Workshop on Argumentation Mining*, pages 29–38.

Chris Reed and Glenn Rowe. 2004. Araucaria: Software for argument analysis, diagramming and representation. *International Journal on Artificial Intelligence Tools*, 13(4):961–979.

Patrick Saint-Dizier. 2012. Processing natural language arguments with the <textcoop> platform. *Argument and Computation*, 3(1):49–82.

Ágnes Sándor and Anita de Waard. 2012. Identifying claimed knowledge updates in biomedical research articles. In *Proceedings of the Workshop on Detecting Structure in Scholarly Discourse*, pages 10–17.

Christian Stab and Iryna Gurevych. 2017. Parsing argumentation structures in persuasive essays. *Computational Linguistics*, 43(3):619–659.

Christian Stab, Christian Kirschner, Judith Eckle-Kohler, and Iryna Gurevych. 2014. Argumentation mining in persuasive essays and scientific articles from the discourse structure perspective. In *Proceedings of the Workshop on Frontiers and Connections between Argumentation Theory and Natural Language Processing (ArgNLP2014)*, volume 1341 of *CEUR Workshop Proceedings*.

Manfred Stede and Jodi Schneider. 2018. *Argumentation Mining*. Synthesis Lectures on Human Language Technologies. Morgan & Claypool Publishers.

Simone Teufel and Marc Moens. 2002. Summarizing scientific articles: Experiments with relevance and rhetorical status. *Computational Linguistics*, 28(4):409–445.

Simone Teufel, Jean Carletta, and Marc Moens. 1999. An annotation scheme for discourse-level argumentation in research articles. In *Proceedings of the Ninth Conference of the European Chapter of the Association for Computational Linguistics*, pages 110–117.

Simone Teufel. 2010. *The Structure of Scientific Articles: Applications to Citation Indexing and Summarization*. CSLI Studies in Computational Linguistics. Center for the Study of Language and Information.

Simone Teufel. 2014. Scientific argumentation detection as limited-domain intention recognition. In *Proceedings of the Workshop on Frontiers and Connections between Argumentation Theory and Natural Language Processing (ArgNLP2014)*, volume 1341 of *CEUR Workshop Proceedings*.

Stephen E. Toulmin. 2003. *The Uses of Argument*. Cambridge University Press.

Henning Wachsmuth, Benno Stein, and Yamen Ajjour. 2017. "PageRank" for argument relevance. In *Proceedings of the 15th Conference of the European Chapter of the Association for Computational Linguistics: Volume 1, Long Papers*, pages 1117–1127.

Douglas Walton, Chris Reed, and Fabrizio Macagno. 2008. *Argumentation Schemes*. Cambridge University Press.

Annotating argumentation in Swedish social media

Anna Lindahl
Språkbanken Text
University of Gothenburg
Sweden
`anna.lindahl@svenska.gu.se`

Abstract

This paper presents a small study of annotating argumentation in Swedish social media. Annotators were asked to annotate spans of argumentation in 9 threads from two discussion forums. At the post level, Cohen's κ and Krippendorff's α 0.48 was achieved. When manually inspecting the annotations the annotators seemed to agree when conditions in the guidelines were explicitly met, but implicit argumentation and opinions, resulting in annotators having to interpret what's missing in the text, caused disagreements.

1 Introduction

In recent years, argumentation mining has grown into a central research topic within the field of computational linguistics. With the aim of automatically identifying and analyzing argumentation in text, its envisioned applications are many, from more effective document retrieval to learning aids (Lawrence and Reed, 2020). There are many different approaches to how argumentation can be modeled and annotated and there are now many data sets of different size and level of annotation, with domains ranging from legal documents to social media. However, in many of the existing data sets, inter-annotator agreement is not very high and it is because annotating argumentation turns out to be a quite challenging task. There is still a need of more annotated data, as well as investigating how to reliably annotate data. It is also important to investigate other languages than English. Because of this, we have conducted a small annotation study on Swedish social-media data where the focus has been on identifying instances of argumentation but not analyzing them further.[1] This is both to select documents for further analysis of the identified argumentation instances but also in order to investigate how reliably annotators can agree on what is argumentation or not.

2 Related work

Annotating with the aim to distinguish what is argumentative from what is not argumentative has not been the most common goal in argumentation mining, although it is necessarily part of studies that annotate components of argumentation, either implicitly or explicitly as a first step in an argumentation mining pipeline. When it comes to documents from the web, the annotation of argumentation is usually done with respect to a topic. For example Habernal et al. (2014), annotated comments and blog posts as argumentative with respect to a topic in order to select documents for further annotation. On this they reach a 0.51 Fleiss κ and 0.59 Cohen's κ. Similarly, Habernal and Gurevych (2017) annotated documents from web discourse as 'non-persuasive' and 'on topic persuasive' before moving on to annotate microstructure. They reached Fleiss κ of 0.59 on this task. In some studies presence of argumentation has been annotated together with the stance or the type of the argumentation. For example, Stab et al.

---

[1]In the literature it seems that the assumption is made that argumentation is universally present in all languages and that its form is comparable across languages. This is obviously subject to empirical verification, but we have not seen any literature addressing this question. Impressionistically, descriptions of the kinds and structure of argumentation made for English seem to apply also to Swedish, but more thorough studies of this would be needed.

Proceedings of the 7th Workshop on Argument Mining, pages 100–105
Barcelona, Spain (Online), December 13, 2020.

(2018) annotated sentences from the web for supporting or opposing argument, or not an argument with respect to a topic. They reached Cohen's κ 0.72 and an observed agreement between 0.86–0.84. More recently, Trautmann et al. (2020) annotated sentences from the web with both expert and crowd-sourced annotators. The sentences were annotated with argument spans, and the spans were marked with stance with respect to a topic. The reached 0.6 Krippendorff's α_u and the crowd-sourced annotators reached 0.71 α_u.

3 Data

The data in this study is from two of Sweden's largest online discussion forums, Familjeliv ("Family life" FM), and Flashback (FB). Familjeliv is generally considered to be more about relationships and family life and Flashback more about politics, although both forums cover a broad range of topics. Both forums have a simple thread structure, where a thread is started with a post by a user and then other users reply with subsequent posts, shown in chronological order. There is a possibility for the users to cite each other, but there is no visually explicit tree structure as for example on Reddit. For this study, nine threads were randomly chosen among the threads which had a length of about 30 posts. These threads are shown in table 1. Threads 1–5 are from Familjeliv and threads 6–9 are from Flashback.

Thread	no. posts	no. users	no. tokens	no. cite tokens	tot no. tokens	Thread title
1	25	7	1426	562	1988	Corona at my kid's preschool
2	51	17	5795	442	6237	Thinking about cheating on my partner?
3	28	17	2627	45	2672	The stepchildren don't want to stay with us
4	20	8	1549	89	1638	To you who made the Trip, mainly Slovakia
5	33	25	1425	461	1886	Abolish home economics
6	32	28	1407	658	2065	The government wants to establish a new department "for psychological defence"
7	22	12	2032	725	2757	Tehran vs. Pyongyang.
8	25	19	1442	822	2264	Who will name their son Anders in the future?
9	30	17	3589	3369	6958	It was right to keep the schools open
Tot	266	150	21292	7173	28465	

Table 1: Thread statistics

4 Annotation

4.1 Annotation guidelines and setup

We employed 8 annotators in this study: one expert (the author) and 7 with linguistic background. For the annotation, the annotation tool WebAnno (Eckart de Castilho et al., 2016) was used. The annotators were asked to annotate spans of argumentation, the spans could not overlap but otherwise there was no restriction on span length. Argumentation was only to be annotated within posts. The annotation guidelines[2] provide the annotators with a definition of argumentation, inspired by a simplified version of the definition given in Van Eemeren et al. (2013). The definition also includes persuasiveness, as this is a fundamental part of argumentation, as discussed in Habernal and Gurevych (2017) among others. The definition is seen below, and says that argumentation should include:

---

[2]Please note that the guidelines were written in Swedish, which means some of the nuances of the following descriptions might be lost in translation.

1. A standpoint/stance.

2. This standpoint is expressed with claims, backed by reasons.

3. There is a real or imagined difference of opinion concerning this standpoint which leads to:

4. the intent to persuade a real or imagined other part about the standpoint.

What is considered as argumentation or an argument in argumentation mining tasks varies and is often adjusted to fit the task or the domain, see for example Bosc et al. (2016) who annotated tweets containing opinions as arguments due to the implicit argumentation on Twitter. In some studies a definition of argumentation is not given, but rather definitions of what is being annotated, for example argumentative components such as premises or claims. The definition described here is not meant to cover all phenomena which could be considered argumentative, the intent is to describe something which hopefully annotators can apply successfully and agree on. From this definition above these three questions were derived:

- Does the poster's text signal that he or she is taking a stance / has a standpoint?

- Does the poster motivate why?

- Do you perceive the poster as trying to persuade someone?

If the annotator considered the answer to be affirmative for all the questions for some span of text, they were instructed to mark it as argumentation. In addition to these questions two tests were supplied in order to aid in answering the questions. The first test asked the annotator to reformulate the argumentation as "A, because B", in order to answer the first two questions. The second test asked the annotator to insert "I agree/I don't agree" into the text. If doing so would not change the meaning of the text, this might indicate that the poster is arguing, and was intending to persuade. These two tests were not meant to give a definite answer but rather to guide the annotators. The guidelines also included examples of argumentation from the forums, as well as examples on how to apply the tests. Four of the annotators were also asked to write down the reformulation of the "A because of B" test in the annotation tool. We've chosen to treat the results from the all the annotators equally in this study as we've yet to analyze the reformulations.

4.2 Annotation statistics

The annotators took between 4.5 and 12 hours each to annotate all the threads. The annotators which had to write down a reformulation took the longer time. Table 2 shows annotation statistics for each annotator. Annotator A is the expert annotator and seems not to diverge from the others. The annotators annotated mostly one argument per post, in some cases two arguments per post (compare number of arguments and number of posts in table 2). The annotators differ in how many argument spans they have annotated. The annotators also differ in how many sentences on average they have included in the argumentation spans, which is reflected in how many of the total tokens they have annotated. The annotators usually marked spans respecting sentence boundaries, but sometimes annotated half a sentence. When a post was annotated with a span, all but one annotator annotated at least half the post on average.

4.3 Inter-annotator agreement

When calculating inter-annotator agreement (IAA) sentences were considered as being argumentative if at least half of the tokens in it were labeled as argumentation, posts were considered as being argumentative if they contained at least one argument span. Observed agreement for tokens are 25%, for sentences 40% and 39% for posts. If we include posts where all but one annotator agree, observed agreement is 60% and if we include posts were all but two agree it's 86%. 70% of all the posts are labeled with an argument span by at least one of the annotators; 47% of those posts are annotated with a span by at least 6 of the annotators. Cohen's κ was measured pair-wise for all annotators and, as used in Toledo et al. (2019), averages from Cohen's κ were calculated and are shown in table 3. Annotator F has the highest

Annotator	no. arg spans	no. arg tokens	no. arg sents	no. of arg posts	% of tokens annotated	avg no. sent / arg span
A	135	9346	601	124	46%	4.45
B	174	11721	765	149	57%	4.40
C	81	6049	414	79	30%	5.11
D	109	6755	451	97	33%	4.14
E	75	2094	140	70	10%	1.87
F	141	5704	367	114	28%	2.60
G	167	12578	821	153	61%	4.92
H	134	7118	495	121	35%	3.39

Table 2: Annotation statistics for each annotator.

average κ, 0.55, and annotator E has the lowest average. Values between 0.21 and 0.40 are considered fair agreement, values between 0.41 and 0.61 are considered moderate agreement (Landis and Koch, 1977). Table 4 shows Krippendorff's α, for each thread and in total. α varies between threads. IAA is the highest for posts.

Annotator	A	B	C	D	E	F	G	H	Task-average
Average Cohen's κ - sents	0.44	0.42	0.30	0.33	0.30	0.38	0.38	0.35	0.35
Average Cohen's κ - posts	0.52	0.53	0.42.	0.46	0.39	0.55	0.48	0.52	0.48

Table 3: Average Cohen's κ for each annotator.

Krippendorff's α Thread	1	2	3	4	5	6	7	8	9	All
Tokens	0.311	0.187	0.419	0.118	0.355	0.358	0.31	0.166	0.166	0.296
Sents	0.365	0.22	0.434	0.112	0.486	0.462	0.398	0.299	0.327	0.356
Posts	0.525	0.363	0.676	0.425	0.437	0.412	0.573	0.309	0.369	0.482

Table 4: Krippendorff's α.

In order to compare the annotators observed agreement and α were calculated holding out each annotator. Holding out annotator E had the largest effect, changing observed agreement on post level from 0.39 to 0.45 and post level α from 0.48 to 0.52.

4.4 Analysis of the annotation results

A manual inspection of the annotation of posts was done on the two threads with highest α, thread 6 and 4, and the two threads with lowest α, threads 5 and 7. These four threads cover different topics, but the ones with lower α have fewer tokens and shorter posts. High agreement was deemed to be when 6 or more annotators agreed, otherwise the agreement was considered low. High agreement seemed to occur when the poster is very explicit with his or her opinion and writes it in terms of "I" and not "one". Explicitly addressing a previous user, using confrontational language and contradicting also seems to occur within high agreement posts. Below is an example of a post were all annotators agreed it contained argumentation. The poster is clearly taking a stance, and is also signaling that they think the person they are addressing doesn't know what they are talking about.

"So? And how do you think the children are feeling right now? That it's so hard to live with their dad that they'd rather refrain from doing it altogether? It doesn't matter that you thought it was boring to not live with your boyfriend. I agree with the others in this thread that you should stop living together. For the sake of the children. You can't just think of yourself."

Disagreements between the annotators seemed to occur when a poster is not explicit with his or her stance or opinion, as well when the poster is using irony. Implicit argumentation (if there is any) such as that will force the annotator to interpret what's not being said in the text and this probably caused disagreement. General statements that are not tied explicitly to the opinion of the poster also seem to cause disagreements. The post below has a similar message as the previous example, but this poster is more sarcastic, and the argumentation is more implicit, if there is any. Here the annotators disagreed.

> "A three-year old should be grateful because you split up his parents? Oh my god! Are you for real?"

Another example of disagreement is seen in the post below where the user could be interpreted as speculating, rather than arguing.

> "The popularity of first names is varying over generations. Names that were popular in the 1900's first half such as Albin, Arvid etc ., have returned a bit. Names which were common a few decades ago, Johan, Andreas, Magnus, and Anders seem to have completely disappeared now. I think Anders is or was at least a few years ago the most common name for persons in high positions in the business world."

The guidelines asked for a stance or standpoint, which might be why posts where the author is clearly taking a stance have high agreement. The third condition, the intent to persuade, might be the reason posts with confrontational (and sometimes condescending) language have high agreement —if someone strongly disagrees with someone they might also intent to persuade them that they are wrong.

5   Conclusions & future directions

IAA values such as the ones reported here are not uncommon in argumentation mining tasks. Still, both the Cohen's κ of 0.48 and the Krippendorff's α 0.48 are lower than the previously reported studies, (for example 0.59 Cohen's κ in Habernal et al. (2014) or 0.71 Krippendorff's α_u in Trautmann et al. (2020)). However, as opposed to those studies, the annotators were not asked to annotate with respect to a topic, so the results are not fully comparable. Annotating only 9 threads might have affected the IAA, especially since the IAA varied between the threads. When manually inspecting the annotations, it seemed as when the conditions asked for in the guidelines were very explicitly met, annotators agreed. When the argumentation (or not argumentation) was more implicit the annotators disagreed. This is something which has to be considered when further developing the guidelines. Another thing to consider when annotating complex phenomena such as argumentation is that even though the annotators disagree, it might not be the case that one is right and the other is wrong. As shown in for example Lindahl et al. (2019) there are cases where two different annotations could both be considered correct. If one allows for several annotations to be correct, this would need to be reflected in both the guidelines and evaluation.

In the future we plan to test the guidelines in a domain where one can assume that people are more explicit with their argumentation, such as newspapers. We also plan to extend the guidelines to annotate components of argumentation to see how this affects the annotation.

Acknowledgements

The work presented here has been partly supported by an infrastructure grant to Språkbanken Text, University of Gothenburg, for contributing to building and operating a national e-infrastructure funded jointly by the participating institutions and the Swedish Research Council (under contract no. 2017-00626). We would also like to thank the anonymous reviewers for their constructive comments and feedback.

References

Tom Bosc, Elena Cabrio, and Serena Villata. 2016. DART: a dataset of arguments and their relations on Twitter. In *Proceedings of the Tenth International Conference on Language Resources and Evaluation (LREC'16)*, pages 1258–1263, Portorož, Slovenia, May. European Language Resources Association (ELRA).

Richard Eckart de Castilho, Éva Mújdricza-Maydt, Seid Muhie Yimam, Silvana Hartmann, Iryna Gurevych, Anette Frank, and Chris Biemann. 2016. A web-based tool for the integrated annotation of semantic and syntactic structures. In *Proceedings of the Workshop on Language Technology Resources and Tools for Digital Humanities (LT4DH)*, pages 76–84, Osaka, Japan, December. The COLING 2016 Organizing Committee.

Ivan Habernal and Iryna Gurevych. 2017. Argumentation mining in user-generated web discourse. 43(1):125–179.

Ivan Habernal, Judith Eckle-Kohler, and Iryna Gurevych. 2014. Argumentation mining on the web from information seeking perspective. In *ArgNLP*.

J. Richard Landis and Gary G. Koch. 1977. The measurement of observer agreement for categorical data. *Biometrics*, 33(1):159–174.

John Lawrence and Chris Reed. 2020. Argument mining: A survey. *Computational Linguistics*, 45(4):765–818.

Anna Lindahl, Lars Borin, and Jacobo Rouces. 2019. Towards assessing argumentation annotation - a first step. In *Proceedings of the 6th Workshop on Argument Mining*, pages 177–186, Florence, Italy, August. Association for Computational Linguistics.

Christian Stab, Tristan Miller, Benjamin Schiller, Pranav Rai, and Iryna Gurevych. 2018. Cross-topic argument mining from heterogeneous sources. In *Proceedings of the 2018 Conference on Empirical Methods in Natural Language Processing*, pages 3664–3674. Association for Computational Linguistics.

Assaf Toledo, Shai Gretz, Edo Cohen-Karlik, Roni Friedman, Elad Venezian, Dan Lahav, Michal Jacovi, Ranit Aharonov, and Noam Slonim. 2019. Automatic argument quality assessment - new datasets and methods. In *Proceedings of the 2019 Conference on Empirical Methods in Natural Language Processing and the 9th International Joint Conference on Natural Language Processing (EMNLP-IJCNLP)*, pages 5625–5635. Association for Computational Linguistics.

Dietrich Trautmann, Johannes Daxenberger, Christian Stab, Hinrich Schütze, and Iryna Gurevych. 2020. Fine-grained argument unit recognition and classification. In *AAAI*, pages 9048–9056.

Frans H Van Eemeren, Rob Grootendorst, Ralph H Johnson, Christian Plantin, and Charles A Willard. 2013. *Fundamentals of argumentation theory: A handbook of historical backgrounds and contemporary developments*. Routledge.

Style Analysis of Argumentative Texts by Mining Rhetorical Devices

Khalid Al-Khatib [1]   **Viorel Morari** [2]   **Benno Stein** [1]
[1] Bauhaus-Universität Weimar, Weimar, Germany, `<first>.<last>@uni-weimar.de`
[2] Averbis, Freiburg, Germany, `viorel.morari@averbis.com`

Abstract

Using the appropriate style is key for writing a high-quality text. Reliable computational style analysis is hence essential for the automation of nearly all kinds of text synthesis tasks. Research on style analysis focuses on recognition problems such as authorship identification; the respective technology (e.g., n-gram distribution divergence quantification) showed to be effective for discrimination, but inappropriate for text synthesis since the "essence of a style" remains implicit. This paper contributes right here: it studies the automatic analysis of style at the knowledge-level based on *rhetorical devices*. To this end, we developed and evaluated a grammar-based approach for identifying 26 syntax-based devices. Then, we employed that approach to distinguish various patterns of style in selected sets of argumentative articles and presidential debates. The patterns reveal several insights into the style used there, while being adequate for integration in text synthesis systems.

1 Introduction

The decision for an adequate writing style plays a crucial role for an author who wants to achieve a particular goal, such as persuading the readers (Burton, 2007). "Style" is an elusive concept which covers a wide range of techniques an author can follow, including justifying a conclusion by anecdotal evidence, using regular repetition of the same phrase, or raising questions and then answering them. In the literature on the subject, these techniques are called *rhetorical devices* (Johnson, 2016).

The automatic analysis of style has been addressed mostly by developing a set of style features (aka style indicators) such as the percentage of function words (Ganjigunte Ashok et al., 2013; Bergsma et al., 2012). Those features have proven to be effective in various analysis tasks, such as genre classification and author recognition. However, they are not appropriate for typical text synthesis and writing assistance tasks, since they cannot reveal the "essence of a style" in an explicit and describable manner.

By contrast, analyzing the writing style based on rhetorical devices provides a mechanism to describe *where*, *what*, and *how* specific techniques are used. This kind of analysis is not only important for exploring content in social science (Niculae and Danescu-Niculescu-Mizil, 2014), but it can also serve text synthesis systems by improving the quality of automatically generated texts (Hu et al., 2017). Moreover, it can form the backbone of style suggestion tools. For example, when writing a text for which the desired specification (e.g., the genre) is given, adequate style techniques can be suggested to improve the text quality. In such a manner, new writers can learn to improve their texts and approach the quality of masterpieces written by top writers. Figure 1 illustrates the described connections.

Rhetoric has been the subject of investigation amongst scholars since the time of ancient Greece. Meanwhile, a considerable number of rhetorical devices were developed and discussed in the literature. The most well-known collected lists of devices contain more than 500 devices (Lawrence et al., 2017). Though various of them, such as irony and sarcasm, is hard to be computationally identified (Java, 2015), there is still a sufficiently large portion of popular and—for our purpose—highly useful devices whose identification can be tackled with the current state of the art. Basically, rhetorical devices can

Proceedings of the 7th Workshop on Argument Mining, pages 106–116
Barcelona, Spain (Online), December 13, 2020.

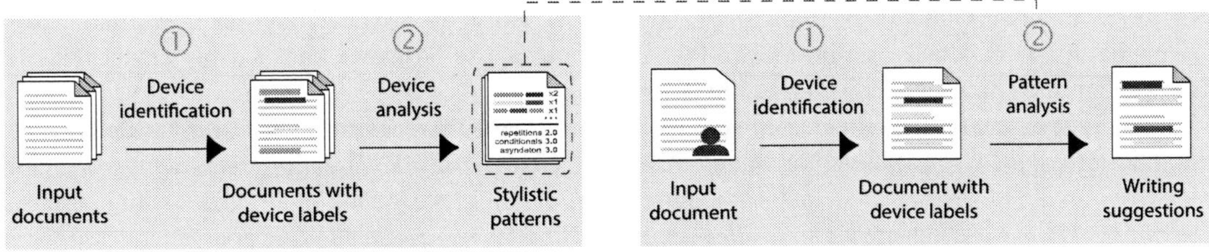

Figure 1: Envisioned tool for style checking and suggestion.

be categorized according to different principles, where an important one is a linguistic level (lexical, syntactic, semantic, and pragmatic). For the time being, we will deal with syntax-based devices.

Against the above background, this paper addresses three research questions. (1) How to identify syntax-based rhetorical devices in a text? (2) What are the most common patterns of using these devices? (3) To which degree differ these patterns across different monological and dialogical argumentative texts? Within and across the texts' genres, topics, and authors? And across different opponent debaters?

To answer these questions, we develop a grammar-based approach for the identification of 26 rhetorical devices. The grammars are built on top of the outputs of a probabilistic context-free grammar parser, PCFG. For evaluation purpose, we create a corpus of 1718 texts which are labelled for rhetorical devices. The evaluation results show that our approach is able to identify the devices with an average of 0.70 in terms of F_1. Based on the developed approach, we quantify and discuss the usage of devices in monological texts within and across different genres, topics, and authors using a subset of the New York Times annotated corpus (Sandhaus, 2008). We also analyze the devices usage patterns in dialogical texts using a set of presidential debates from the American presidency project (Woolley and Gerhard, 2017).

We consider the gained qualitative and quantitative insights about the usage of rhetorical devices as step forward to a new generation of semi-automated argumentative text generation and writing tools. All developed resources in this paper are made publicly available at `www.webis.de`

2   Related Work

Recently, Investigating rhetorical devices for style analysis has been considered in computational linguistics. Various devices at the semantic and pragmatic levels have been addressed singly such as irony (e.g., (C. Wallace et al., 2014)), sarcasm (e.g., (Ghosh et al., 2015)), evidence (e.g., (Rinott et al., 2015)), and means of persuasion (e.g., (Duthie et al., 2016)). In a notable work, Strommer (2011) work on identifying 'epanaphora'. They try to distinguish between accidental and intentional use of this device.

Other studies target identifying a mix of syntax, and semantic devices. Gawryjołek et al. (2009) addressed four rhetorical devices: 'anaphora', 'isocolon', 'epizeuxis', and 'oxymorons'. These devices were utilized to recognize the author of a set of documents. Java (2015) identified the four devices mentioned above in addition to nine new devices belonging to parallelism, repetition, and trope. The primary purpose of that work is to use the presence of a rhetorical device as a feature in machine learning models for authorship attribution. Since the authors consider syntax-based devices, we already considered five of their devices in our study. Regarding argumentaion, Lawrence et al. (2017) analyzed eight devices, six belong to the syntax and lexical levels, and two to the trope (i.e., semantic or pragmatic). Mainly, a pilot study was conducted to study the relation between argumentation structure and the identified devices.

Few resources for rhetorical devices are publicly free. Up to our knowledge, the code of the previous studies is not available anywhere on the web. Hence, researchers often have to write a new piece of code every time they need to analyze style based on rhetorical devices. This paper resolves this problem considerably by providing a tool for identifying 26 different rhetorical devices. Our developed resources, including the code, will be made freely available.

PCFG outputs have been employed for different tasks including response generation in dialogue (Yuan et al., 2015), multiword expression identification (Green et al., 2011), and the task at hand: identifying rhetorical devices (Gawryjołek et al., 2009; Java, 2015). However, we develop a set of original heuristic rules that map the devices' definitions to PCFG grammars. As far as we know, many devices from the 26 we identified have not been considered in any other study.

Writing style analysis has been studied widely. The authorship recognition has been tackled in a large number of papers (e.g., (Sundararajan and Woodard, 2018)). Besides, quality assessment research has involved applying several style analysis features (e.g., (Ganjigunte Ashok et al., 2013)). In comparison to our analysis, we conducted a *controlled* analysis using 'matching' technique and we covered various aspects of monological and dialogical texts such as genre, topic, author, and debate opponent.

3 Identification of Rhetorical Devices

Rhetorical devices are the techniques of using the language to produce an effect on the target audience or readers (McKay and McKay, 2010). For example, repeating particular phrases can produce effects such as emphasizing a certain argument, or evoking a specific emotion (Corbett, 1990).

This paper targets syntax-based rhetorical devices. Particularly, we aim to identify 26 devices belonging to two main categories: (1) **figurative syntax**, which is referred as *schemes* in literature, and (2) **ordinary syntax**, which concerns the rules of well-formed structuring texts. The effect of the first attributed to using an artful deviation from the ordinary arrangement of words, while the effect of the second is coming from using a specific arrangement of words among other arrangements.

In the next subsections, we detail the figurative and ordinary syntax devices and describe our approach for identifying them.

3.1 Figurative Syntax Devices

Figurative devices center on arranging words artfully (Burton, 2007). They are divided into four types: *balance, inversion, omission* and *repetition*.

- The *balance* devices involve arranging the rhythm of thoughts. Hence, they can produce a sense of equivalence among the proposed ideas, or emphasize ideas' differences. For example, we can notice the contrast between ideas in the famous quote of Neil Armstrong: "That's one small step for man, one giant leap for mankind".

- The *inversion* devices concern changing the order of words, either to stress some ideas or to avoid the monotonous flow of a sentence. For example, "Everybody's got troubles" could be reordered to "Troubles, everybody's got.".

- The *omission* devices deal with removing words that readers can reveal intuitively. They are often used to imply unfinished thoughts or to keep a fast rhythm, such as: "He came, he saw, he conquered.".

- The *repetition* is the most frequent, and arguably, the most powerful. According to Aristotle, repetition is the key to a persuasive speech (Fahnestock, 2003). Typically, repetition devices aim at influencing the emotional state of the reader by emphasizing or implicating a specific idea (Burton, 2007; Corbett, 1990). An example which illustrates the emotional impact of repetitions is the famous line from King Lear written by Shakespeare: "Never, never, never, never, never." (Müller, 2006).

Table 1 shows an overview of the identified figurative devices in our work. The overview covers a definition, a formalization, and an example for each device belongs to balance, omission, or repetition [1]. Our formalization is grounded on the devices' definitions which are taken from a set of reliable sources such as 'Silva Rhetoricae': a comprehensive source for rhetoric on the web (Burton, 2007).

The formalization elements are: 'Cl' for clause, 'Phr' for phrase, 'W' for word, 'N' for noun, 'Vb' for verb, 'CC' for conjunction, 'COMMA' for comma, ...for arbitrary intervening material, [...] for word boundaries, {...} for phrase or clause boundaries, $_{a=b}$ for identity , and $_{a \neq b}$ for nonidentity. The elements of formalization are adopted from Harris and DiMarco (2009).

Notice that we essentially concentrate on identifying the devices at the sentence-level, or across consecutive sentences. Besides, some rhetorical devices, according to their definitions, might overlap with

---

[1]The inversion is left to future work due to its complexity.

Device definition	Formalization	Example

(B1) Enumeration: Lists a series of details, words or phrases.

```
< ...W [CC | COMMA] W ...>
```

Diligence, talent and passion will drive anybody to success.

(B2) Isocolon: Similarly structured elements with the same length.

```
< ...<Phr>ₐ <Phr>ₐ ...<Phr>ₐ ...>
```

Fill the armies, rule the air, and pour out the munitions.

(B3) Pysma: Asking multiple questions successively.

```
< ...< Cl? > < Cl? > ...>?
```

Ex: Who are you? Why are you doing here

(O1) Asyndeton: Omission of conjunctions between clauses.

```
<Clₐ> COMMA <Cl_b> COMMA <Cl_c> ... )
```

I came, I saw, I conquered.

(O2) Hypozeugma: Placing last, in a construction containing several elements of equal value, the word(s) on which all of them depend.

```
< ...[W]ₐ , [W]_b , [W]_c ...Vb >
```

Friends, Romans, countrymen, lend me your ears...

(O3) Epizeugma: Placing the verb that holds together the entire sentence either at the very beginning or the very ending of that sentence.

```
< Vb ...> or, < ...Vb >
```

Neither a borrower nor a lender be.

(R1) Epanalepsis: Repetition at the end of a line, the word(s) that occurred at the beginning of the same line.

```
< [W]ₐ ...[W]ₐ >
```

Believe not all you can hear, tell not all you believe.

(R2) Mesarchia: Repetition of the same word(s) at the beginning and middle of successive sentences.

```
< [W]ₐ ...[W]_b ...> < [W]ₐ ...[W]_b ...>
```

I was looking for a paper. I was anxious for a paper.

(R3) Epiphoza: Repetition of the same word(s) at the end of successive sentences.

```
< ...[W]ₐ > < ...[W]ₐ >
```

O apple! wretched apple! Miserable apple!

(R4) Mesodiplosis: Repetition of the same word(s) in the middle of successive sentences.

```
< ...[W]ₐ ...> < ...[W]ₐ ...>
```

There's no time like the future! There's no time like the past!

(R5) Anadiplosis: Repetition of the last word(s) from the previous sentence at the beginning of the next.

```
< ...[W]ₐ > < [W]ₐ ...>
```

We ordered a pizza pie. A pizza pie that changed our lives.

(R6) Diacope: Repetition of a word with one or more in between.

```
< ...[W]ₐ ...[W]ₐ ...>
```

The horror! Oh, the horror!

(R7) Epizeuxis: Repetition of words with no others between.

```
< [W]ₐ [W]ₐ >
```

Awake, awake and stand up O Jerusalem.

(R8) Polysyndeton: Several conjunctions in close succession (mainly between clauses).

```
<Clₐ> CC <Cl_b> CC <Cl_c> ...
```

He ran and jumped and laughed for joy.

Device definition	Formalization	Example

(C1) If-cond. Zero: Conditionals which express general truths.

```
If [VB/VBP/VBZ], then [VB/VBP/VBZ]
```

If you heat ice, it melts.

(C2) If-cond. One: Express situations which are very likely to happen in the future.

```
If [VB/VBP/VBZ/VBG], then [MD+VB]
```

If it rains, you will get wet.

(C3) If-cond. Two: Expresses consequences that will not likely happen in the future.

```
If [VBD], then [MD+VB]
```

If it rained, you would get wet.

(C4) If-cond. Three: Used to explain that present circumstances would be different if something different had happened in the past.

```
If [VBD+VBN] , then [MD+VBN]
```

If I had worked harder, I would have passed the exam.

(C5) If-Counterf.: Statements that examine how a hypothetical change in a past experience could have affected the outcome of that experience.

```
If [VBD+VBN], then [past modals]
```

If I were you, I wouldn't come.

(C6) Unless-cond.: Restricted version of if-conditional (its intrinsic meaning is narrowed down to "Q in the case other than P").

```
<... unless ...>
```

You can't go on vacation unless you save some money.

(C7) Whether-cond.: Expresses alternative (disjunctive) conditions.

```
<... whether ... or ...>
```

Whether you are overweight or not, it is always better to watch your diet.

(CS) Comp./Super. Adj. and Adv.: Used to compare differences between the two objects/states they modify.

```
<... [JJR/JJS/RBR/RBS] ...>
```

(comp. adjective): My house is larger.

(PV) Passive Voice: Occurs when the object of an action is changed into the subject of a sentence.

```
<... [to be] ... [VBN] ...>
```

The problem is solved.

Table 1: An overview of the (B) Balance, (O) Omission, and (R) Repetition figurative devices, and the (C) Conditionals, (CS) Comparatives and Superlatives, and (PV) Passive Voice ordinary devices.

other devices in some special cases. This overlap is rare and partial. Nevertheless, we consider minimizing the possible overlaps among devices as much as possible in our formalization.

3.2 Ordinary Syntax Devices

From the ordinary syntax devices, we select *conditionals, comparatives and superlatives,* and *passive voice.* This selection is based on the impact of these devices on the readers (Martinet, 1960).

- The *conditional* devices entail the causality aspect of the language, and causality, in turn, could imply explaining an event. But it can also be used to argue about positive/negative consequences of a specific action such as "If we were elected him, we would not have achievements".
- The *comparatives and superlatives* devices might be used to emphasize the superiority of an entity or idea, e.g., "I will be the greatest jobs president that God ever created".
- The *passive voice* might be used to hide the subject of a negative action, or to stress the importance of an event, e.g., "many mistakes were made, but the future will be great".

Table 1 provides an overview of the conditionals, comparatives and superlatives, and passive voice devices. The overview is analog to the one of the figurative category. The formalization is based on definitions from the same set of resources used in the figurative category. The elements of formalization are taken from The Penn Treebank POS Tag Set (Marcus et al., 1993).

3.3 Experiments and Results

Device	Instances	Prec.	Recall	F1	Device	Instances	Prec.	Recall	F1
(B1) Enumeration	60	0.76	0.93	0.84	(C1) If-cond. Zero	60	0.71	0.76	0.73
(B2) Isocolon*	180	0.57	0.83	0.68	(C2) If-cond. One	60	0.78	0.78	0.78
(B3) Pysma	60	1	1	1.00	(C3) If-cond. Two	60	0.82	0.75	0.78
(O1) Asyndeton	60	0.25	0.93	0.39	(C4) If-cond. Three	60	0.86	0.65	0.74
(O2) Hypozeugma	60	0.61	0.8	0.69	(C5) If-Counterf.	60	0.84	0.87	0.85
(O3) Epizeugma	60	0.65	0.7	0.67	(C6) Unless-cond.	60	1	1	1.00
(R1) Epanalepsis	60	0.63	0.83	0.72	(C7) Whether-cond.	60	1	0.83	0.91
(R2) Mesarchia	20	0.45	0.85	0.59	(CS1) Comp. Adj.	68	0.51	0.61	0.56
(R3) Epiphoza	60	0.58	0.93	0.71	(CS2) Comp. Adv.	70	0.6	0.62	0.61
(R4) Mesodiplosis	40	0.27	0.68	0.39	(CS3) Super. Adj.	70	0.62	0.73	0.67
(R5) Anadiplosis	60	0.76	0.73	0.74	(CS4) Super. Adv.	70	0.63	0.5	0.56
(R6) Diacope	60	0.73	0.73	0.73	(PV) Passive Voice	60	0.78	0.98	0.87
(R7) Epizeuxis	60	0.79	0.77	0.78	Other [†]	60	0.23	0.23	0.23
(R8) Polysyndeton	60	0.77	0.7	0.73					

* including samples of bicolon (60), tricolon (60) and tetracolon (60).
[†] we applied the 26 classifiers on the 'other' instances. If any of them labels an instance with its device, we consider the instance as wrongly classified.

Table 2: The precision, recall, and F_1-score for identifying the 26 rhetorical devices.

Category	Instances	Prec.	Recall	F1
(B) Balance	300	0.67	0.88	0.76
(O) Omission	180	0.4	0.81	0.54
(R) Repetition	420	0.6	0.77	0.67
(C) Conditionals	420	0.85	0.8	0.82
(CS) Comp.&Super.	278	0.59	0.62	0.60
(PV) Passive voice	60	0.78	0.98	0.87

Table 3: The precision, recall, and F_1-score for identifying the rhetorical devices by category.

Here, we discuss the evaluation experiments of our approach for identifying the syntax-based rhetorical devices. First, we describe the newly created evaluation dataset. Then, we talk about the experimental settings and report on the obtained results. Finally, we address the limitations of our approach and perform an error analysis for its output.

Evaluation Dataset: Creating a dataset for rhetorical devices using manual annotation, even with crowd-sourcing, is extremely expensive and time consuming (Java, 2015); The reason behind this is the big number of devices, the potential overlaps between them, and the possibility for some devices to be spread across phrases, sentences, or even paragraphs. Thereby, we decided to follow a bunch of related research studies (e.g., (Java, 2015)) and build the evaluation dataset as follows: We first identify a set of trustworthy sources on the web, which address the rhetorical devices, and have credibility as being developed by experts in rhetoric. Most of the selected sources are either mentioned or already used in some research studies, which speaks for their trustworthiness. From those sources, we use meta-data information (e.g., "Example of Pysma:") to collect a set of instances for our rhetorical devices. We found that targeting about 60 examples for each device is reasonable considering the size of content in the selected sources. We verified all the examples and ensured that there are no duplicated ones. Additionally, we accounted for the possible overlaps between the devices and minimized them adequately, i.e., all the examples for a device belong solely to this device. Unfortunately, two devices turned out to be considered only from few sources, and hence, we got less than 60 examples for them. We also collected 60 examples where none of the devices covered by our work is used. Overall, we collected 1718 examples: 1658 example distributed among the 26 devices and around 60 examples that belong to 'other'. The distribution is shown in Table 2. This dataset, despite its relatively small size, is significantly larger than those that have been used for rhetorical devices in related work (Java, 2015).

Experimental Settings: The implementation of our approach was carried out using Apache Ruta^{TM} (Rule-based Text Annotation) (Kluegl et al., 2016). This tool provides a flexible language for identifying patterns in text spans intuitively. Thus, it facilitates identifying sophisticated patterns with a few lines of code. The implementation is performed on top of the outputs of Stanford Parser (Manning et al., 2014), the version of 3.8.0. We evaluated our approach using the one-vs.-rest classification. That means we performed one classification experiment for each device; The instances of this device in the evaluation dataset is considered as the *positive* class, and the instances of the remaining devices as well as the 'other' as the *negative* class. The classifiers' effectiveness is reported in terms of precision, recall, and F_1-score.

Classification Results: Table 2 shows the results of our experiments. Overall, we manage to identify the 26 devices with an average of 0.70 F_1-score., which indicates a high effectiveness of our approach.

As for the "figurative" devices, the approach got high scores for the *balance* devices, including F_1-score of 1.00 for 'pysma'. The 'isocolon' is the most challenging with F_1-score of 0.68. As for the *omission* devices, the F_1-scores range from 0.39 for 'asyndeton' and 0.69 for the 'hypozeugma'. These results are a bit lower than the other types. Most of the *repetition* devices have F_1-score of about 0.73, except 'mesarchia' with 0.59, and 'mesodiplosis' with 0.39. Besides, "ordinary" devices got scores between 0.56 and 1.00. Interestingly, despite their simple syntax, *comparatives and superlatives* devices got the lowest scores.

Table 3 shows the results of our approach regarding the six rhetorical categories that group the 26 devices. The F_1 scores range from 0.54 to 0.87. The best result is obtained for passive voice (0.87) and conditionals (0.82). Omission and repetition are the hardest to identify with 0.54 and 0.67 F_1.

Figure 2 shows an excerpt from a news editorial along with several rhetorical devices that our approach manages to identify.

Error Analysis: Despite the high effectiveness of our approach, it is subject to fail in some cases.

Concerning the "figurative" category, identifying the *balance* devices seems to be precise except for 'isocolon'. The identification of this device is based on the outputs of the syntax parser (i.e., POS tags) which are sometimes inaccurate, especially for long sentences. This has a negative impact on the precision score; for instance, "It looks like the Libertarian candidate is racking up the percentage points in recent polls. As far as I can see the Libertarian candidate has over . . . .". Here, the 'Libertarian candidate' makes the classifier of 'isocolon' treats it wrongly as a valid instance. For the *omission* devices, our approach manages to get 0.93 recall score for 'asyndeton' device, but only 0.25 for precision. We found that the abundance of commas, which we use as an indicator of the lack of conjunctions is insufficient to distinguish 'asyndeton' from other devices, especially 'enumeration'. For example, "Old McDonald

Title: HEALTH; Salk's Injectable Polio Vaccine May Be Revived — Rhetorical Device

Health officials are considering a major change in the strategy of polio vaccination, using a new, more potent version of the injectable Salk vaccine that helped eradicate polio in the United States almost 30 years ago. — Comp. Adv.

The injectable " killed-virus " vaccine was largely replaced by an oral vaccine made from live viruses, which is still being given to millions of American children. — Passive Voice

The development of the new form of the Salk vaccine opens the way for it to be used in combination with other childhood vaccinations. — Passive Voice   Some health officials, noting that it has been used in Europe and tested in the developing world, believe that it can be an effective way to reduce immunizations and associated costs. — Passive Voice / Asyndeton

However, other experts say the current reliance on the Sabin oral live-virus vaccine has worked so well that great care should be taken before changing policies. — Passive Voice

Study Under Way The Institute of Medicine, an adjunct of the National Academy of Sciences, is studying polio policy and is expected to submit recommendations to the Federal health authorities by April. — Passive Voice / Asyndeton / Enumeration / Hypozeugma   At a recent public meeting in Washington, the committee heard suggestions for bringing back the inactivated-virus vaccine by combining it with the diphtheria, tetanus and pertussis shots. — Enumeration

Dr. Frederick C. Robbins of Case Western Reserve University, chairman of the panel, said early attempts at the combined vaccine were abandoned in this country because of potency problems. — Asyndeton / Hypozeugma / Passive Voice   Later successes with this approach in Europe, using an enhanced polio vaccine, have rekindled the idea of a combination approach, including the possibility of using both types of polio vaccines to merge their benefits, he added. — Asyndeton / Hypozeugma

Figure 2: An excerpt from a NYT news editorial. The rhetorical devices in each sentence are identified using our approach.

had a pig, a dog, a cow and a horse." is identified as 'asyndeton', while it is actually 'enumeration'. As regards *repetition*, two devices there got low scores: the 'mesarchia' and 'mesodiplosis'. These devices have the least number of instances in our evaluation dataset. We also observed that our heuristic rules for defining the beginning and middle of sentences are the reason for some errors.

For the "ordinary" category, the approach has promising results. However, the scores for the 'comparatives and superlatives' are moderate. Observing the errors there, we found that the main reason is again the inaccurate POS tags. For example, in the sentence 'the airport is *further* than the train station.', 'further' is tagged as comparative adverb instead of comparative adjective.

The 'other' class got a low F_1- score. In addition to its restrictive way of evaluation that we followed, this score indicates that some devices' classifiers tend to have a lot of false positives.

To have a better idea regarding the effectiveness of our approach, we performed a manual inspection of the classifiers' outputs on a set of ten newspaper articles. We found that some devices such as 'isocolon' and 'asyndeton' indeed have many false positives. Besides, we found that the classifiers make more mistakes with very long sentences.

4   Analysis of Rhetorical Devices

We rely on our identification approach to analyze the usage patterns of rhetorical devices in argumentative newspaper articles and presidential debates. First, we describe the acquisition and sampling of the *analysis datasets*. Then, we discuss the distribution of rhetorical devices there along with different article and debate aspects. The computed distributions illustrate various patterns of rhetorical devices and lead to several interesting insights.

Analysis Datasets: To conduct insightful analysis, we constructed two datasets for newspaper articles and presidential debates.

(1) Newspaper dataset: to construct this dataset, we used the NYT annotated corpus (Sandhaus, 2008). The corpus comprises more than 1.8 million high-quality articles written by professional writers. It comes with many types of meta-data labeled by NYT staff, including the type of material (e.g., editorial), the author name, and the topic (e.g., sport). From this corpus, we sampled three subsets, each of which represents one of the three properties of genre, topic, and author. To conduct a *controlled analysis*, the sampling should account for the confounding variables. For example, studying the style in articles with

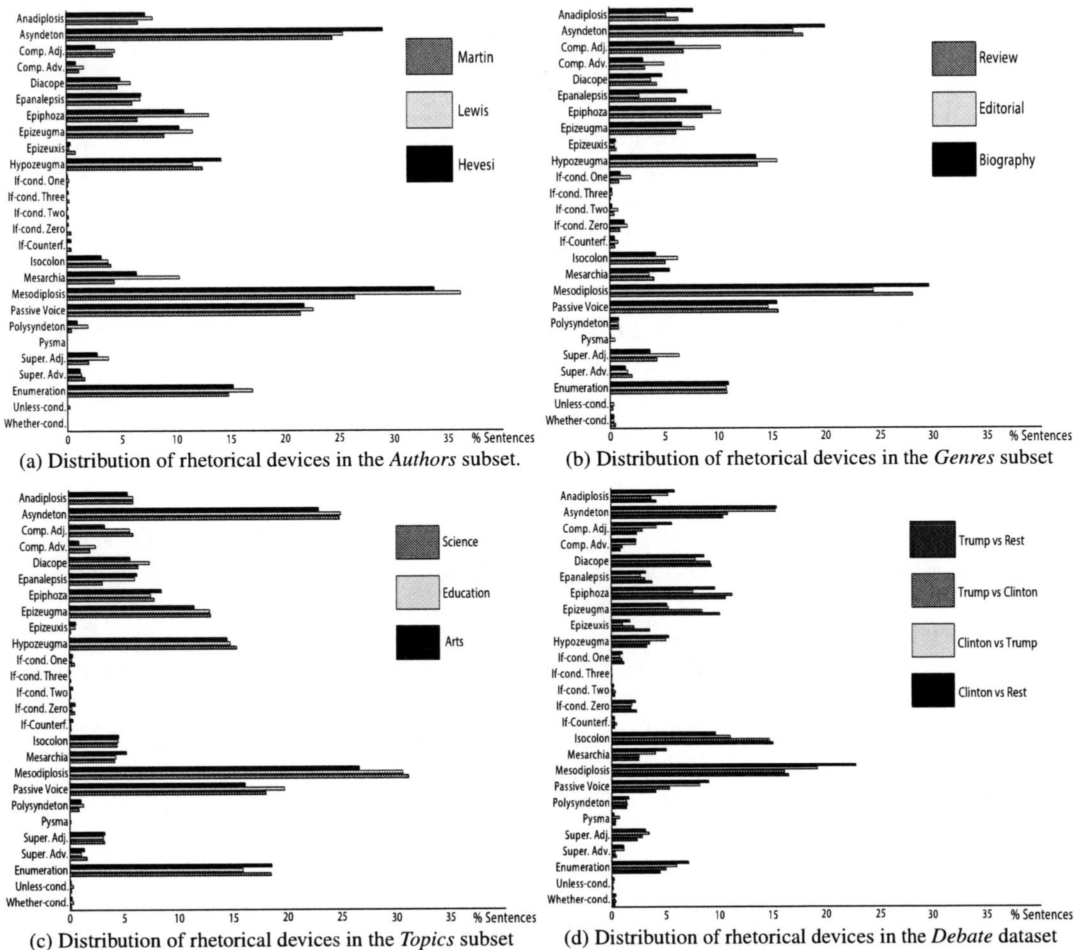

(a) Distribution of rhetorical devices in the *Authors* subset.

(b) Distribution of rhetorical devices in the *Genres* subset

(c) Distribution of rhetorical devices in the *Topics* subset

(d) Distribution of rhetorical devices in the *Debate* dataset

Figure 3: The distribution of rhetorical devices among the authors (a), the genres (b), and the topics (c) in the newspaper articles dataset, and the distribution of rhetorical devices in the debate dataset (d).

a specific 'topic' can be influenced by their genres and authors. Hence, we first tried to resolve this issue with the stratification method (Tripepi et al., 2010), which turned out to be not successful; despite the large size of the corpus, we found no information about the authors of about 40% of articles. Also, the distribution of articles in texts belong to the three properties are very skewed. The corpus includes much more reviews than editorials, for example. Many articles are written for 'politics' and few for 'sport', and some authors wrote tens of articles while others wrote only one. Therefore, we tried the matching technique (de Graaf et al., 2011), where we managed successfully to sample the three subsets. To preserve the balance between the subsets, we consider three *instances* for each propriety, i.e., the 'topic' subset includes 114 articles belong to science, education, and art. The 'genre' subset includes 89 articles belong to biography, editorial, and review. Finally, the 'authors' subset includes 159 articles written by Martin, Lewis, and Hevesi.

(2) Debate dataset: we acquired this dataset based on the presidential debates from the American presidency project (Woolley and Gerhard, 2017). In particular, we extracted the entire set of debates that involve Donald Trump or/and Hillary Clinton. We think that these two characters are different in many aspects such as ideology, background, experience, opinions on different topics, etc. This difference could be reflected in their styles leading to interesting patterns. We created three subsets of the dataset: 'Trump vs. Clinton,' 'Trump vs. Not-Clinton', and 'Clinton vs. Not-Trump'. In this way, we can analyze the style of the two characters, and also address the question of whether they change their styles according to

the debate opponent. In total, Clinton has 226 turns in her debates with Trump, and 1216 in her debates with the other candidates. Trump, on the other side, has 342 turns in his debates with Clinton, and 778 in his debates with the rest of candidates.

Analysis Method: Basically, we applied our Identification approach (see Section 3) to the analysis datasets. In particular, a classifier for each device is applied to the articles or debates turns, resulting in the frequency of the device there. However, since our identification approach is not perfect, it is crucial to account for its errors. Hence, we followed the method used in (Al-Khatib et al., 2017): for the frequency n of a rhetorical device rd in an instance i in a dataset. We computed a confidence interval for n, where the $lowerbound = n * precision(rd)$, and the $upperbound = n/recall(rd)$. Ultimately, The mean of the upper and lower bounds is the new frequency, which is normalized by the number of sentences in the articles/debate-turns belong to i. Accordingly, we computed the distributions of rhetorical devices in the analysis datasets and their subsets. The chi-squared test with 0.01 significant level is used to check whether the difference in the usage of rhetorical devices in the datasets and across their instances is significant, and the Cramer's V test is used to measure the effect-size of the distributions' difference.

Analysis Results: Figure 3 shows the distribution of rhetorical devices among the three authors (a), the three genres (b), the three topics (c), and the debate subsets (d). As expected, the style in newspaper articles (monologue) are significantly different than in debates (dialogue). Some analysis results for each of the datasets are as follows.

(1) Newspaper dataset: In addition to the significant difference among the three properties under studied, the results show a significant difference among the three authors. For example, Lewis and Hevesi use more *repetition* than Martin. Also, Lewis barely considers conditionals, in contrast to the other two authors. The results also show a significant difference between 'biography' and 'editorial' as well as 'editorial' and 'review', but not between 'review' and 'biography'. The reason might be that the articles in these two genres are written mainly to describe an entity. Interestingly, there is no significant difference between the three topics. Overall, our analysis suggests that the "style" identified by syntax-based rhetorical devices is primarily influenced by the 'author', and 'genre', while 'topic' has the least impact.

(2) Debate dataset: Interestingly, the results show that Clinton is more fond of 'comparatives' and 'passive voice' than Trump, which actually contradicts a widespread assumption (Gingell, 2016; Raskin, 2016). However, our findings are mainly related to the debate genre. The style could be different in speeches, for example. We also found that Clinton uses 'asyndeton' more often than Trump. Since this device is very effective for making the turns easier to grasp, our finding this time is in line with (Raskin, 2016), where they find that Clinton's language is 13% clearer and more direct than Trump's. The results indicate a significant difference between Clinton and Trump styles. More interestingly, while Clinton's style is significantly different when she debates with Trump than when she debates with the rest, Trump's style has no significant difference between his debates with Clinton and his debates with the rest. Apparently, unlike Clinton, Trump does not change his style depending on the opponent.

5   Conclusion and Future Work

Writing style analysis has become a mature discipline, but it is mostly tackled from the recognition perspective. I.e., it can give strong classification results that, because of their intrinsic nature, cannot be transferred to constrained text generation or computational writing assistance. We address this shortcoming by proposing an approach for the *explicit* encoding and identification of rhetorical devices. In carefully designed experiments, we study the usage of these devices in different argumentative articles and presidential debates. The distributions show different patterns of style among three text's properties and provide new insights regarding style usage within the studied topics. The achieved F_1 classification performance (0.70) can be considered as very good for concrete multi-class classification setting; it shows that the applied approach has the potential to find its way into real-world argumentative text synthesis tools. We plan in the future to improve our grammars to minimize mistakes and increase the number of devices considering the *inversion* type of figurative syntax devices.

References

Khalid Al-Khatib, Henning Wachsmuth, Matthias Hagen, and Benno Stein. 2017. Patterns of Argumentation Strategies across Topics. In *Proceedings of the 2017 Conference on Empirical Methods in Natural Language Processing (EMNLP 17)*, pages 1362–1368. Association for Computational Linguistics.

Shane Bergsma, Matt Post, and David Yarowsky. 2012. Stylometric analysis of scientific articles. In *Proceedings of the 2012 Conference of the North American Chapter of the Association for Computational Linguistics: Human Language Technologies (NAACL HLT 12)*, pages 327–337. Association for Computational Linguistics.

G. Burton. 2007. The forest of rhetoric (silva rhetoricae). Accessed on 16.08.2017.

Byron C. Wallace, Do Kook Choe, Laura Kertz, and Eugene Charniak. 2014. Humans Require Context to Infer Ironic Intent (so Computers Probably do, too). In *Proceedings of the 2014 Annual Meeting on Association for Computational Linguistics (ACL 14) - Volume 1*.

E. P. J. Corbett. 1990. *Classical rhetoric for the modern student*. USA: Oxford University Press, 3 edition.

M A de Graaf, K J Jager, C Zoccali, and F W Dekker. 2011. Matching, an Appealing Method to Avoid Confounding? *Nephron Clin Pract*.

R. Declerck and S. Reed. 2001. *Conditionals: A Comprehensive Empirical Analysis*. Beitrage Zur Alexander-Von-Humboldt-Forschung. Mouton de Gruyter.

Rory Duthie, Katarzyna Budzynska, and Chris Reed. 2016. Mining Ethos in Political Debate. In *6th International Conference on Computational Models of Argument (COMMA 16)*, pages 299–310.

Jeanne Fahnestock. 2003. Verbal and Visual Parallelism. *Written Communication*, 20(2):123–152.

Vikas Ganjigunte Ashok, Song Feng, and Yejin Choi. 2013. Success with Style: Using Writing Style to Predict the Success of Novels. In *Proceedings of the 2013 Conference on Empirical Methods in Natural Language Processing*, pages 1753–1764. Association for Computational Linguistics.

Jakub J. Gawryjołek, Randy A. Harris, and Chrysanne DiMarco. 2009. An annotation tool for automatically detecting rhetorical figures. In *Proceedings, CMNAIX (Computational Models of Natural Argument)*.

Debanjan Ghosh, Weiwei Guo, and Smaranda Muresan. 2015. Sarcastic or Not: Word Embeddings to Predict the Literal or Sarcastic Meaning of Words. In *Proceedings of the 2015 Conference on Empirical Methods in Natural Language Processing (EMNLP 15)*.

James Gingell. 2016. Why superlatives are the absolute worst (unless you're Donald Trump). https://www.theguardian.com/media/mind-your-language/2016/apr/15/. visited on 24.10.17.

Spence Green, Marie-Catherine de Marneffe, John Bauer, and Christopher D. Manning. 2011. Multiword Expression Identification with Tree Substitution Grammars: A Parsing Tour De Force with French. In *Proceedings of the Conference on Empirical Methods in Natural Language Processing*, EMNLP '11, pages 725–735. Association for Computational Linguistics.

R. Harris and C. DiMarco. 2009. Constructing a Rhetorical Figuration Ontology. In *In Symposium on Persuasive Technology and Digital Behaviour Intervention*.

Zhiting Hu, Zichao Yang, Xiaodan Liang, Ruslan Salakhutdinov, and Eric P. Xing. 2017. Toward Controlled Generation of Text. In *Proceedings of the 34th International Conference on Machine Learning*, volume 70 of *Proceedings of Machine Learning Research*, pages 1587–1596. PMLR.

James Java. 2015. *Characterization of Prose by Rhetorical Structure for Machine Learning Classification*. Ph.D. thesis.

R. Johnson. 2016. *The Alphabet of Rhetoric*. BiblioLife.

Peter Kluegl, Martin Toepfer, Philip-Daniel Beck, Georg Fette, and Frank Puppe. 2016. Uima ruta: Rapid development of rule-based information extraction applications. *Natural Language Engineering*, 22:1–40.

Johna Lawrence, Jackya Visser, and Chris Reed. 2017. Harnessing rhetorical figures for argument mining. *Argument & Computation*, 8:289–310.

Christopher D. Manning, Mihai Surdeanu, John Bauer, Jenny Finkel, Steven J. Bethard, and David McClosky. 2014. The Stanford CoreNLP Natural Language Processing Toolkit. In *Association for Computational Linguistics (ACL) System Demonstrations*, pages 55–60.

Mitchell P. Marcus, Mary Ann Marcinkiewicz, and Beatrice Santorini. 1993. Building a Large Annotated Corpus of English: The Penn Treebank. *Comput. Linguist.*, 19(2):313–330.

André Martinet. 1960. *Elements of General Linguistics.* Faber and Faber Ltd., London.

Brett McKay and Kate McKay. 2010. Classical Rhetoric 101. Accessed on 14.08.2017.

Wolfgang G. Müller. 2006. Style. In Thomas O. Sloane, editor, *Encyclopedia of Rhetoric.* Oxford University Press, February.

Vlad Niculae and Cristian Danescu-Niculescu-Mizil. 2014. Brighter than gold: Figurative language in user generated comparisons. In *Proceedings of EMNLP*, October.

Robin Raskin. 2016. Hillary clinton's acceptance speech as seen by the algorithms. the huffington post. `https://www.huffingtonpost.com/robin-raskin`. visited on 18.11.17.

Ruty Rinott, Lena Dankin, Carlos Alzate Perez, M. Mitesh Khapra, Ehud Aharoni, and Noam Slonim. 2015. Show Me Your Evidence - An Automatic Method for Context Dependent Evidence Detection. In *Proceedings of the 2015 Conference on Empirical Methods in Natural Language Processing (EMNLP 15)*, pages 440–450. Association for Computational Linguistics.

Evan Sandhaus. 2008. The new york times annotated corpus ldc2008t19. dvd. *Philadelphia: Linguistic Data Consortium.*

Claus W. Strommer. 2011. *Using rhetorical figures and shallow attributes as a metric of intent in text.* Ph.D. thesis, University of Waterloo, Waterloo, Ontario, Canada.

Kalaivani Sundararajan and Damon L. Woodard. 2018. What represents "style" in authorship attribution? In *Proceedings of the 27th International Conference on Computational Linguistics, COLING 2018, Santa Fe, New Mexico, USA, August 20-26,2018*, pages 2814–2822.

Giovanni Tripepi, Kitty J Jager, Friedo W. Dekker, and Carmine Zoccali. 2010. Stratification for confounding – part 1: The mantel-haenszel formula.

John T. Woolley and Peters Gerhard. 2017. American Presidency Project. `http://www.presidency.ucsb.edu/`. visited on 18.11.17.

Caixia Yuan, Xiaojie Wang, and Qianhui He. 2015. Response Generation in Dialogue Using a Tailored PCFG Parser. In *Proceedings of the 15th European Workshop on Natural Language Generation (ENLG)*, pages 81–85. Association for Computational Linguistics.

Creating a Domain-diverse Corpus
for Theory-based Argument Quality Assessment

Lily Ng[1]*, Anne Lauscher[2]*, Joel Tetreault[3], Courtney Napoles[1]

[1]Grammarly
[2]Data and Web Science Group, University of Mannheim, Germany
[3]Dataminr, Inc.
[1]first.last@grammarly.com, [2]anne@informatik.uni-mannheim.de,
[3]jtetreault@dataminr.com

Abstract

Computational models of argument quality (AQ) have focused primarily on assessing the overall quality or just one specific characteristic of an argument, such as its *convincingness* or its *clarity*. However, previous work has claimed that assessment based on theoretical dimensions of argumentation could benefit writers, but developing such models has been limited by the lack of annotated data. In this work, we describe GAQCorpus, the first large, domain-diverse annotated corpus of theory-based AQ. We discuss how we designed the annotation task to reliably collect a large number of judgments with crowdsourcing, formulating theory-based guidelines that helped make subjective judgments of AQ more objective. We demonstrate how to identify arguments and adapt the annotation task for three diverse domains. Our work will inform research on theory-based argumentation annotation and enable the creation of more diverse corpora to support computational AQ assessment.

1 Introduction

The notion of *Argumentation Quality (AQ)* plays an important role in many existing argument-related downstream applications, such as argumentative writing support (Stab and Gurevych, 2017), automatic essay grading (Persing and Ng, 2013), and debate systems (Toledo et al., 2019). For some of these applications, the idea is to automatically give feedback to users to help them improve their writing skills or assess their writing capabilities. For others, assessing AQ is an important step in a more complex pipeline for retrieving high-quality arguments.

While grading overall AQ (Toledo et al., 2019) or a specific conceptualization of AQ, such as *prompt adherence* (Persing and Ng, 2014) is relatively well explored, researchers have noted the lack of work in so-called *theory-based AQ*[1] (Wachsmuth et al., 2017b), which can be represented with a taxonomy characterizing overall AQ into several subdimensions and aspects, for instance, as *logic* and *rhetoric*, which therefore provides a more informative and targeted perspective. However, this holistic approach comes with the downside of higher complexity, especially when it comes to annotating textual corpora, which are required for training and developing common computational approaches (see, e.g., Gretz et al. (2020)). In a small study, Wachsmuth et al. (2017a) demonstrate that theory-based AQ annotations can be done both by trained experts and by crowd annotators, though the authors acknowledge the high complexity and subjectivity of the problem and call for the simplification of theory-based AQ annotation in order to reliably create larger-scale corpora. To date, no work has tackled this challenge and accordingly, no larger-scale and no domain-diverse corpus of this kind exists. We aim to close this gap by describing our efforts to create Grammarly Argument Quality Corpus (GAQCorpus) (Lauscher et al., 2020), the largest and the only domain-diverse corpus consisting of 5,285 English arguments annotated with theory-based AQ scores across four dimensions.

---

[1]In the following, we adopt the term "theory-based AQ," which was proposed by Wachsmuth et al. (2017b) to indicate that the conception of AQ is specifically grounded in argumentation theoretic literature (and not in CL or NLP).

Proceedings of the 7th Workshop on Argument Mining, pages 117–126
Barcelona, Spain (Online), December 13, 2020.

Building on Wachsmuth et al. (2017a), in this work, we modify the annotation task to be suitable for both experts and the crowd while preserving the theoretical basis of the taxonomy. We collect and annotate argumentative texts from web debate forums, as well as community questions and answers forums (CQA), and review forum texts, which are still understudied in computational AQ. The latter domains can consist of rather non-canonical arguments in that they exhibit a lack of explicitness of certain argumentative components; are topic-wise more subjective; or consist of longer, more convoluted text. This makes assessing the quality of such arguments even more challenging, but downstream can result in a more robust model of computational AQ.

Given all these challenges, we work closely with trained linguists to adapt the annotation task, iterating over how best to approach these novel domains and simplify the annotation guidelines for crowdsourcing, allowing us to collect a large number of judgments efficiently. We hope that our work fuels further research on theory-based computational AQ. Our approach to building GAQCorpus can inspire and inform AQ annotation in new domains, enriching the domain-diversity of linguistic resources available in this space and consequently expanding computational approaches to AQ.

Structure. We start by surveying previous AQ annotation studies (§2). Next, we describe our efforts to adapt and simplify the annotation task (§3), which is followed by a discussion of the data domains (§4). §5 presents an analysis of the resulting corpus. Finally, we conclude our work and provide directions for future research (§6).

2 Related Work

Most argumentation annotation studies have been conducted on student essays or web debates. Student essays have been annotated for thesis clarity (Persing and Ng, 2013), organization (Persing et al., 2010), and prompt adherence (Persing and Ng, 2014), and Persing and Ng (2015) model argument strength rated on a 4-point Likert scale. Similarly, Stab and Gurevych (2016) annotate the absence of opposing arguments and Stab and Gurevych (2017) predict insufficient premise support in arguments. For web debates, Habernal and Gurevych (2016) conduct an annotation study in which they present debate arguments pairwise to crowd annotators, who then can choose the more convincing argument. Persing and Ng (2017) also annotate the reasons why an argument receives a low persuasive power score.

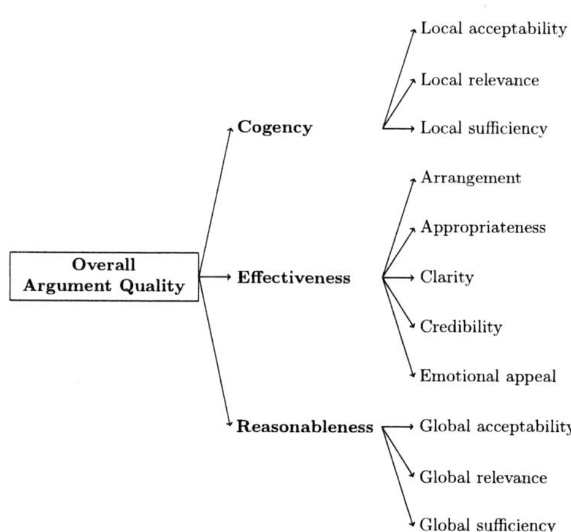

Figure 1: The taxonomy of theory-based argument quality aspects (Wachsmuth et al., 2017b).

Wachsmuth et al. (2017b) developed a taxonomy of AQ synthesized from traditional works in argumentation theory, such as Aristotle (trans 2007). The full taxonomy is depicted in Figure 1, and defines the Overall AQ to consist of the following three subdimensions, each of which is itself defined by several finer-grained AQ aspects:

(1) Cogency relates to the logical aspects of AQ, for instance, whether the an argument's premises are acceptable (local acceptability) or whether they can be seen as relevant for the conclusion (local relevance).

(2) Effectiveness indicates the rhetorical aspects of an argument. Aspects of effectiveness include, for instance, its clarity or its emotional appeal.

(3) Reasonableness reflects the quality of an argument in the overall context of the discussion, as, for instance, its relevance towards arriving at a resolution of the issue (global relevance).

Wachsmuth et al. (2017a) conducted a study in which crowd workers annotated 304 arguments for all 15 quality dimensions (Figure 1), and demonstrated that the theory-based and practical AQ assessments

118

match to a large extent. Their findings indicate that theory-based annotations can be crowdsourced and that theory-based approaches can inform the practical view, especially. Most importantly, the authors conclude that the annotation task should be simplified to guarantee a reliable crowd-annotation process.

Most recently, Toledo et al. (2019) and Gretz et al. (2020) crowdsourced overall argument quality by presenting pairwise arguments to annotators, who then had to select the argument "they would recommend a friend to use that argument as is in a speech supporting/contesting the topic." This is an extreme simplification of the task, which does not seem to lead to better agreement: the authors (Gretz et al., 2020) report an average inter-annotator agreement of $\kappa = 0.12$ and attribute the low score to the high subjectivity of the task. The authors conducted a theory-based annotation study in the spirit of Wachsmuth et al. (2017b) on a subset of the data (100 arguments) which indicated the highest correlation of the annotations with the effectiveness dimension. Later on, Lauscher et al. (2020) empirically confirmed this observation using computational model predictions across the whole corpus.

Building on this large body of work, we aim to facilitate the annotation of theory-based AQ in diverse domains of real-world argumentative writing and compare expert vs. crowd annotations. Our study results in the largest English corpus annotated with theory-based argumentative quality scores.

3 Annotation Study

In this section, we detail how we developed and designed our annotation task to enable efficient, reliable collection of theory-based AQ judgments with crowdsourcing. We validate Wachsmuth et al. (2017a)'s hypothesis that crowdsourced annotation of theory-based AQ is possible if the task is simplified.

3.1 Simplifying the task

Before collecting any crowdsourced annotations, we conducted 14 pilot experiments with a group of four "expert" annotators, simplifying the TvsP task design through their feedback and observations, as they provided both a deep understanding of the argumentation theory and practical experience annotating the arguments. Each expert annotator was a fluent or native English speaker with an advanced degree in linguistics. Experts underwent training, which included studying guidelines and participating in calibration tasks to analyze debate arguments from three sources: Dagstuhl-ArgQuality-Corpus-V2[2], originally from UKPConvArgRank (Habernal and Gurevych, 2016); the Internet Argument corpus V2[3] (IAC) (Abbott et al., 2016); and ChangeMyView,[4] a Reddit forum. Through the pilots and subsequent debriefs with the experts, we made the following modifications to the annotation task of Wachsmuth et al. (2017a):

(1) Reduce taxonomy complexity. While TvsP defined the task to score all 11 AQ subaspects (Local Acceptability, Local Relevance, etc.), 3 dimensions (Cogency, Effectiveness, Reasonableness), and overall AQ, we reduced the number of qualities scored by only focusing on the 3 higher-level dimensions plus overall AQ. As a result, annotators assessed an argumentative text in terms of 4 scores instead of 15 scores, and instead of 3 different AQ levels, the simplified taxonomy is reduced to 2.

(2) Instruction Modifications. We reworded the TvsP dimension descriptions and added several examples to make the guidelines more understandable. As the annotators were not rating the 11 AQ subaspects, we experimented with different methods to incorporate the subaspects into the guidelines. Instead of explaining the subdimensions in the guidelines and trusting crowd annotators to bear them in mind, we represented each subdimension as a yes/no question in the annotation task itself (Table 1). Our pilot experiments showed that presenting the questions without asking for a response eased the perceived complexity of the task while not affecting agreement.

(3) Five-point scale. While TvsP collected judgments with a three-point rating scale (low, medium, high), we employ a five-point scale (very low, low, medium, high, very high, plus *cannot judge*) to allow for more nuanced judgments, as the expert annotators found too great of a distance between the items on a three-point scale. Scales with 5–9 items have been shown to be optimal, balancing the informational

---

[2]http://argumentation.bplaced.net/arguana/data
[3]https://nlds.soe.ucsc.edu/iac2
[4]https://www.reddit.com/r/changemyview/

Dimension	Subdimension	Question
Cogency	Local Acceptability	Are the justifications for the argument acceptable/believable?
	Local Relevance	Are the justifications relevant to the author's point?
	Local Sufficiency	Do the justifications provide enough support to draw a conclusion?
Effectiveness	Credibility	Is the author qualified to be making the argument?
	Emotional Appeal	Does the argument evoke emotions that make the audience more likely to agree with the author?
	Clarity	Does the author's language make it easy for you to understand what they are arguing for or against?
	Appropriateness	Is the author's argument and delivery appropriate for an online forum?
	Arrangement	Did the author present their argument in an order that makes sense?
Reasonableness	Global Acceptability	Would the target audience accept the argument and the way it is stated?
	Global Relevance	Does the argument contribute to the resolution of the given issue?
	Global Sufficiency	Does the argument address and adequately rebut counterarguments?

Table 1: Subdimensions represented as questions in the annotation task of debates.

needs of the researcher and the capacity of the raters (Cox III, 1980). We experimented with both three- and five-point scales and found that the larger scale did not negatively affect inter-annotator agreement.

3.2 Validating the Task Design

Our finalized task design is as follows. First, annotators decide whether a text is argumentative. If *yes*, the three high-level dimensions are scored on a five-point scale and subaspect questions are presented to guide the annotator's judgment. The Overall AQ is scored last, also on a five-point scale.

Before collecting annotations from the crowd, we validated our modifications subjectively and objectively. First, we ran a series of pilot tasks with our expert annotators. They initially annotated using the TvSP guidelines and next worked with the simplified taxonomy. In follow-up discussions, the experts confirmed that the new task design reduced the time and cognitive load necessary to rate arguments, and that the guidelines were more understandable. These modifications make the task more approachable, which is vital when presenting it to (untrained) crowd-workers for larger-scale annotation.

	Cogency	Effectiveness	Reasonableness	Overall
Ours	**0.46**	**0.48**	**0.48**	**0.55**
TvsP	0.27	0.38	0.13	0.43

Table 2: Agreement Dagstuhl "gold" annotations and our crowdsourced annotations (Ours) compared to TvsP.

We validated the simplifications quantitatively by reproducing the study of TvsP, which compared their crowd and "expert" annotations. To this end, we randomly sampled 200 arguments from Dagstuhl-ArgQuality-Corpus-V2, which come with author-annotated "gold" ratings. We collected ratings from a crowd (10 ratings per item), following our simplified design[5] (§3.1). All crowd contributors were native or fluent English speakers engaged through Appen (formerly Figure Eight). Crowd contributors did not participate in calibration meetings and all feedback was relayed to contributors through a liaison.

We average the crowd ratings to obtain a single score for each argument and computed the inter-annotator agreement (IAA) with the "gold" annotations using Krippendorff's α (Krippendorff, 2007) (Table 2). Even though the annotation scores are not strong, the IAA between our crowd annotators and the gold annotations generally surpasses the agreement scores reported by TvsP. This is a highly nuanced and subjective task, which is reflected in the agreement levels. Based on these results and annotator observations, we conclude that our task guidelines and design allow for better (or at least comparable) quality crowdsourcing of theory-based AQ annotations.

---

[5]The only difference is that we used a 3-point scale to more fairly compare to the gold.

4   Data Domains

In this work, we consider three domains: *Debate* forums, *CQA* forums, and *Review* forums. While Debates are generally well-explored in computational AQ, we are unaware of any work involving CQA and Reviews. For each of these domains, we first identified items likely to be argumentative and then adjusted the guidelines in consultation with expert annotators, as described below.

Debate forums.   Of these three domains, *Debates* is the most straightforward to annotate. Given a topic or motion, users can define their stance (*pro*/*contra*) and write an argument which supports it. We included data from two online debate forums. ConvinceMe (CM) is a subset of the IAC, where users share their *Stance* on a topic and discuss their point of view, with replies aiming to change the view of the original poster. Change My View (CMV) is a Reddit forum in which participants post their opinion on a topic and ask others to post replies to change their mind. We sampled original posts from CMV, skipping any moderator posts, and the first reply to an original post from CM, in order to limit the context that annotators must consider when evaluating arguments. CMV posts always include the author's perspective in the title, while CM posts may or may not include a stance in the title. In the guidelines, we instruct annotators to judge a post by how successfully it justifies the author's claim.

CQA.   In community questions and answers forums, users post questions or ask for advice, which other users can address. We experimented with arguments from Yahoo! Answers[6] (YA). When posting a question, a user can provide background information for their question (*context*) and can later indicate which response is the *best answer* to their question. The forum's looser structure provides for a wide variety of content, which is appealing as a potential source of non-standard arguments, but challenging as many of the posts do not contain any arguments. Through manual analysis, we identified three categories that frequently contained controversial topics, hypothesizing they would have a higher incidence of debates: *Social Science > Sociology*, *Society & Culture > Other*, and *Politics & Government > Law & Ethics*. We empirically selected the category with the highest proportion of arguments in a study on Amazon Mechanical Turk (MTurk). Qualified annotators[7] decided if question and best-answer pairs were argumentative. We collected 10 judgments for 100 pairs from each category and aggregated judgments with a simple majority. *Law & Ethics* had the most argumentative posts (70%, compared to *Sociology* with 40% and *Society & Culture* with 34%), so we sampled posts from this category to annotate.

In the guidelines for this domain, we asked annotators to judge the argumentative strength of an answer with respect to how well it addressed the given question. The guidelines and subdimension questions were altered to encourage this. One obstacle in pilot studies with expert annotators was posts offering, as many users solicited legal advice in the Law & Ethics forum. We decided to consider advice as argumentative as long as the author supported the advice with justification, which mirrors our general approach to the Argumentative dimension.

Reviews.   The third domain consists of restaurant reviews from the Yelp-Challenge-Dataset[8]. On Yelp, users write reviews of businesses and rate the quality of their experience from 1 (low) to 5 (high) stars. Unlike the Debate and Q&A forums, the format of Yelp does not support dialogue between users (i.e., users cannot directly reply to other users or posts), and so it is possible to present each post in isolation as a self-contained argument. As most posts do not explicitly state a claim, we pose the star rating as a claim the user is making about the business, and the review as the argument supporting it.

Yelp reviews can be highly subjective in that each review is based on a single user's experience. For instance, a user may rate a restaurant as 5-stars and write only *The food was delicious* in their review. To address this subjectivity, we asked annotators to judge the argumentative quality of each review with respect to how well it supported the rating provided. Another challenge was defining what constituted a counterargument, as these have a very different character than counterarguments in debates (for example, *Everyone says that the pizza crust is too thin here but that's authentic!*). In consultation with our experts,

---

[6] https://answers.yahoo.com/
[7] HIT approval rate >= 97; HITs approved > 500; Location = US
[8] https://www.yelp.com/dataset

Domain	Cogency	Effectiveness	Reasonableness	Overall
CQA	0.16	0.31	0.36	0.29
Debates	0.22	0.33	0.20	0.33
Reviews	0.41	0.19	0.21	0.34

Table 4: Agreement (Krippendorff's α) between experts on pilot studies for CQA, Debates, and Reviews (146, 150, and 50 arguments, respectively).

	Cogency	Effectiveness	Reasonableness	Overall
CQA	0.42	0.52	0.52	0.53
Debates	0.14	0.11	0.21	0.19
Reviews	0.32	0.32	0.31	0.33

Table 5: IAA between the mean expert and crowd scores for Cogency, Effectiveness, Reasonableness, and Overall AQ.

we defined counterarguments by the following characteristics: 1) addressing and rebutting the viewpoints of other reviews, 2) addressing and rebutting points that discredit the author's rating, and 3) bringing up favorable points in an unfavorable review and vice versa.

Experts completed a series of pilots before each domain was presented to the crowd, using the task design described in §3.1. Expert agreement on novel domains (YA and Yelp) are shown in Table 4. Feedback on the task and guidelines was gathered during calibration meetings with experts, and they were iteratively altered to be more clear and specific.

5　A Theory-based AQ Corpus

Applying the annotation task design and data selection described above, we created `GAQCorpus`, containing 5,285 arguments across three domains, annotated for theory-based dimensions. All arguments were limited to have a length between 70 and 200 characters. Ratings were provided by the two groups of annotators

	Crowd	Experts			Overlap	
# Annotators	10	1	2	3	11–13	**Total size**
CQA	1,334	626	–	625	500	**2,085**
Debates	1,438	600	–	600	538	**2,100**
Reviews	600	200	400	–	100	**1,100**

Table 3: Number of arguments annotated by experts and the crowd and the number of overlapping instances (annotated by both experts and the crowd) by domain.

described above, Experts (§3.1) and the Crowd (§3.2). Each group judged 3,000 arguments, with about 1,000 arguments annotated by both groups for comparison. The size of the corpus is described in Table 3. Annotators worked with the domains in the following order: Debate forums, CQA forums, and Review forums. Before switching to a new domain, annotators completed a small study for calibration. All data and guidelines are available from `https://github.com/grammarly/gaqcorpus`.

5.1　Inter-annotator Agreements (IAA)

We assessed the quality of the crowd annotations by calculating the agreement between the experts and crowd workers on the overlapping portions of `GAQCorpus` using the mean scores (Table 5).

For debate forums, the agreement is weak with $\alpha \leq 0.21$, while for the CQA forums, the agreement is higher: 0.42–0.53. These results suggest that the difficulty of the task is highly dependent on the domain. While our Debates data and the DS data both consist of web debate arguments, the difference in IAA is high, which might be attributed to different complexities of the web debates data. While TvsP only look at single arguments in isolation, often consisting of a single sentence only.

One area of disagreement centered on arguments which were sarcastic, ironic, or included rhetorical questions. Consider the argument given in Figure 2, over which the expert annotators expressed

	Cogency	Effectiveness	Reasonableness	Overall
Annotator 1	4	1	1	2
Annotator 2	4	5	3	4
Annotator 3	2	2	2	2

Figure 2: Example argument exhibiting disagreement in the Effectiveness dimension.

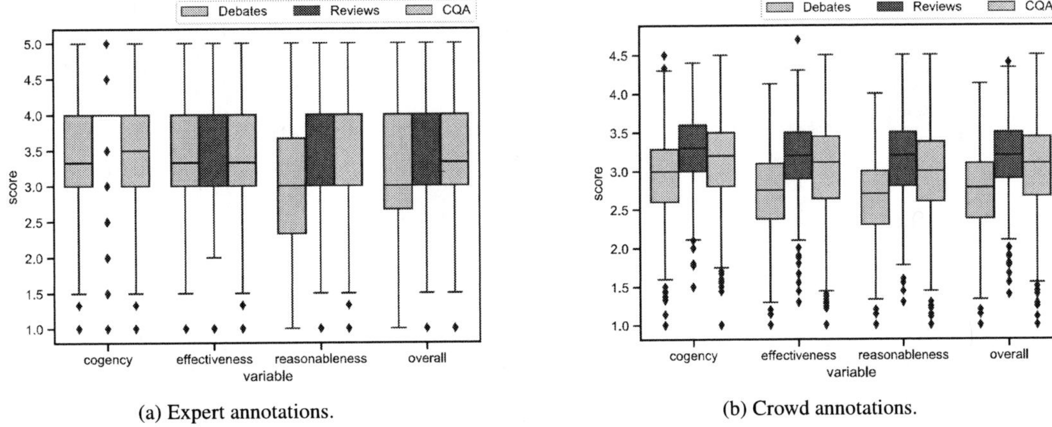

<table>
<tr><td align="center">(a) Expert annotations.</td><td align="center">(b) Crowd annotations.</td></tr>
</table>

Figure 3: Score distributions by domain for expert and crowd annotators.

disagreement. This argument appears to support the stance that a government has the right to censor speech, but several linguistic cues indicate that the argument might be ironic: (a) Punctuation: ellipsis indicates thinking/searching for justifications; similarly, (b) the filler *um*; (c) capitalization: the noun phrase *Our Leader* is capitalized, indicating hyperbolic apotheosis; and finally, (d) the phrase *(...) so I have to argue for this side.* acts like an apologia, which is put in front of the actual argument. Annotators 1 and 2 based their judgments on an interpretation of this text that related to the estimated degree of irony in the post. While Annotator 1 did not perceive irony and judged the argument as *very weak* in *Effectiveness*, Annotator 2 considered it to be highly effective as in their view, the irony positively underlined the perceived stance. Annotator 3 gave medium scores across the board. Such disagreements were regularly discussed and usually revealed that multiple opinions may exist according to how the texts were interpreted, highlighting the high subjectivity of the task.

Another area of disagreement was how to judge arguments on topics that were deemed "less worthy" of being discussed, and which usually were humorous in nature or had trivial consequences, such as *Batman vs Superman*, in which users argued for the the superiority of either superhero. In pilots, some experts provided lower ratings of arguments on a topic that they considered less worthy Others thought that writing a strong, serious argument on a less worthy topic was especially difficult, and thus provided higher ratings for such arguments.

5.2 Analysis of Scores

The distributions of mean scores across domains and annotator groups in GAQCorpus are depicted in Figures 3a and 3b. In general, the interquartile range of the expert scores was higher than the crowd, suggesting that experts were more specific when scoring items, which is also reflected in the medians: while the crowd exhibits a tendency to score variables equally, expert annotations exhibit more differentiation.

To understand the interrelations between Overall AQ and the dimensions, we compute Pearson correlations between the mean scores (Figure 4). Generally, the trends are similar across all three domains. For instance, for Debates (Figures 4d and 4a), the crowd annotations exhibit stronger correlations between the different dimension scores than the experts, with $0.83 \leq r \leq 0.96$. Interestingly, the variance among the Pearson scores is lower, indicating that the crowd tends to distribute ratings for a single instance more consistently while the experts seem to put more weight on differentiating the dimensions.

Expert ratings of Overall AQ have substantially stronger correlation with the dimensions than any of the dimension scores with each other, further indicating that experts are more discerning in their scores than the crowd. Across both annotator groups and all domains, the correlation between Overall AQ and Reasonableness is highest, which is consistent with earlier observations (Wachsmuth et al., 2017b).

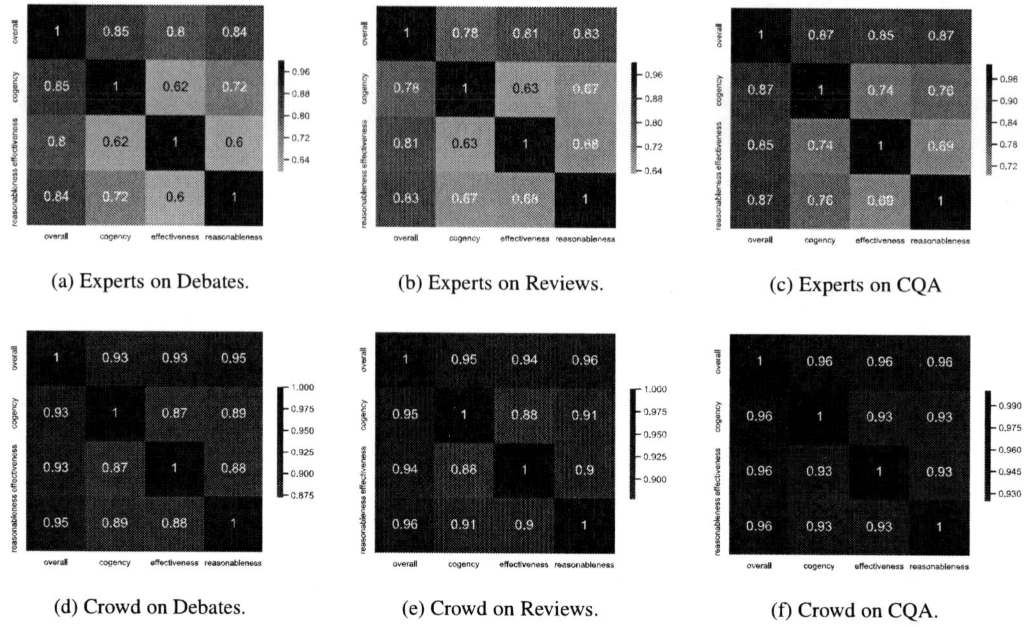

(a) Experts on Debates.   (b) Experts on Reviews.   (c) Experts on CQA

(d) Crowd on Debates.   (e) Crowd on Reviews.   (f) Crowd on CQA.

Figure 4: Mean score correlations between the different dimensions for expert and crowd annotators across the three domains (Pearson's r).

5.3 Qualitative Analysis

We next examine low-scoring arguments from all domains to understand how AQ is perceived differently, focusing on the *Reasonableness* dimension. Table 6 shows a low-scoring argument from each domain. The Debate argument raises a counterargument but does not rebut it and additionally neglects to address an obvious counterargument (i.e., the many ethical implications of such a policy). On the other hand, the CQA and Review arguments do not raise or address any counterarguments and are not judged Reasonable for other reasons: the CQA argument jokes about the original poster's question and accuses the poster of malignant behavior, while the Review argument delves into a personal experience that does not contribute to the discussion about the quality of the business.

6 Conclusion

Theory-based AQ assessment provides a holistic and targeted perspective on AQ, but its high complexity makes annotation difficult. In this work, we describe our efforts to create `GAQCorpus`, a multi-domain corpus of 5,295 arguments annotated for quality along theory-based AQ dimensions. We demonstrate that it is possible to collect complex annotations with crowdsourcing in three domains: Debate, CQA, and Review forums. Drawing from the initial study of Wachsmuth et al. (2017a), which suggested the general feasibility, we relied on the intuition of trained linguists to simplify the task and guidelines while preserving the theoretical basis of the task. The agreement between experts and the crowd was higher than the agreement in earlier studies (Wachsmuth et al., 2017a), validating our approach and indicating that it is possible to collect complex ratings using a crowd.

`GAQCorpus` and the findings of our annotation study will serve as a basis for future corpus development and computational model development in theory-based AQ. They are available for download from `https://github.com/grammarly/gaqcorpus`.

Debates		
Cogency	2.0	**Title:** Should you need to pass an IQ test to have kids?– **Stance:** Dumb parents lead to more dumb
Effectiveness	1.7	kids. **Text:** I have a strong opinion that before having children, the prospective parents should have to
Reasonableness	1.0	pass a series of background and IQ tests. Kids being brought into this world need a good foundation to
Overall	1.3	start a successful life with. You may have that limited case where the parents are morons and the kids
		strive to be different then their failure parents, but in most cases it is an endless line of parasites on our
		world. We need more smart people.

CQA		
Cogency	2.7	**Question:** Bounced CHECK? **Context:** Does the company holding the bounced check have to send
Effectiveness	2.0	you a certified letter before issuing a warrant for your arrest. I feel almost certain that they do but i am
Reasonableness	1.7	not sure. **Answer:** I always make sure my checks are not printed on rubber. they are just too expensive
Overall	2.0	and not worth it. We all make a mistake from time to time, and usually it is no big deal except for the
		extreme annoyance and all the bounced check fees. But if you are worried about an arrest warrant then
		I am sure you are doing this deliberately and trying to defraud the company. You have probably sent
		them a couple of bad checks already in an attempt to string them along so your guilt is probably pretty
		well established. You can hope that you do not have to share a jail cell with a gross deviate of some
		sort.

Reviews		
Cogency	1.0	**Title:** Business review: 2.0 Stars. **Business name:** Cook Out. **City:** Charlotte. **Categories:** Restau-
Effectiveness	1.0	rants, Desserts, Food, Fast Food, American (Traditional), Hot Dogs, Burgers **Review:** Burgers are good
Reasonableness	1.0	but I like those other 5 guys burgers instead oh and I guess if your not from around here don't even think
Overall	1.0	about going thru the drive thru it's like the biggest most unreadable confusing hurried crazy thing ever
		if I ever go again hell with drive thru until I've lived here for at least 5 maybe 10 years and can be a
		veteran drive thru person I'm walking in it's like if I mix up all the letters in this review and give you 1
		minute to read it and figure it out then you gotta move on.

Table 6: Low-scoring arguments from all domains

Acknowledgements

The work of Anne Lauscher is supported by the Eliteprogramm of the Baden-Württemberg Stiftung (AGREE grant). We thank our linguistic expert annotators for providing interesting insights and discussions as well as the anonymous reviewers for their helpful comments. We also thank Henning Wachsmuth for consulting us w.r.t. his previous work and Yahoo! for granting us access to their data.

References

Rob Abbott, Brian Ecker, Pranav Anand, and Marilyn Walker. 2016. Internet argument corpus 2.0: An SQL schema for dialogic social media and the corpora to go with it. In *Proceedings of the Tenth International Conference on Language Resources and Evaluation (LREC 2016)*, pages 4445–4452, Portorož, Slovenia, May. European Language Resources Association (ELRA).

Aristotle. trans. 2007. *On Rhetoric: A Theory of Civic Discourse.* Oxford University Press, Oxford, UK. Translated by George A. Kennedy.

Eli P. Cox III. 1980. The optimal number of response alternatives for a scale: A review. *Journal of Marketing Research*, 17(4):407–422.

Shai Gretz, Roni Friedman, Edo Cohen-Karlik, Assaf Toledo, Dan Lahav, Ranit Aharonov, and Noam Slonim. 2020. A large-scale dataset for argument quality ranking: Construction and analysis. In *Proceedings of AAAI2020*.

Ivan Habernal and Iryna Gurevych. 2016. Which argument is more convincing? analyzing and predicting convincingness of web arguments using bidirectional LSTM. In *Proceedings of the 54th Annual Meeting of the Association for Computational Linguistics (Volume 1: Long Papers)*, pages 1589–1599, Berlin, Germany, August. Association for Computational Linguistics.

Klaus Krippendorff. 2007. Computing krippendorff's alpha-reliability. Technical report, University of Pennsylvania, Annenberg School for Communication.

Anne Lauscher, Lily Ng, Courtney Napoles, and Joel Tetreault. 2020. Rhetoric, logic, and dialectic: Advancing theory-based argument quality assessment in natural language processing. In *Proceedings of the 28th International Conference on Computational Linguistics (COLING 2020)*.

Isaac Persing and Vincent Ng. 2013. Modeling thesis clarity in student essays. In *Proceedings of the 51st Annual Meeting of the Association for Computational Linguistics (Volume 1: Long Papers)*, pages 260–269, Sofia, Bulgaria, August. Association for Computational Linguistics.

Isaac Persing and Vincent Ng. 2014. Modeling prompt adherence in student essays. In *Proceedings of the 52nd Annual Meeting of the Association for Computational Linguistics (Volume 1: Long Papers)*, pages 1534–1543, Baltimore, Maryland, June. Association for Computational Linguistics.

Isaac Persing and Vincent Ng. 2015. Modeling argument strength in student essays. In *Proceedings of the 53rd Annual Meeting of the Association for Computational Linguistics and the 7th International Joint Conference on Natural Language Processing (Volume 1: Long Papers)*, pages 543–552.

Isaac Persing and Vincent Ng. 2017. Why can't you convince me? modeling weaknesses in unpersuasive arguments. In *Proceedings of the 26th International Joint Conference on Artificial Intelligence*, IJCAI'17, pages 4082–4088. AAAI Press.

Isaac Persing, Alan Davis, and Vincent Ng. 2010. Modeling organization in student essays. In *Proceedings of the 2010 Conference on Empirical Methods in Natural Language Processing*, EMNLP '10, pages 229–239, Stroudsburg, PA, USA. Association for Computational Linguistics.

Christian Stab and Iryna Gurevych. 2016. Recognizing the absence of opposing arguments in persuasive essays. In *Proceedings of the Third Workshop on Argument Mining (ArgMining2016)*, pages 113–118.

Christian Stab and Iryna Gurevych. 2017. Recognizing insufficiently supported arguments in argumentative essays. In *Proceedings of the 15th Conference of the European Chapter of the Association for Computational Linguistics: Volume 1, Long Papers*, pages 980–990, Valencia, Spain, April. Association for Computational Linguistics.

Assaf Toledo, Shai Gretz, Edo Cohen-Karlik, Roni Friedman, Elad Venezian, Dan Lahav, Michal Jacovi, Ranit Aharonov, and Noam Slonim. 2019. Automatic argument quality assessment-new datasets and methods. In *Proceedings of the 2019 Conference on Empirical Methods in Natural Language Processing and the 9th International Joint Conference on Natural Language Processing (EMNLP-IJCNLP)*, pages 5629–5639.

Henning Wachsmuth, Nona Naderi, Ivan Habernal, Yufang Hou, Graeme Hirst, Iryna Gurevych, and Benno Stein. 2017a. Argumentation quality assessment: Theory vs. practice. In *Proceedings of the 55th Annual Meeting of the Association for Computational Linguistics (Volume 2: Short Papers)*, pages 250–255, Vancouver, Canada, July. Association for Computational Linguistics.

Henning Wachsmuth, Nona Naderi, Yufang Hou, Yonatan Bilu, Vinodkumar Prabhakaran, Tim Alberdingk Thijm, Graeme Hirst, and Benno Stein. 2017b. Computational argumentation quality assessment in natural language. In *Proceedings of the 15th Conference of the European Chapter of the Association for Computational Linguistics: Volume 1, Long Papers*, pages 176–187, Valencia, Spain, April. Association for Computational Linguistics.

Association for Computational Linguistics
209 N. Eighth Street
Stroudsburg, Pennsylvania 18360

ISBN 978-1-7138-2822-8